WATSON COLLECTION OF INDIAN MINIATURES

AT THE ELVEHJEM MUSEUM OF ART

Watson Collection of Indian Miniatures at the Elvehjem Museum of Art

A DETAILED STUDY OF SELECTED WORKS

Gautama V. Vajracharya

Elvehjem Museum of Art UNIVERSITY OF WISCONSIN–MADISON 2002

800 University Avenue, Madison, WI 53706-1479. *www.lvm.wisc.edu*
Distributed by The University of Wisconsin Press, 1930 Monroe St,. Madison, WI 53711-2059. *www.wisc.edu/wisconsinpress*

On the front cover: *Potrait of a Nobleman*, Mughal style, ca. 1780, cat. no. 23 (detail).

On the back cover: *A Prince and Princess*, Indo-Persian style, mid-16th century, cat. no. 11.

Library of Congress Cataloging-in-Publication Data
Elvehjem Museum of Art
Watson collection of Indian minatures at the Elvehjem Museum of Art : a detailed study of selected works / Gautama V. Vajracharya.
p. cm.
Includes bibliographical references and index.
ISBN 0-932900-89-5 (pbk.)
1. Miniature painting, Indic—Catalogs. 2. Watson, Jane Werner, 1915– —Art collections—Catalogs. 3. Miniature painting—Private collections—Wisconsin—Madison—Catalogs. 4. Miniature painting—Wisconsin—Madison—Catalogs. 5. Elvehjem Museum of Art—Catalogs. I. Vajracharya, Gautamavajra. II. Title.

ND1337.I5 E42 2002
751.7'7'095407477583—dc21 2002029713

Patricia Powell, editor
Rebecca Giménez, designer
American Printing Company, Madison, Wisconsin, printer

Contents

Rajasthani Style

Director's Foreword

One of the delights of the Elvehjem collection is a group of Indian paintings, dating from the thirteenth through the nineteenth centuries, donated to the museum by a native Wisconsinite and alumna of the university, Jane Werner Watson. These are miniature paintings; originally they appeared as illustrations in palm-leaf manuscripts, and in the conservative tradition of the subcontinent, they retained this format for many years after the introduction of paper. Numerous examples of illustrated manuscripts of the *Rāmāyaṇa*, the *Mahabharata*, and other religious and epic works, even love poems such as the *Rasikapriyā* of Keśavadāsa are extant, with examples represented in this collection. The paintings are intimate, intended to be viewed and studied by one person. They sometimes come from portfolios gathered for a particular ruler or important person, such as the early Mughal emperor Akbar, who established an atelier of painters and at his death in 1605 left a library of 24,000 illuminated manuscripts. The early Mughal paintings are realistic, while the Rajput painting in the same periods was consistently metaphorical and symbolic examples of both appear in this collection. By the early seventeenth century various regional styles were developing among Hindu miniature paintings, and most styles are represented in this collection.

The donor of these works, Jane Werner Watson, was born in Fold du Lac in 1915. She graduated from the University of Wisconsin in 1936 with a bachelor's degree in English. She worked as editor and writer for Western Publishing Company from 1938 to 1958. She wrote more than a hundred Golden Books such as *The World of Science*, *Dinosaurs*, *Wonders of Nature*, which were translated into several languages, and numerous children's books under various pseudonyms. She was named Woman of the Year in Literature by the *Los Angeles Times* in 1958.

Jane and her late husband Earnest collected these paintings in India when he was assigned as science attaché to the United States Embassy in New Delhi in 1960–62 and on visits to India for the next few years. In a catalogue of the complete collection published by the Elvehjem in 1971, Jane Watson gives a fascinating account of their introduction to the world of Indian art and their increasingly interested forays into the little world of Krishna, the wonder world of Indian miniatures. According to Jane:

> It was curiosity that made us expose ourselves to miniatures by the hundred and thousands in the museums of India, curiosity that led me to leaf attentively through paintings by the score—more often the hundred—in the frequently dusty and unpromising packs of dealers who, alerted by the grapevine of their trade, found their way to our door, if we did not find our way to theirs. . . . As we became increasingly interested in these local styles, interrelated but distinct, we reached another conclusion. Surely, we told ourselves, it was only sensible to put together while they were still readily available in the Delhi market samplings of all these schools, representing wherever possible the major stages in their development—and even decline.
>
> Sensible or not, that is what we tried to do through the two and a half years of our residence in Delhi from early 1960 until 1962. On each of our half dozen return trips during the years since [until 1970], we have tried to fill some of the gaps in the coverage. Here is the result. We most warmly hope that it will provide for many of our friends a pleasant introduction to an enchanted land, in which we have spent countless happy hours—the little world of Krishna in Indian miniatures.

Anticipating the opening of the Elvehjem Museum of Art, Jane and her husband Earnest Watson began donating their collection of Indian paintings to the University of Wisconsin in 1964. The first donation consisted of an Indian folk painting and six Tibetan Than-kas and was followed in 1965 by four illuminated manuscripts. Their donations have continued over the years until the collection now contains well over 250 outstanding Indian miniatures. Sadly, Earnest Watson passed away before the first catalogue on the collection, which was dedicated to him, was published.

The entire Watson collection of 271 works was catalogued in the early 1970s by Professor Pramod Chandra, then of the University of Chicago, and the Elvehjem published his research in *Indian Miniature Painting* (182 pp. 10 color, 89 B&W illus.) in 1971. Chandra was the first scholar to recognize the significance of the collection, and his preliminary research established the basic style and date for each work with a brief paragraph analyzing the subject and basis for the attribution for the style. Chandra was also able to establish the manuscript from which many folios came and to provide translations of text on several paintings. According to museum records, other scholars who examined collection and conferred with Chandra include Stuart C. Welch, Robert Skelton, W. G. Archer, G. N. Goswamy, Chaudary Muhammad Naim, and Edwin Binney III. This catalogue was and is the cornerstone of our understanding of the Watson collection. However, as ever in the field of scholarship, new discoveries lead to new insights in any given field. The present publication represents years of thought and research by yet another scholar and, we hope, will provide much food for thought for future generations of scholars and UW students regarding the style, subject matter, and cultural significance of a selection of paintings from the Watson collection.

Gautama V. Vajracharya has taught Indian civilization and art history in the Departments of South Asian Languages and Cultures and Art History here at the University of Wisconsin since 1987. Dr. Vajracharya began actively researching and documenting the Watson collection soon after arriving at the university. He has drawn heavily on this collection for his teaching and has steadily been accumulating his own more extensive research on the Watson collection. No scholar knows this collection better than Vajracharya or is in a better position to give us an extended analysis of 129 works from this collection. His deep knowledge of Sanskrit as well as the art historical tradition gives him a unique perspective on these works.

Gautama V. Vajracharya did his undergraduate work in his native Nepal at the Samsodhana-Mandala in Sanskrit literature and philology. He came to the United States in 1975 as a visiting research scholar at the Los Angeles County Museum of Art, funded by a three-year John D. Rockefeller fellow grant.

There he worked with Pratapaditya Pal, a preeminent scholar of art of the Indian subcontinent. He received his M.A. from Claremont Graduate School in California and his Ph.D. from the University of Wisconsin–Madison. He has published widely on stone and metal sculpture in Nepal and in recent years has been publishing on the continuity of ancient art traditions of the subcontinent. It is this focus that he brings to bear on the Watson collection of Indian miniature painting.

In the introductory essay, Vajracharya analyses ancient Indian art as a reflection of the belief system in place that continued well into the nineteenth century and continued to be expressed, whether consciously or not, in the artistic traditions found in the Indian miniature paintings. He goes on to explicate the gradual development and interrelationship between two of the most prominent styles of Indic miniature painting: one commissioned by Muslim rulers, mainly the great Mughals and their descendants (sixteenth to eighteenth centuries); and the other by Hindu Rajput princes who ruled various northwest Indian principalities during the same period. Since the Watson collection includes excellent examples of almost all aspects of these Mughal and Rajput paintings, the introduction presents a brief history of Indic painting of this period, comparing this collection with other well-known examples of miniature art. He concentrates on the interaction of different styles rather than focusing on a singular style. The main section of the catalogue employs this methodology by grouping individual paintings by style while also exploring the uniqueness of each work, the important differences within each style, and the interrelationship between various styles.

Each entry includes a description of the painting and a detailed stylistic analysis and reviews the basic information on date, region, and artist. Where Gautama Vajracharya's findings differ from the 1971 conclusions of Pramod Chandra, we have placed the earlier material in brackets, for example the Pratisarā, folio from the *Aṣṭasāhasrikā Prajñāpāramitā* manuscript [formerly an unidentified manuscript], Nepal [formerly Eastern Indian style], 13th century.

We are grateful to the E. Rhodes and Leona B. Carpenter Foundation and the National Endowment for the Arts, a federal agency, for supporting this publication project.

And finally, I wish to once again reaffirm the gratitude of the Elvehjem Museum of Art to Jane Werner and Ernst Watson for their forethought, generosity, and dedication to the teaching of the arts at the University of Wisconsin–Madison.

Madison
August 2002
Russell Panczenko

Preface and Acknowledgement

Pramod Chandra's 1971 catalogue *Indian Miniature Painting: The Collection of Earnest C. and Jane Werner Watson* is the initial study of the Watson collection of over 300 paintings. This important work provided me with valuable guidelines, without which I would not have been able to carry out further study. The main focus of my study, however, differs from that of the initial work. I studied the collection to detect the underlying links between earlier Indian art of the classical period and miniature painting, about which scholars have debated for years. In the course of my investigation, I became aware that both stylistic elements and the subject of the painting are helpful for such a study. Accordingly, I have analyzed 129 miniatures of many styles and subjects that are directly or indirectly related to my investigation. I give a detailed explanation of my approach in the introductory essay.

I am delighted to acknowledge my indebtedness to several scholars: Dr. Pratapaditya Pal, my first tutor in America, for giving me the benefit of his broad knowledge, and Joanna Williams, for kindly reading my first draft of the introductory essay. Her thoughtful comments and suggestions encouraged me to proceed with confidence. Similarly I would like to express my gratitude to Catherine Glynn for her critical reading of some sections of my work. Needless to say, however, I take responsibility for the use or misuse I have made of all suggestions and comments.

It is also a matter of great pleasure to acknowledge the help I have received at the Elvehjem Museum of Art, University of Wisconsin–Madison, from my colleagues, in particular curator of prints and drawings Andrew Stevens, curator of education Anne Lambert, and development specialist Kathy Paul, who assisted me in many different ways such as providing me with better photographs, preparing grant proposals, and most important, giving me their valuable time whenever I approached to them for help. Furthermore, I would like to express my special gratitude to editor Patricia Powell, who helped me not only in correcting my English and style of writing but also gathering illustrations. The success story of this project, indeed, greatly depended on her professional skill and experience.

Finally, I would like to dedicate this work to Russell Panczenko, director of the museum, without whose vision and inspiration this project would not have germinated, let alone come to fruition. This catalogue is a part of his bigger project, which has provided Madisonians, for last two decades, with an unprecedented opportunity to enjoy the spectrum of artistic expressions of a variety of cultures ranging from the Indus valley civilization in South Asia to Yoruba culture in West Africa.

Madison
June 2002
Gautama V. Vajracharya

Foreword

Early in 1970, soon after I arrived in Los Angeles, I received a telephone call from Jane Watson, who was then living in Santa Barbara with her husband. She informed me that they had a collection of Indian paintings, which they invited me to see and to catalogue. Because of other commitments I was unable to accept the invitation. A year later, the collection was exhibited at Madison, and the catalogue written by my distinguished colleague Pramod Chandra, now the George P. Bickford Professor of Indian and South Asian Art at Harvard University (Chandra 1971). Subsequently, a small group from the collection was published in another exhibition catalogue (Raducha). So it is especially gratifying to be associated with yet another salutary publication on the collection over three decades after that first conversation with Jane Watson.

Even a better reason for accepting the invitation to write this introduction is the involvement of Gautamvajra Vajracharya with the project. I have known him since the mid-seventies when I first met him in Nepal. He was already well-known in his country as a young scholar of promise and had published several articles and a book in Nepali on the history of Hanumandhoka, the royal palace. At the time, he was not an art historian but an accomplished Sanskritist and epigraphist. Subsequently he came to this country to work with me both at the Los Angeles County Museum of Art and at the University of Southern California, Los Angeles, thereafter taking his master of arts degree at the Claremont

Only when we have been convinced that a work [of art] answered to intelligible and reasonable needs, tastes, interests, or aspirations, whether or not these coincide with our own (a matter of no significance, where censorship is not in view), only when we are in a position to take the work for granted as a creation which could not have been otherwise than it is, are conditions established which make it possible for the mind to acknowledge the splendor of the work itself, to relish its beauty, or even its grace.—Ananda K. Coomaraswamy (1977)

Graduate School and moving on to Wisconsin to complete his doctorate. He has been an esteemed colleague since, and I have benefited in many ways from his extensive knowledge of the Newar culture of Nepal as well as his facility with both Newari and Sanskrit languages.

The great savant of the last century, Ananda K. Coomaraswamy (1877–1947), once said that "iconography is the constant essence and style the variable accident" of art. In keeping with that sagacious observation, Vajracharya has probed deeply into the meaning of the paintings' contents rather than their styles. In so doing he has not concentrated simply on descriptive iconography and identification of the subject matter but has also dilated on the symbolic significance of the rich array of motifs as well as the forms of Indian paintings, especially of the Rajput Schools, both of the plains and hills. No matter how technically sophisticated the Mughal pictures are and how seductive their appeal to Western viewers has remained (as is evident from the art market), the essence of Indian aesthetics continued to be expressed with renewed energy and spontaneity in Rajput pictures. The motifs used in Rajput art are not merely descriptive but also connotative. As Coomaraswamy stated in his essay on the theory of art in Asia, "It should be hardly necessary to point out that art is by definition essentially conventional (*saṃketita*); for it is only by convention that nature can be made intelligible, and only by signs and symbols, *rūpa*, *pratīka*, that communication is made possible" (1956: 24).

One of the key Sanskrit words that expresses the essence of Indian culture is *svasti*, meaning auspicious, or *subhamastu* (let it be auspicious). This was the most common expressions uttered in greeting when two educated people met. Not only has Vajracharya convincingly demonstrated the fundamental importance of the concept of auspiciousness generally in Indian culture but also in the country's arts and how they continued to influence the Rajput artists consciously or unconsciously.

For instance, both in the ancient temple art and in Rajput paintings, trees are represented conceptually rather than naturalistically as healthy plants with a circular dome of densely packed leaves and fruit, inhabited by birds and animals, all of which symbolize fullness and hence auspiciousness. A water-filled pot (*purṇaghaṭa*) or a beautiful and buxom woman (*divayanārī*) are considered auspicious signs, seeing which before undertaking a journey will result in success. The idea of fullness or completeness is expressed ubiquitously in Indian and religious art as well as in Rajput paintings by such motifs as lovers (*mithuna*) or a generously endowed woman standing below a fruit-laden tree. As the *Bṛihadāraṇyaka Upaniṣad* eloquently states,

The world there is full;
The world here is full;
Fullness from fullness proceeds.
After taking fully from the full,
It still remains completely full.
(*Upaniṣads*: 72)

It is now well known that both the Gandhara and Mughal schools of art were strongly influenced by European aesthetics, particularly in their insistence on realistic observation and images. The two most graphic examples of this attitude are the representations of the starving, emaciated, meditating Buddha in Gandhara and the well-known Mughal painting showing the death of Inayat [Enayat] Khan, a Mughal dandee and an opium addict, discussed by Vajracharya (see pp. 18–19). It should not surprise anyone that the rest of India generally avoided representing the haggard and gaunt Buddha as it was not an auspicious theme. The emaciated goddess of dread Chamunda is rarely worshiped at home by Hindus. For the same reason it would not have occurred to a Rajput patron or artist to portray a dying man realistically, which would be considered inauspicious and hence not to be looked at (*adarśaniya*).

Indeed, *darśan* is a keyword in Indian culture whose wide significance, as noted by Vajracharya, is yet to be fully realized, despite the appearance of a slim volume on the subject (Eck). That "Truth" can be seen or beheld, as in "Behold, I have seen the glory," is fundamental to Indian philosophy from the earliest times, and hence the poets who composed the Vedic verses are called seers and the Sanskrit expression for philosophy is *darśan*. But at the most mundane level, the word or its synonym *drishti* is used to denote a wide variety of situations both auspicious and inauspicious. As we noted, to see a full water pot or a beautiful woman is considered to have auspicious consequences, but to see a snake or a monk before a journey is considered to be an ill omen. For both seeing a friend and the image of a deity, the word *darśan* is used with equal facility. A frequently employed expression is *darśaniya*, used to imply pleasure or satisfaction as well as auspiciousness on beholding a work of art. This attitude had important implications for the arts, for even though some theoretical texts such as the *Chitrasūtra* of the seventh-century *Viṣṇudhamottara Purāṇa* asserts that everything in the three worlds is suitable for representation, in point of fact strict limitations are placed on what subjects are appropriate for temples and homes.

In a divine residence or in the memorial shrines of past kings, all subjects are appropriate; but in homes, only the erotic *śṛṅgāra*, a word commonly used in discussions of aesthetics but explained in a novel way by Vajracharya on page 15), the comical (*hāsya*), and the tranquil (*śānta*) themes should be represented. By all means, homes should avoid cremation grounds, scenes of battle, pathos and tragedy, corpses, suffering, misery, and all things ugly and inauspicious. Incidentally, it may be recalled that the young Siddhartha saw a sick man, an ascetic, and a corpse, which persuaded him to renounce his family and home, conventionally regarded as an inauspicious act from the householder's standpoint.

A similar emphasis on the concept of auspiciousness also dominates the act of judging a work of art:

> Those who desire auspiciousness should avoid pictures depicting a figure with defective limbs, stained, dispirited and incidence by persons overcome with fear and disease and with disheveled hair. . . . A painting done by the experts, well-versed in *śāstras*, brings prosperity and removes adversity. A painting purifies and removes anxiety and brings forth prosperity and causes unequalled and pure delight, kills the bad dreams and pleases the house-deity. (*Viṣṇudharmottara Purāṇa*: 135, 137)

It is doubtful if in any other culture the purpose of painting has been so expansively described. It is remarkable how these observations of an unknown savant in seventh-century Kashmir have continued to influence the artists who worked for the Hindu courts in seventeenth- to nineteenth-century India, as is clear from the themes of the pictures.

As I demonstrated in the introduction of a catalogue of another private collection almost a generation ago, the first scholar to emphasize the continuity of the ancient Indian intellectual and spiritual traditions in Rajput painting was its "discoverer," Ananda Coomaraswamy (Pal 1978). As early as 1926 he wrote, "It is interesting to recognize in Rajput paintings a great variety of motifs, compositions, and formulas that occur commonly in much older Indian works or correspond to the phraseology of classical rhetoric (Pal 1978: 9). The continuity is in fact much more substantive and deeper than the survival of simply perceptual elements and aesthetic language. A perusal of texts on artistic theories and the instructions for artists make such continuities clear. This is all the more astonishing considering how radically different the society was due to the presence of Muslims from west Asia who had continuously occupied northern India since the eleventh century. Islamic cultures exerted enormous influence on the Hindu civilization, to a far greater extent than that following the encounter with Alexander and the classical civilization in the fourth century B.C. This influence was particularly profound in texts and in the arts: culinary, sartorial, musical, architectural, and visual.

What is extraordinary is that despite profound religious and cultural differences, such synthesis and rapprochement was possible. Although the Mughal and Rajput pictorial traditions differ significantly, both are products of this synthesis in different ways. Strong belief in their religions was fundamental to both Hindus and Muslims, but in encouraging the arts of painting the Mughal and the Rajput patrons harbored different attitudes. Except for the nonfigurative decoration of the Koran, Mughal painting is concerned with little that is religious. For that matter, most religious books illustrated for the Mughals are Hindu rather than Islamic texts. On the contrary, Rajput art is permeated with religiosity, even when the themes are ostensibly secular. Apart from religious books, Rajput patrons and artists delighted in depicting mythological themes and images of gods in their houses and in the portable pictures of the type collected by the Watsons. That tradition thrives in modern India, although not in the form of exquisitely rendered, delicate pictures like the ones discussed with such erudition and insight in this catalogue, but in the form of prints and chromolithographs that are equally at home in bazaars, temples and, more recently, in digitized versions.

Plus ça change, plus c'est la même chose.

Los Angeles
August 1, 2002
Pratapaditya Pal

WATSON COLLECTION OF INDIAN MINIATURES

AT THE ELVEHJEM MUSEUM OF ART

Auspicious Sight *Link between Classical Art and Indian Miniature Painting as Reflected in the Watson Collection*

The entire universe consisting of movables and immovables emanated from a painting. . .the universe is a [macro] painting and a painting is the [micro] universe.—Aparājitapṛcchā

The Watson collection of Indian art in the Elvehjem Museum of Art consists of miniature paintings that come from the foothills of the Himalayas to the tip of the Indian peninsula, including Orissa on the east coast and Gujarat on the west coast. It ranges in time from the thirteenth century to the nineteenth century. Thus it includes over half of the medieval period (ca. 750–1750) of Indic history. Various schools, each with its own distinctive style, developed within this time and space and can be classified roughly as traditional, Sultanate, Mughal, Rajput, Deccani, or South Indian. Collected by Jane Werner Watson, a connoisseur of Indian paintings, and her late husband Earnest C. Watson, this collection provides us with valuable examples of the South Asian manuscript illuminations and miniature paintings of seven centuries (1200–1900). This period in the history of South Asian painting is significant mainly because it witnessed the germination and blossoming of the world-renowned Mughal and Rajput styles. Most of the paintings of the Watson collection belong to these two contemporaneous styles, with a majority being Rajput and further broken down into eleven regional schools.

The evolution of each artistic school and its prominent stylistic features are discussed under the heading of each school immediately before the relevant series of entries of the catalogue. In this introduction, we hope to enrich the catalogue by showing some examples of where the classical tradition continues in miniature painting. After briefly describing political events as the historical background for the collection, we discuss the conceptual aspects of Indic art associated with religions and culture, followed by a study of their expression in symbols and the pictorial representations of musical modes. We pay special attention to the concept of "seeing" known as *darśana* in Sanskrit and its close relationship with the belief system of the typical monsoon culture of India. We show how understanding this concept and belief system helps distinguish the artistic expression of the mainstream of India from that of other traditions. Finally we study the stylistic evolution of Indian paintings in order to understand the relationship of the collection to the earlier history of Indian paintings.

Historical Background

In the history of India Persian, Greek, Kuṣāṇa, and Muslim invaders always approached from across the Hindu Kush mountain range in the northwest, never from other directions. Each invasion introduced some new cultural elements first in the northwest, then throughout the country. As India became culturally enriched, the invaders gradually adapted an Indic style of life and became assimilated with native Indians as they lost their foreign identity.

This political pattern is also closely associated with Indian art, particularly because the art history of India is characterized by the side-by-side development of two different schools—one exposed to foreign artistic traditions and willing to learn from international sources, the other less familiar with international activities and reluctant to break from earlier Indian traditions. For instance, due to the Persian and the Greek invasion around 419 B.C. and 327 B.C. respectively, India came in contact with foreign artistic traditions that enriched the imperial art of the Maurya period (ca. 321–185 B.C.). But in several localities such as Bharhut, Sanchi, and Amāravatī, traditional Indian art continued to flourish with little foreign influence even in the second century B.C. and the first century A.D. Likewise, during the Kuṣāṇa, period (A.D. 50–320) the artists of the northwest of modern Pakistan incorporated Greco-Roman and Persian artistic features, thereby creating a syncretic art known as Gandharan art, which does not strictly follow the norms of the mainstream of Indic art. But the contemporaneous artists of Mathura showed very little interest in assimilating foreign artistic elements in their work particularly if the elements did not agree with their belief system. The same phenomenon, which appeared again when Indo-Persian, Mughal, and Rajput art flourished side by side, is what we examine through the Watson collection.

The Indo-Persian style of painting flourished during the rule of the Delhi sultans (1206–1526). This period was not a uniform whole, but consisted of several Islamic dynasties of different ethnic groups, including Afghans, Turks, and Persians. The period of the great Mughals (1526–1540, 1555–1707), however, was ruled by a single dynasty, which was founded by a descendant of Timurlane and Chinghaiz Khan. The word Mughal is derived from Mongol. Even after the Mughals uprooted the sultans ruling from Delhi, the Deccani sultans continued ruling independently in the south for several generations.

Despite their different historical and geographical origins, the sultans and Mughals shared several prominent features. First, they were Muslims and came from the Middle East. Second, they appreciated the Islamic art and culture of Turkey, Persia, and other cultural centers of the Middle East and initially considered indigenous Indian art and culture to be inferior. Third, they eventually modified their attitude toward the native culture of their new homeland, and following an earlier pattern of South Asian history, partially accepted Indianization even as they continued fighting with Rajputs and other native rulers. Islam, however, remained almost untouched by Indic religious beliefs.

THE SULTANS

The Sultanate period began with Qutb-ud-din Aibak's enthronement as a first sultan of Delhi in 1206. He had been a general of the Muslim invaders from their capital city Ghor, located in modern Afghanistan. The invaders had been fighting with Indian kings for several decades. Toward the end of the twelfth century, a decisive battle was fought near Delhi, where the Muslim army defeated Prithviraj Chauhan, the Rajput king of Delhi and Ajmer. This victory helped the invaders to move further east, where they uprooted the kingdom of the Pāla dynasty of Bihar, the last Buddhist kingdom in India. During the invasion, many famous Buddhist monasteries such as Nalanda, Vikramaśīla, and Odāntapurī were destroyed. Universities and libraries associated with the monasteries were burned down, and thousands of Buddhist monks were killed. Some Buddhist monks fled to Nepal and Tibet. It is fortunate that some manuscripts that they carried with them have been preserved along with the preexisting collections of those Himalayan countries. Catalogue numbers 1 and 2 remind us of one such collection.

Because Qutb-ud-din Aibak served the sultan of Ghor as a slave for many years, the dynasty that he established around Delhi is known as the slave dynasty. Toward the end of his rule, he employed local artists to build a mosque that included the famous tower Qutb Minar in Delhi. Although this was the beginning of the Indo-Islamic art, no painting from the slave dynasty has been found. The slave dynasty is followed by four other Sultanate dynasties: the Khalji (1290–1320), Tughlaq (1321–1388), Sayyid (1414–1450), and Lodi (1450–1526) (Bhattacharya: 796). Thus the Muslim rule in India continued to expand.

During the second quarter of the fourteenth century, Muhammad Bin, a Delhi sultan of the Tughlaq dynasty, was able to rule almost the entire Indian subcontinent. The Rajput rulers of Rajasthan, however, maintained their independence. Only those nearest to Delhi were forced to pay tribute. These Rajput rulers who considered themselves kṣatriyas, the Hindu warriors, continued fighting Muslim power in India even in the Mughal period.

Muhammad Bin's Tughlaq empire did not last long. Even in his lifetime his empire began to disintegrate, and his successors could not recover the imperial territories. Thus Muslim and Hindu rulers refused to acknowledge the domain of the Delhi sultanate and began to establish an independent kingdom. It is in this milieu that significant sultanate paintings made a dramatic appearance. The paintings were commissioned not by the Delhi sultans but by the sultan of Malwa who ruled from the capital city, Mandu. These Malwa paintings (ca. 1500–1505) are the illuminated folios of the *Ni'mat-nama*, a sumptuously illustrated cookbook. The Watson collection fortunately includes a rare example of a *Ni'mat-nama*-style painting (cat. no. 9), although it is not a part of the cookbook.

Also in the Indian peninsula, as a result of the disintegration of the sultanate empire of Delhi, the Bahmani kingdom in Deccan and the Vijayanagara kingdom in South India were established. The Deccan was ruled by a Muslim dynasty and South India by Hindu kings, ensuring an inevitable struggle between these two neighboring kingdoms. The Bahmani kingdom further disintegrated into four Muslim kingdoms: Ahmednagar, Bidar, Golkunda, and Bijapur. These Muslim kingdoms were rivals, but they united against the rising Hindu power. They invaded the Vijayanagara kingdom as a unified force and successfully uprooted the last Hindu kingdom on the peninsula. The Deccan and South India remained under the rule of various sultans until the Mughal invasions in the sixteenth and seventeenth centuries. Each of these Muslim kingdoms of the Deccan developed a distinct style of miniature painting that lasted long after the kingdoms were gone. Thus the Deccani schools flourished side by side with Mughal and Rajput schools even in the nineteenth century. The Watson collection provides us with sumptuous examples of such Deccani miniature paintings (cat. nos. 124–128).

THE MUGHALS AND RAJPUTS

Babur (r. 1526–1530 in India), the founder of the Mughal dynasty, inherited a small kingdom around Samarqand as a descendant of Timurlane. Because of the rise of the Safavis in Persia and the Usbegs in central Asia Babur experienced difficulties ruling Samarqand. He lost his original homeland, but he firmly established himself in Kabul, a city in modern Afghanistan, not far from the Indian subcontinent. From there he invaded the northwestern part of the subcontinent and in 1526 defeated the last sultan of the Lodi dynasty. Threatened by this Mughal advance, Rana Sanga, the Rajput king of Mewar, invaded the newly established Mughal domain without much success. This was the first encounter between the Mughals and Rajputs. Even after the Mughal emperors successfully expanded their territory in the Gangetic valley by defeating the Afghan chiefs of Bihar and Bengal, the Rajput king who ruled Rajasthan and neighboring area remained a constant danger to the Mughal dynasty.

The word Rajput literally means "the prince." Historians believe them to be the descendants of the Huns, the seminomadic immigrants from central Asia who were responsible for weakening the Gupta empire (ca. 320–647). During the medieval period, they established themselves throughout northwest India. Gradually they became members of Hindu society and took responsibility for protecting the northwest of the subcontinent from the Muslim invaders. Although most of the time they were not militarily superior to Islamic forces in India, they never voluntarily accepted the suzerainty of either the sultans or the great Mughal emperors. Thus, in the political history of India, the Rajputs became famous for bravery and national pride. Socially, as kṣatriyas, Hindu warriors, they enjoy very high status in Indian society even today. In the artistic tradition, on the other hand, the word "Rajput" became synonymous with the particular style of painting that developed in their kingdom and neighboring regions.

Despite all these praiseworthy qualities, the Rajputs were unable to unify against their common enemy. The third Mughal emperor, Akbar (r. 1556–1605), understood this defect of Rajput power, and unlike his predecessors, Akbar made a diplomatic approach to the Rajputs. A shrewd monarch, he understood that he needed the support of the Rajputs and the Hindus in his empire to rule peacefully. Thus when the emperor established the Mughal atelier, he hired not only Muslim painters but also many Hindu and Jaina painters.

Akbar planned to reward the Rajputs who accepted his suzerainty and use them for the advantage of the empire. In accordance with his plan, he married the daughter of Bihar Mall, a prominent Rajput king of Jaipur (Amber) and received into his imperial service several members of the Jaipur royal family. The Rajput princess became the mother of Prince Salim, later to become the fourth great Mughal emperor, Jahangir (r. 1605–1627). This was the beginning of a trend that continued for several generations of the Mughal dynasty. "The happiness of marriage and the excellence of the Rajputs' loyal services led to the adoption by Akbar of the position of ruler over both Hindus and Muslims alike" (Smith: 340). After Jaipur, several other Rajput states such as Bundi, Bikaner, and Jodhpur submitted to the Mughal emperor without much resistance. The Rajput kings and other members of royal family were appointed to high positions, and Rajput princesses were received into the imperial harem with great respect. The princesses were allowed to practice Hindu rituals in the palace. Thus a new palatial culture began to emerge.

The Rajput kings of Mewar, however, continued fighting with the Mughals. Even after they lost their original capital, Chitor, and the second capital, Udaipur, the kings of Mewar resisted the Mughals. Akbar was unable to bring them into submission nor make them allies through intermarriage. The Mewar kings found nothing more repugnant than submitting to foreigners and allowing Mewar blood to be polluted by intermarriage with Mughals (Barrett and Gray: 133). Akbar's son Jahangir, with great military and diplomatic efforts, finally brought the Mewars under control. Even after defeating the Mewars in the battle, Jahangir wisely did not request Mewar princesses for the imperial harem and treated the prince Karan Singh with great honor when he visited the Mughal palace in 1614. Following this memorable visit the Mewars established friendly relations with the Mughals and began to enjoy a peaceful and luxurious life under the imperial support. The Mewar paintings in the Watson collection reflect this later phase of their history (cat. nos. 29–41).

The peaceful relationships between the Mughals and Rajputs significantly promoted the growth and wellbeing of both Mughal and Rajput cultures. Yet the last great Mughal emperor, Aurangzeb (r. 1658–1707), completely underestimated the value of such relationships. A devout Muslim, he dreamed of converting his entire empire to Islam and therefore his policies demonstrated his intolerance: He reimposed *jizya*, a tax on the non-Muslim subjects, which Akbar had abolished. Moreover, he forbade the employment of Hindus in high offices and destroyed many Hindu temples. As a result, even before Aurangzeb's death, the Mughal empire began to disintegrate. Not only the Rajputs but also other Hindu powers, such as the Marathas in the Deccan and the Sikhs in the Punjab, began to revolt.

Despite Aurangzeb's anti-Hindu policy, the merging process of Islamic and native artistic tradition continued even in the eighteenth century (cat. nos. 22, 24). Meanwhile Europeans were exploring the Indian subcontinent through the newly discovered sea route. Attracted by the wealth of India, first the Portuguese, then the Dutch, the English, and the French arrived in the subcontinent. The Mughal emperors from Akbar to Aurangzeb did not foresee the consequences of the European discovery of a sea route, although they were curious about European art and culture. For a time, the Mughal artists working for Akbar and Jahangir became fascinated with the European artistic tradition. They borrowed European elements such as chiaroscuro and other illusionistic techniques. Contemporary Rajput artists also adopted such European elements as a solar nimbus and flying angels through Mughal painting. Politically, however, the Mughals, Rajputs, and other Indian rulers never realized how the naval power and political ambition of the European countries would affect their own status in India. This weakness eventually paved the way for the British Raj in India.

Religion and Culture

The Watson collection consists of both religious and secular paintings. Even the secular paintings are created carefully to avoid conflict with religious belief system. Thus directly or indirectly, the paintings of the collection are associated with three Indian religions, Hinduism, Buddhism, and Jainism, and with Islam. I will describe these religions briefly, devoting special attention to the religious aspects that are closely related to the artistic tradition.

HINDUISM

Unlike many other religions, Hinduism, the most popular religion of India, does not have a particular founder. It originated in the beliefs of agrarian people and evolved, like a language, over a long period, gradually incorporating many elements from different sources, indigenous and foreign alike. But it has remained, throughout history, close to the agrarian society of India by showing great respect to the needs of the society. The agrarian elements of Hinduism are pan-Indic, shared by other Indian religions.

An important aspect of Hinduism, which brings the artistic tradition very close to religious culture, is the *pūjā* ritual in which a devotee stands or kneels in front of the icon of a deity and greets him by joining both hands in supplication. This ritual also involves bathing the image of the deity, circumambulating the shrine, and offering flowers and other items to a divine image. Without an image or symbol of a deity this ritual cannot be performed. Thus Hinduism is always interested in representing religious concepts in art. The main purpose of the ritual is to express devotion to the deity.

The *pūjā* ritual is also intertwined with the concept of *darśana*. Literally *darśana* simply means "an act or instance of seeing" and can be translated into English as "sight." It is, however, based on the deeply rooted Indic belief that a sight of something causes it to happen. A human being perceives a wide range of things not only in reality but also in dreams, mental pictures, chance appearances, and artistic representations. Irrespective of different media of appearances, a scene or a picture could be either auspicious or inauspicious. These phenomena are beyond human control; however, a human being can make the situation better by creating artistic representation of auspicious scenes, images of divine saviors and their legends. During the *pūjā* ritual, a devotee sits in front of the image and consciously observes the iconographical features of the deity with an expectation of good luck and blessing from the god. Such ritual observation is also known as *darśana*, a concept confusing even to scholars, who misunderstand its original significance and development. In a recent work Eck (Eck: 6–7) interprets the meaning of *darśana* as both the gaze of the god from heaven and the eye contact between a devotee and divine figure during the *pūjā* ritual. This view is partially correct, but the concept of *darśana* is not always confined within the boundary of religious belief or ritual. Even the sight or *darśana* of a secular scene such as a lotus blossom or a dying figure may affect the future of a viewer. Thus the desire for seeing auspicious things and avoiding inauspicious elements from a scene became the main focus of *darśana*. With this desire the concept of *darśana* became an integral part of the *pūjā* ritual. This is indeed a secondary development. It is even possible that *pūjā* is the ritualization of the *darśana* theory, on which a reader will find more in the section "Auspicious Symbols." The original significance of *darśana* never disappeared even after such ritualization.

In addition to *pūjā* and *darśana*, yet another important concept frequently depicted in Indian art is the theory of reincarnation. According to this theory, Viṣṇu, the protector of the universe, incarnates in the earth whenever he senses that the world is endangered. Once he incarnated as Rāma (cat. nos. 66, 129) because he learned that the ten-headed demon Rāvaṇa was harassing innocent people. Although Hindus believed that Buddha Śākyamuni was the fifth incarnation of Viṣṇu, Buddhists did not accept it. In a sense, the theory of incarnation is not only a religious belief but also a mechanism for incorporating divergent belief systems into Hinduism. Furthermore, the political history of India reveals that sometimes politicians used the concept of reincarnation as propaganda. The Gupta emperors considered themselves incarnations of Viṣṇu by relating their imperial career to a Vaisnavite myth in which Viṣṇu incarnated himself as a boar to protect the Earth Goddess when she was drowned in the deep ocean. The Guptas claimed that just as the boar Viṣṇu had saved the Earth

Goddess, they had saved the entire world from drowning into the ocean of chaos.

After the Gupta period (ca. 320–647) the story of Kṛṣṇa became more popular than other legends of Viṣṇu's incarnation. Although the nucleus of Kṛṣṇa's cult can be found even in the Vedic texts, it went through many stages of development before Kṛṣṇa was adopted in his classic form—that of a divine flute-player who dallies with milkmaids in a pastoral setting.

The *Bhagavadgītā*, a work composed around the first century A.D. consisting of Kṛṣṇa's teaching, relates that he is the cosmic man who represents not only space and time but also the cosmic soul designated as *brahman*. He controls and regulates every activity of the universe including human destiny, *karma*. According to later texts, such as the *Harivaṃśa* (ca. 500) and the *Bhāgavata Purāṇa* (ca. 900), Kṛṣṇa's was also a great hero fighting against demons and a romantic lover who actively participated in the spring festival Holi, which is a main subject of many Rajput paintings (cat. no. 63). These elements are completely missing in the early text.

In ancient India, spring festivals were celebrated in the honor of Kāma, the god of love. In the medieval period, the romantic aspect of Kṛṣṇa's character became so popular that he replaced Kāma as the god of love. With this development, the vernal festival of Holi became a part of Kṛṣṇa's dalliance with milkmaids. This does not mean that Kṛṣṇa gave up his earlier role; he was still believed to be the cosmic soul. This created a contradiction: How could the romantic lover also be the supreme god? Hindu texts resolve this problem by considering the cosmic soul masculine, and the human soul, which is inferior to the cosmic soul, feminine. Thus Kṛṣṇa's dalliance with milkmaids is interpreted as the symbolic expression of the union of the masculine cosmic soul with the feminine human soul. Therefore, in the cult of Kṛṣṇa , a devotee often expresses his devotion to the god just as a Hindu wife does to her husband.

The Rajput rulers of Rajasthan and the Punjab hills found this Kṛṣṇa cult appealing for several reasons. Like Kṛṣṇa , they were warriors constantly fighting with neighboring kings and Muslim rulers. When they were free from warfare, they spent most of their free time in their harem, a life that was similar to Kṛṣṇa's affairs with milkmaids. Male polygamy was accepted. The expression of devotion to a king as if he were a divine figure was another aspect of Rajput culture that resembled Kṛṣṇa's cult in which *bhakti* or "devotion" always plays primary role. Because of this connection between devotion or *bhakti* and royal cult, the concept of *darśana* also became part of palatial culture. A loyal subject regularly visited the palace gate or the audience hall to express devotion by doing *darśana* of the ruling monarch, who made a ritual appearance. This ancient palatial custom continued even in the medieval period and was adopted by both the Mughals and Rajputs.

The Rajput kings never directly claimed themselves to be the incarnation of Viṣṇu, as the Gupta emperors did. But in their miniature paintings, Kṛṣṇa is often depicted as a Rajput king, and the reflection of Rajput lifestyle is always clearly visible even though the paintings are supposedly based on Kṛṣṇa's legend.

In addition to Vīṣṇu and his incarnation, the cult of Śiva and Pārvatī also plays an important role in Hinduism. According to popular Hindu belief, the Vedic god Brahmā is the creator, Viṣṇu the protector, and Śiva the destroyer. However, the worshipers of Śiva believe that he is all: creator, protector, and destroyer. The duality of creation and destruction of the world, which are happening simultaneously, make up his cosmic dance. This Saivite concept is very popular in the Deccan and South India. Śiva's cosmic dance is the main theme of these regions. But it is rarely seen in north Indian art, and this author does not know any example of a dancing Śiva in Rajput painting.

Different Saivite stories were prevalent in northern India, including the Punjab hills where Śiva and his consort Pārvatī are depicted as an auspicious loving couple living happily in the caves of the Himalayan mountains (cat. no. 120). Śiva is a great god endowed with supreme power and capable of reducing the entire universe into ashes just by opening his third eye. In northern Saivism, however, Śiva is not always superior to Pārvatī. She is the embodiment of *śakti*, the cosmic energy, considered to be the female principal. Without *śakti*, Śiva—the male principal—is nothing but a corpse (cat. no. 111). This concept is much more frequently depicted in the art of the Punjab hills than in the works of Rajasthan. For an unknown reason, the Rajputs of Rajasthan did not find this concept as appealing as the cult of Kṛṣṇa, perhaps because the Rajputs appreciated the masculine quality of Kṛṣṇa more than the feminine energy of the *śakti* cult.

BUDDHISM AND JAINISM

The gradual decline and disappearance of Buddhism from mainland India and continuity of Jainism in the subcontinent play significant roles as a prologue to the history of Mughal and Rajput painting. Fortunately the Watson collection does have some examples of Buddhist and Jaina paintings. Therefore we will briefly discuss Buddhism and Jainism to show their impact, or lack of impact, on the development of Mughal and Rajput painting.

Both Buddhism and Jainism were established toward the end of the sixth century A.D. by two princes of the Gangetic valley who abandoned their luxurious lives residing in palaces to become homeless wanderers in search of truth beyond the phenomenon of this world. They were contemporaneous and shared many aspects of an Indian way of thinking. Buddhism was, however, more flexible than Jainism. For unknown reasons, even before the Gupta period (ca. 320–647), the popularity of Buddhism began to decline in India. After the Muslim invasions in Bihar and Bengal in the late twelfth century and early thirteenth century, Buddhism almost completely disappeared from the Indian plains. However, it managed to survive in remote Himalayan regions such as Ladakh and Nepal. Jainism, on the other hand, did not spread even in the Himalayan region, perhaps because it was too cold for naked or scantily dressed Jaina monks. But in many parts of tropical areas of the subcontinent, such as Gujarat and Malwa, Jainism continues to flourish even today.

These events of religious history are related to the history of Indian paintings either directly or indirectly. When the Mughal emperor Akbar enthusiastically hired local artists from many different regions to work in his newly established atelier, he employed Jaina artists. Their prominent stylistic features are visible in the early works of the Akbari atelier. By this time, the Buddhist tradition of wall, manuscript, or thanka paintings had been completely forgotten in the Indian plains. Muslim authors of the Mughal period made no reference to Buddhist artists. However, in Himalayan regions such as Ladakh and Nepal, the Buddhist artistic tradition affiliated with the earlier tradition of Buddhist art was still active. The Mughal emperor Akbar, who was not familiar with this Buddhist tradition, hired no Buddhist artists for his atelier. Thus, the establishment and development of the Mughal school of art is unrelated to Buddhist art. If the Mughal school has any link with the ancient art of India, that link could be only Jaina art. The Rajput artists of Rajasthan were not familiar with Buddhist art either because the most popular Indic religions during the thirteen to the nineteenth centuries in India were Hinduism, mainly the cult of Kṛṣṇa, and Jainism. It was in this ambiance that Islam made its forceful presence known and remained an effective religious force in many areas of the subcontinent.

ISLAM

The people of the Arabian town of Mecca were worshipers of 360 idols and a huge black stone, the Kabba. When Mohammad, founder of Islam, preached against the idols, he so angered the people of the region he eventually had to flee from the town in 622 A.D. This flight is known as Hijrat in Arabic, and the Muslim calendar begins from this date.

This event seems to contain the core explanation for the Islamic prohibition of making images. However, the Koran itself does not contain any clear statement about this prohibition. According to some scholars only later Islamic texts such as the *Hadith* pronounced that an artist should not represent a living creature because making a representation is almost like creation, and only God has that right. For this reason Islamic art concentrates more on ornamentation such as arabesques and floral scrolls than iconography.

When Akbar established his atelier and encouraged artists to represent mythical and real events, mullahs, Muslim religious teachers, were not happy with this imperial interest. Akbar, who was not an orthodox Muslim, tried to establish a new religion called the Din Ilahi, "Divine Faith." Only when Aurangzeb came into power did he reverse the process and cease supporting the artists of the Mughal atelier in order to show his belief in Islam. Conflict between Islam and artistic creation can be found in other countries as well. However, Islamic artists found many different ways to express their ideas in art without directly confronting the Islamic rules.

This brief discussion on Islam may suffice to show the difference between the Islamic approach to art and Indic concept of *darśana* and *pūjā*.

Auspicious Symbols

Archer and some other art historians think that Indian miniatures are filled with hidden sexual symbolism such as a peacock that represents an absent lover and entwining trees that signify lovers embracing intimately (Archer 1976: 103). In opposition to this view, Barrett and Gray believe the paintings have an explicit sexual purpose:

> They [sexual moods and temperaments expressed in a miniature] appealed, one supposes, to the owner of the zenana, whose interest in women must have required continuous stimulation, and even more to the women who were presumably required to study a variety of moods to secure the casual attention of their lords. . . . The content of the picture has of course to be experienced: it cannot be explained and can so easily be explained away. It is important however to emphasize that the miniatures are not to be 'read' by symbolism, sexual or any other. . . (Barrett and Gray: 16).

Because this view has prevailed, studying the symbolism of miniature painting has been virtually abandoned, and in recent years more attention has been given to stylistic analysis than symbolic significance. Admittedly Indian miniatures do reflect contemporaneous life style and palatial culture as Barrett and Gray suggested. However, a comparative study of these miniatures and ancient Indian art reveals that many aspects of Rajput art and concepts were not an innovation of the time. Instead they were either a direct inheritance or gradual development of an earlier tradition in which even stylistic elements are intertwined with symbolism. Sexual symbolism, indeed, played an important role throughout the history of Indian art, although not so much as Archer suggested but as an expression of opulence, fertility, and happiness. I believe that the expression of Indian miniatures can be understood more correctly if we see them not from our modern perspective but from the viewpoint of the old agrarian culture of traditional India.

THE CONCEPT OF *DARŚANA*

The agrarian people of the Indian subcontinent believed that everything related to fertility was auspicious. They also believed that the indications of the growing seasons, such as the croaking of frogs and the growth of fresh vegetation, were not the effects of, for example, the arrival of the rainy season but the causes. This belief is first mentioned in the fifteenth century B.C. Vedic Sanskrit work. It also appears in fifth-century and eighteenth-century A.D. astrological texts. These texts clearly tell us that the appearance of the frogs on the ground and their croaking brings rain and the sight of a fresh green tree causes adequate rainfall and successful harvest (Vajracharya 1997: 4–20; *Bṛhatsaṃhitā* 24.19; 29.14). Similarly people thought the playful behavior of elephants and peacocks at the beginning of the rainy season caused the seasonal rain. This reverse perspective is the origin of the *darśana* theory positing that seeing is the cause and happening is the effect. Such reverse perspective is technically designated in Sanskrit literature as *nimittadarśana*, "seeing cause." Thus the sight of a fresh and green tree in reality or in artistic representation is auspicious.

Thus a believer of this concept of *darśana* expects to see auspicious things not only inside the shrine but everywhere. Indian art is created with this expectation. Because of this, quite often, Indian art cannot be classified either as religious or as secular. (See Dehejia: 18–19, 64-66 for contrasting view). A voluptuous female figure that stands seductively on the walls of the Buddhist, Jaina, and Hindu shrines or at the both edges of Jaina manuscript illumination does not have anything to do with those Indic high religions. But it is closely associated with the *darśana* concept of the agrarian society. As we will see shortly, this society believed that an artistic representation of a skinny female figure (instead of the familiar voluptuous figure) caused scarcity and drought.

The earliest epigraphic evidence for such a concept of *darśana* is found in the third century B.C. Aśokan inscription, which refers to the auspicious sight of a sculptural representation of an elephant. The exact word given in the Aśokan inscription is *hassida(sa)na,* a compound word synonymous with Sanskrit *hastidarśana* "seeing an elephant" (Vajracharya 1999: 72, 76). Apparently this was a generic term applicable to other auspicious animals as well. The display of sculptures of such animals is designated in the same inscription as *divya rūpa* "divine figure." The term *rūpa* has the double meaning "appearance" and "artistic representation." As we know from Pāli literature, an art student goes to school to learn *rūpa*.

There is an ancient verse, which also helps us understand the significance of "seeing" in Indian tradition. The verse is found both in Sanskrit and Pāli literature and is still popular in most parts of the Indian subcontinent. It can be translated loosely in the following words:

> May all be happy. May all be healthy. May all see auspicious scenes (*bhadrāṇi*) so that nobody will suffer.

Mainstream Indic art, including the early Buddhist stone sculptures and the Rajput miniature paintings, is executed with great deal of attention paid to the significance of such auspicious scenes. Except for the main symbol or icons in the Buddhist or Hindu shrine, most of the artistic representations such as the sensuous happy couple, an elephant emerging from a lotus pond, or a dancing peacock around the shrine are not necessarily created for worship. But they are certainly for *darśana*. This statement, however, should not give the readers an impression that Indian art is nothing but a collection of good omens. Judging from available artistic examples, which include a wide range of subjects, we should understand the word *darśana* more correctly as a sight devoid of inauspicious element rather than auspicious sight. Thus visual motifs and compositions that can not be classified by the dichotomy of auspicious or inauspicious scenes were permitted to be included in the artistic repertoire of classical art and Rajput painting.

Illuminated manuscripts of omens did provide guidance to the Indian artists. During the medieval period, when the Mughals and Rajputs were ruling India, the intellectuals of the subcontinent became more intrigued with the concept of *darśana*. Unknown Rajput authors and artists compiled illustrated manuscripts comprising an elaborate list of auspicious and inauspicious sights. Although several copies of such manuscripts have been found from Rajasthan to Nepal, they are not published yet. One illustrated folio of such a manuscript from Rajasthan was published more than two decades ago (Portland: 22). An entire text from Nepal is currently preserved in the Los Angeles County Museum of Art (Pal 1985: 222). In this text, just as in the third century B.C. Aśokan inscription, the word *darśana* is used to indicate the significance of seeing. More important is the fact that here the word does not imply the *pūjā* ritual; hence the text is helpful in understanding the wider concept of *darśana*. Guided by such a concept, just like the classical artists the Rajput painters constantly attempted to avoid the inauspicious element in their works. Rajput paintings are not intended for *pūjā,* but they are for *darśana*. This is the main link between classical Indic art and Rajput painting. Because of this unbroken link, in the entire history of mainstream Indian art the representation of old age, suffering, scarcity, emaciated figures, and death is difficult to find. Compare this phenomenon of Indian art with the statement from the well-known Sanskrit text *Viṣṇudhamottara Purāṇa:*

> An auspicious painting brings good fortune to the country, the artist, and the king. . . . The scenes associated with a battle, a cremation ground, pitiful condition, death, suffering, and arousing contempt are inauspicious. They should not be depicted in a house. (34. 14)

This Sanskrit text, which is actually a manual of Indian art and iconography, was compiled around seventh century A.D. Some ideas recorded in the text, however, remained popular throughout history. Readers may find yet another passage from the same manual equally interesting and informative regarding the Indian view about a painting:

> An auspicious painting . . . promotes long life, leads to glory or distinction, brings prosperity, and increases the harvest. (38. 24–25)

Such expressions repeatedly appear in this text and in other art manuals of India. It is, indeed, difficult for us to see the relationship of a painting with longevity and harvest, for we consider a painting an artistic representation rendered mainly for viewing pleasure. But this textual evidence testifies that traditional India created a painting not simply as a representation but a powerful expression that could alter the future of a viewer. Indian artists believed that a work of art, directly or indirectly associated with harvest, fertility, and happiness is worth seeing. In accordance to this reverse perspective the representation of lush vegetation, vivacious life, and the dalliance of an amorous couple that we see both in classical art and Rajput painting are considered auspicious and worth seeing. Likewise kingship and royal insignia are also listed in Sanskrit texts as auspicious. The main reason again is fertility. An Indian king is a supernatural being capable of providing his subjects with prosperity. He is a rainmaker and everything associated with rain is divine and auspicious.

Admittedly, there are some exceptions in Rajput painting. Of them are the scenes of hunting and occasional representation of battle with a noticeable emphasis on bloodshed, both of which are almost unknown to classical Indian art. They began to appear in Rajput painting (cat. no. 51) only after the local artists came in close contact with foreign and sophisticated Indian art such as Persian and Mughal. Art is like a living language, full of rules and exceptions partially as a result of ongoing exchange of ideas with other artistic traditions.

Figure 1. The Niranjana River, on the east gateway pillar of the Great Stupa, Sanchi, ca. 1st century B.C. After photographs by Messrs Johnston and Hoffman in Benjamin Rowland, *The Art and Architecture of India: Buddhist, Hindu, Jain* (Baltimore: Penguin Books, 1974), fig. 47.

Rajput painters, like native speakers, expressed their views intuitively and beautifully without thinking what grammatical rule guided their language of artistic expression. Most Rajput paintings, however, remained closely associated with the concept of *darśana*.

LOTUSES, BANANA PLANTS, MANGO TREES, AND LUSH VEGETATION

Perhaps the most popular Indic symbol is a lotus, which is ubiquitous in Buddhist, Jaina, and Hindu art. Just as in the first-century B.C. stone relief (fig. 1) so also in the eighteenth-century Rajput art we see the symbolic lotus flower blooming in the river (cat. no. 32), although in reality it is a perennial flower that grows in the mud and water. During the dry summer season it remains dormant, but starts growing immediately after the monsoonal rain and flowers when the rice is ready to harvest. The main symbolic significance of the lotus is the availability of rainwater for crops, which in traditional Indian culture always means prosperity and wealth. This is why in Sanskrit a lotus, Kamalā, means goddess of wealth.

Although this agrarian symbolism originally had nothing to do with the high religious thought of Hinduism and Buddhism, as these religions evolved, the lotus was incorporated into their myth and belief systems. Thus in Hinduism the lotus goddess became Viṣṇu's spouse Lakṣmī; in Buddhism sometimes the lotus represented the Buddha himself while at other times the entire Buddhist universe. Even after these developments, the original symbolism of the lotus never completely disappeared from the Indian mind. Even in eighteenth- or nineteenth-century Rajput paintings, a lotus remained an auspicious symbol. In numerous examples of Rajput miniatures, Kṛṣṇa and Rādhā are shown walking on a bank of a lotus pond holding fresh lotus flower in their hands (cat. no. 73). The shape of the eyes of Kṛṣṇa and Rādhā are rendered in the imitation of a lotus (cat. nos. 41, 73), and the soles of their feet often resemble the color of the flower almost exactly as described in literature. Furthermore, Kṛṣṇa's headgear is often decorated with lotuses, and he wears a garland of lotuses. The reason for such overwhelming attention given to this flower is its original association with fertility, a symbolism that survived unconsciously in the minds of the agrarian society of India. For clarity, let's examine a counter example. Mainstream Indian artists never depicted a dry lake of the summer when the lotuses were still dormant, although such scene can be found described in Sanskrit literature. They believed a scene representing drought to be inauspicious. Its sight, even in the artistic representation, might bring bad luck to the viewer. Because of the potency of such images, conversely, scenes of fertility and prosperity are always auspicious.

The same hidden rule also applies to the representation of banana plants, mango trees, and other green vegetation. Many examples from the Watson collection depict flowering banana plants in the middle of the lush vegetation (cat. nos. 32, 42, 47) and mango trees with fresh leaves turning pink or scarlet (cat. nos. 32, 42). Such depictions of these fruit-trees are not a Rajput invention but date back at least to the first century B.C. Although we do not have any painting from such an early period, in many cases if an artist translates the stone reliefs of Sanchi and Amāravatī into paintings, thematically they would not be much different from Mewar or Bundi paintings reproduced in this catalogue. Both these sculptures and paintings are based on the Indic artistic theory that "the seasonal phenomena should be represented with the depiction of (seasonal) flowers and fruits and [the periodic] sexual excitement (*mada*) of creatures." (The *Viṣṇudharmottara Purāṇa* 42. 80)

In India banana and mango trees grow through the rainy season in June or July, and their fruiting time is toward the end of the season, around September. This is the period often designated as *sahakāra* or *sahakāla*, which has a double meaning, "mango time" or "cooperative time." When food is plentiful, people are friendly. However, during a drought or famine, people become too selfish to cooperate. According to a popular Sanskrit verse called *subhāṣita*, "during the cooperative time when mango trees are weighted down with fruit, everybody is equal in virtue (*samānadharmāṇaḥ*) and everybody is plump." Thus the time of prosperity and abundance is expressed in Indian art as sometimes showing the mango trees either bearing fresh leaves or laden with ripe mangos and at other times as indicating cooperativeness by representing an entire group of human figures with identical physiognomy. Such an approach is a ubiquitous feature of Indian art. It can be seen in the first century B.C. Buddhist sculptures of Bharhut (fig. 2) and also in the seventeenth- or eighteenth-century Rajput paintings (cat. nos. 28, 32, 71, 92). Art historians understand that studying such physiognomy is helpful for classifying styles of Indian art because the artists who belong to a particular school or region utilize the same physiognomy throughout their works. This is not, however, exclusively a stylistic element but also the symbolic expression of the cooperativeness of prosperous times resulting from a successful growth and harvest. In other words, such treatment is not intended to capture earthly phenomena realistically. Instead they are powerful symbols capable of creating prosperous times.

The authors of astrological texts also relate that a luxuriant tree with plenty of leaves without any gap among them (*nicchidrapatra*) forecasts seasonal rain and bountiful harvest (*Bṛhatsaṃhitā* 29. 14). A careful observation of Indian art reveals that such a concept is literally translated into art. To indicate the luxuriant growth of the tree Indian artists often encircle the branches of the tree with a heavy outline or shadelike thick contour. Once again this element is not entirely stylistic but symbolic as well. Such a treatment of a tree is ubiquitous after it appears in the first century B.C. Amāravatī sculpture representing Buddha's bodhi tree (Huntington: fig.

Figure 2. The Buddha's Worship, a railing from Bharhut Stupa, ca. 100–80 B.C. Reddish brown sandstone. Indian Museum, Calcutta. Photograph by John C. Huntington. Compliments of The Huntington Archive, The Ohio State University, Columbus

5.37). It continued not only in eleventh century Buddhist manuscript painting from Nepal (see fig. 10) but also in early seventeenth-century Gujarati painting and nineteenth-century Pahari painting (cat. nos. 27, 123) with very little stylistic variation. On the contrary a leafless tree, which was considered unworthy to be seen, is difficult to find in mainstream Indian art. An interesting example is a painting from the Watson collection that belongs to a series depicting the phenomena of various seasons of India (cat. no. 67). This particular example represents the dry summer season. Since it is inauspicious to show the drought that occurs during this season, the artist represented the drought in the remote background where the trees are dry and animals seek shelter from the sun. But in the middle ground of the painting he shows lush vegetation, including the banana plants, to make scenes of drought acceptable to Rajput viewers. Rajput artists gave more attention to auspicious scenes than to describing the subject as it was.

ELEPHANTS, PEACOCKS, AND CRANES

These creatures have one thing in common. During the dry summer season, they remain inactive, but when the rainy season arrives, they become energetic. The rainy season is also the mating time of these creatures. The appearance of the animals and the playful behavior of their mating time are not, however, considered the effect of the rainy season but the cause of the desirable natural phenomena. In Sanskrit texts an elephant is identified with the elephant-headed Hindu god Gaṇeśa, who is renowned for providing good luck and prosperity to his devotees (cat. no. 2b). The divine quality of the creature, however, is derived from the association of its life cycle with Indian seasons. The thickness of an elephant's skin prevents it from perspiring properly in summer. Therefore, this animal hides itself in mud and water to escape from the summer heat. However, the availability of the mud holes depends on the arrival of the monsoon rain, which is notoriously unpredictable. If the drought continues for an unusually long time, elephants suffer so badly that even their lives are in danger. They patiently endure the pain and anticipate the rainy season. When it finally arrives, they are the happiest creatures in the world. Their happiness reassured the Indian of the routine arrival of the monsoon. Thus the elephant became an auspicious figure capable of making rain, which explains the popularity of animals in Indian art.

In paintings in the Watson collection elephants often appear in the middle of the royal processions (cat. nos. 35, 50, 109). The royal elephant is always the center of attraction, and his huge body dominates most of the painting. Such pictorial representation of a procession is significant for two different reasons, royal presence and the auspicious nature of the elephant.

As we know from the *Hastyāyurveda* 4. 22, a fifth- or sixth-century treatise on elephants' health and wellbeing, people in ancient India worshiped an elephant for rain and successful harvest because they believed that the elephant is a cloud. Therefor, either at the end of the dry summer season or in the very beginning of the rainy season, they organized the annual procession of an elephant, which they identified as Megha, "cloud." For the procession, the elephant was decorated with beautiful cloths and ornaments. The physician of the elephant, king, royal priest, musicians, and dancers took part in the procession and walked around the city chanting indecent words instead of a mantra. The main purpose of the procession was to induce monsoonal rain. The author of the text prescribes that such event should be observed once a year to secure the seasonal rain and the growth of the seeds and to avoid the calamity of a famine.

Originally this was an agrarian ritual, unrelated to any high religious sects. However, in secondary development, the elephant's procession became part of the Buddhist ritual. Therefore, Buddhist authors interpreted its significance in a slightly different way. The *Mahāvaṃśaṭīkā* relates that during the procession when a mahout put the Buddha's reliquary on the elephant's head, the divine animal realized the significance of the event and trumpeted loudly to show his happiness. Then immediately it rained (Sohoni: 339). Likewise, in Rajput painting the original meaning of the elephant became intertwined with the significance of kingship. Indian kings took great pride in their fighting elephants. In the paintings they are often depicted among the various royal paraphernalia such as the umbrella, the flag, and the yak tail. Due to the royal association all these items are considered auspicious (cat. no. 50).

Despite the elephant's association with kingship, the animal's legendary capacity of making rain was never forgotten. The Watson collection has a nineteenth-century example (cat. no. 40) that shows a huge, dark elephant surrounded by the soldiers and retainers holding various regalia. The king and his attendant are seated on their respective howdahs, and the mahout is immediately below the royal seat. A superscription identifies the king as Sambhusyangh (Sambhu Singh) and the elephant as Bādalisanagar (Bādal-śṛṅgāra). The elephant's name Bādal-śṛṅgāra, which literally means "cloud ornament," is significant. He was so named because he was believed to be the symbolic representation of the rain cloud as described in the above-mentioned classical text on elephant's health and wellbeing. In order to indicate its identity with the rain cloud and divine nature, the elephant is shown floating in the air. Since the legs of the elephant are not touching the ground, the feet of the soldiers walking on the other side of the elephant are visible. Actually, the elephant hovers like a dark cloud. Undoubtedly the pictorial representation of the procession was considered auspicious. Although elephants are frequently depicted in Mughal painting, they are not there treated as supernatural animals (cat. nos. 18, 19).

If there are symbolic creatures shown more frequently in Indian paintings than elephants, they are the peacock and white cranes. Peacocks are everywhere: perched on the branches of flowering trees (cat. no. 93), at the corner of a flat roof (cat. no. 81), or dancing on top of the horizontal pole of a swing (cat. no. 92). These birds are indeed very beautiful, but their popularity in Indian art is inspired more by their symbolic significance than their beauty. Archer's view that a peacock or a crane symbolically represents unappeased desire or an absent lover (Portland: 103) is difficult to accept, for no logical explanation supports such interpretation. Besides, these birds are shown not only when the lovesick heroine is alone but also when she is united with her lover. In fact the birds herald the rainy season. Peacocks make loud noises for three months of the rainy season, June, July, and August. In Sanskrit this period is designated as *kālāpaka*, "time of peacock's screech." A viewer who is familiar with this natural phenomenon can hear the loud noise of peacocks as he glances at the Rajput paintings in the collection (cat. nos. 81, 92, 93).

Likewise the white cranes are associated with the rainy season. They are often shown flying in a row immediately bellow the dark monsoon clouds. Such depictions of birds go back to classical period, as we know from the description of a contemporaneous painting given in early Sanskrit drama such as the *Mṛcchakaṭika* "Clay Cart" (5.1–6). In Sanskrit literature, the birds are designated as *valākās* who mate in their flight as they become excited by the sound of thunder of monsoonal cloud. Here it should be pointed out that the *cātaka* birds, identified as *Cucculus melanoleucus*, are not differentiated from the white cranes in Rajput painting. In Sanskrit poetic conventions (*kavisamaya*) the *cātaka* birds are described as unusual creatures, who do not drink ground water but subsist on raindrops. For this reason in literature the rainy season is known as "*cātaka*'s delight." This convention is frequently depicted in Rajput painting where we see white cranelike birds drinking pearl white raindrops in the middle of sky. Moreover, geese and swans of classical art and literature are also depicted in Rajput art as white cranes perhaps because the cranes symbolically represent aquatic birds. Like elephants and peacocks all these aquatic birds are worth seeing because of their association with rain and fertility.

Not every object that is auspicious has to be related to the rainy season. Spring is the other planting season in India. The phenomena of this season are also considered worthy of viewing. Holi, the festival of color, is a vernal celebration, and Rajput painters never tired of describing the scene of the festival in association with Kṛṣṇa. Most of the festivals of the spring such as the swing festival are also celebrated in the rainy season. In Pāli literature the spring season is described as if it is the second autumn that follows the rainy season. However, India gave more attention to the rainy season than the spring season. A prominent feature of Indian life is the custom of *varṣāvāsa* "rainy season retreat," when Hindu, Buddhist, and Jaina monks and devotees perform special rituals for three to four months. Initially this custom was not entirely religious. It also affected the annual cycle of Indian kings and their army who refrained from military activity during the retreat and were allowed to indulge themselves. Thus, for the Rajput warriors the rainy season became almost synonymous with a time for sensual indulgence. The reflection of such a life style can be found even in a statement of a modern Indian artist, trained in the Rajput tradition of painting. The artist describes his own work in following words:

> The man is a prince. As the dark monsoon clouds gather over distant hills he stands on terrace of palace, embracing his lover. Lightning has startled the white cranes and they are flying wildly up into black sky. That peacock roosting beneath the terrace will soon go off and dance joyously in the forest; peacocks always dance at start of the monsoon,

Figure 3. Lovers, Ajanta Cave I, mural on east wall, ca. 6th century. AAAUM, University of Michigan, Ann Arbor

> though, to be honest, I have never seen them do it. Maids carry the prince's fans and rose water pipe. The female musicians downstairs are serenading the rains and also our amorous couple. When the rain begins the couple will retire to the small pavilion and make love; as you see, a bed awaits them, the red counterpane signifying bliss. Down in the garden is a lotus pond and tree filled with birds. Parakeets are eating the ripening mangoes. In the valley, directly beneath the black cloud, stands a small town, part of the prince's estate. On the green hills all around cowherds are hurrying their animals to shelter. . . . But there's no rain. . . . Every single element in the picture is speaking of rain. The rain itself would be superfluous (as quoted in Frater: 165).

Due to such significance of rain the subcontinent itself is named after the rainy season. The Sanskrit name Bhāratavarṣa literally means "the Monsoonal land of the Bhārata dynasty." The spring season is regular, predictable, and taken for granted. But the arrival of the rainy season is extremely unpredictable, requiring rituals to be performed and prayers to be made to divinities. Therefore, the fertility symbols are more closely related with the rainy season than the spring. Either way the hidden symbolism of fertility is the driving force that inspires the Indian artists to represent repeatedly the phenomena of the growing seasons.

THE AMOROUS COUPLE AND THE SENSE OF INNER VITALITY

The popular theme associated with the dalliance of an amorous couple is designated in Sanskrit as *mithuna*, the sense of inner vitality as *prāṇa*, a ubiquitous artistic element often used to enliven the representation of living beings including the amorous couple.

Perhaps the most celebrated pictorial representation of the dalliance of an amorous couple in India is the fifth-century A.D. Ajanta wall painting that depicts a young couple seated on a stone slab. The man holds a goblet and the woman leans languorously on his body (fig. 3). The firm flesh and sensuous bodies of the couple emphasize their youthful appearance. In sculpture, a much earlier representation of this theme appears on the architrave of a gate of the first-century B.C. Buddhist *stūpa* shrine in Sanchi (Kramrisch: fig. 21). It shows a handsome couple in their prime seated on a mountain rock watching antelopes and peacocks. Another Sanchi sculpture represents a landscape of a mountainous region with natural fountain and a lake (Agrawala: fig. 29). In this landscape background, several men and women either rest on a rock or ride elephants in the middle of a lake in the atmosphere of a pleasure excursion. This represents a a prosperous time, perhaps, as a scholar has indicated, a mythical event (Agrawala: 21). It is depicted on the gate of the Buddhist shrine mainly because it symbolizes happiness and prosperity. This we know conversely from the description of a chaotic time mentioned in the well-known Sanskrit epic *Rāmāyaṇa* 2.67. The epic relates that during anarchical chaotic times clouds do not release heavenly water on the earth with lighting and thunder. Agriculture dwindles, people, including spouses, behave strangely, and young men do not go to the forest with their women to spend their leisure time, as they were accustomed to do in better times. Clearly, the scenes depicted on the Sanchi sculptures indicate an unchaotic prosperous time known to Sanskrit authors as *subhikṣa*. This significant term is the creation of the wandering Indian yogis who survived by begging for food; the term literally means "excellent [time] for begging." The antonym for this word is *durbhikṣa*, "the bad time for begging," which is always used in Sanskrit and other Indian languages for scarcity, drought, and famine. Nowhere in Indian art do we see the description of *durbhikṣa*. In a sense, the art of India is the visual expression of abundance.

When the theme of amorous couples was incorporated in the Hindu iconography, it became the auspicious image of the divine couple of Śiva and Pārvatī. A miniature painting from the Punjab hills in the Watson collection depicts the divine couple resting in front of a cave of the Himalayan mountains (cat. no. 120). Because the iconographical elements of Śiva—the trident, bull, and the third eye—are shown there so emphatically, the painting prods us to find out its relation with Saivite legend. But the theme of the amorous couple, although in disguise, is clearly discernable. This view is particularly true because the scene of an amorous couple predates the first appearance of Śiva and Pārvatī in Hindu iconography.

The Sanskrit word for the dalliances of amorous couples is *śṛṅgāra*. During the classical period, in literature and rhetorical compositions the word *"śṛṅgāra"* is used for the erotic sentiment, which is one of nine sentiments such as heroic, comic, terrible, etc. The authors of such literature argue that erotic sentiment is very different from a vulgar description of sex. In spite of this, the original meaning of the word is closely associated with animal reproduction and fertility. An animal becomes mature and capable of producing offspring only when its horns begin to emerge. The animal's sexual behavior indicating maturity is *śṛṅgāra* "having horns." (Compare the English word "horny.") Therefore in several Sanskrit stories we see the close association of *śṛṅga,* "a horn," with sexuality and fertility. For example, the name of the legendary figure Ṛsyaśṛṅga means "antelope's horn." Ṛsyaśṛṅga, a son of an ascetic brought up in his father's isolated hermitage, was totally ignorant about the opposite sex. Such ignorance was considered an abnormality of cosmic order. Because of this cosmic disorder, there was drought in India for a long period. The drought ended only after Ṛsyaśṛṅga was introduced to females (*Vālmikīya Rāmāyaṇa* 1.9–10). Another literary source that supports the relationship between fertility and *śṛṅgāra;* is the mythical ascetic known as *Śṛṅga,* who is still worshiped in many places in the subcontinent for rain and fertility.

For this reason, in the Indian artistic tradition, *śṛṅgāra* does not simply imply erotic sentiment but also sexuality. In the context of Indian symbolism, sexuality is, however, almost always associated with fertility. The agrarian culture of India quite often considers the stark expression of sexuality in speech or art as conducive to rain. Today as in ancient times, toward the end of the dry summer season or in the very beginning of the rainy season, in many places in the Indian subcontinent, people walk around the city or town chanting sexually explicit phrases. This purely symbolic act does not affect the behavior of everyday Indian society, which does not permit even married couples to kiss in public.

According to a widespread ancient Indian belief, human couples symbolically represent the sky father and the earth mother. Rain and fertility are their sexual act and result. In a wedding ritual a groom says to his bride "I am the sky, you are the earth." Although the earliest reference to this view is found in the Vedic texts, it is closely associated with the typical monsoonal culture of India. Therefore, a man who is sexually inactive was known as *varṣavara,* "withholding rain (generative fluid)." In the above-mentioned story, Ṛsyaśṛṅga, in a sense, was a *varṣavara*. He was not impotent, but simply withholding or not releasing the generative fluid just as the cloudy sky does not release the shower of rain as expected. Since he was the microcosm of the sky, his sexual inactivity caused drought. Unequivocally, people in India saw the close relationship between sexuality and drought. In the secondary development of the meaning, the word *"varṣavara"* completely lost its primary significance and became synonymous with a eunuch who is portrayed in Sanskirt drama as an impotent man working in a royal harem.

The concept that sexuality and drought are polar opposites seems to be based on India's experience of repeated disaster of drought and famine. People may have realized that during a severe drought when food is scarce, reproductive energy dwindles. The authors of the early Sanskrit texts frequently refer to the notion that the rain produces food; food turns into semen, *retas,* which makes the young couples fertile (*Śatapathabrāhmaṇa* 2.5.1.6, 6.1.3.12, 14.9.1.13–16.). The *Suparṇādhyāya*, a pre-Christian era text dealing with the story of the sun-bird Garuḍa and serpents, also relates that when the sun-bird Garuḍa created an intense drought women became unable to conceive and cows stopped producing milk. Thus, conversely the *śṛṅgāra* of a healthy couple became the symbol of fertility and prosperity. In ancient Sanskrit texts these ideas are described in words, but in Indian art including Rajput painting they appear in figures. Numerous paintings in the collection are associated with the theme of the dalliance of amorous couples. Sometimes the theme appears in the form of Śiva and Pārvatī (cat. no. 128), other times a mythical king and queen (cat. no. 93, 112) but most frequently Kṛṣṇa and Rādhā (cat. nos. 32, 42, 87, 92) often surrounded by female attendants.

Since the symbolism of the amorous couple is closely associated with the typical meteorological phenomena of the Indian subcontinent, Persian artists who came to India to work for the Mughal emperors were not familiar with the typical Indian theme of the auspicious couple and its symbolism. Therefore we can not expect to see the popularity of this theme in early Mughal art. But within a few decades the approach of Mughal art gradually changed, so that by the seventeenth century, it commonly showed handsome princes amorously embracing their consorts (fig. 4). Catalogue number 24 is an example from the Watson collection that depicts a young couple in an intimate mood. Although this Mughal painting immediately reminds us of the classical theme of the loving couple, it does not mean that original symbolism remained intact. When an artistic element is borrowed from another culture, symbolic significance often is modified. Almost certainly, for Mughal artists the scene of romantic love meant no more than eroticism. In fact even Rajput artists do not seem to be aware consciously of the original significance of the loving couple. Why did India tolerate the overwhelming emphasis of eroticism in art? Why do divinities such as Śiva and Pārvatī, Kṛṣṇa and Rādhā, and many other Indian gods and goddess, who are regarded as father and mother, have to be depicted as romantic couples? Very likely the Rajput artists did not have the answers to these questions. Although they knew that the auspicious sight of the divine couple brings good luck to a devotee, it was not clear to them what grammatical rules guided the language of Indian iconography and symbolism. Only through analytical study based on the methodology of Indian art can one attempt to discern the antidrought notion associated with the dalliance of the amorous couple.

The antidrought notion is discernible also in pneumatic modeling of the romantic couple. A tireless attempt to create warm and firmly fleshed figure enlivened by momentarily inhaled life breath is not, however, confined to the motif of the loving couple, but it is a ubiquitous tendency of Indian art. Like the mainstream artists of the early period, so also the Rajput painters often represented male and female figures swollen with inner vitality (cat. nos. 63, 83, 84, 92, 102, 124). A

Figure 4. Attributed to Govardhan (active ca. 1600–ca. 1640), *Lovers on a Terrace*, ca. 1615 or later, Los Angeles County Museum of Art, Nasli and Alice Heermaneck Collection, Museum Associates Purchase, m.83.1.6

well-known art historian describes such figures in an early nineteenth-century work of a Rajput artist in following words:

> Men and women, to his [artist's] eyes, are heavy-trunked, big-eyed, and comfortable—like bulls and cows. They are pneumatically modeled like the pillows . . . and rise like bubbles toward the patch of hot sky. (Welch: 52)

Note also the fact that the unnaturally swollen chests of the male figures in Jaina and Orissan manuscript illumination (cat.

nos. 7, 8) are the result of the exaggerated representation of such inner vitality or prāṇa. Students of Indian art are familiar with this prominent artistic feature that appears throughout history. However, it is has not been explained properly why Indian artists gave so much attention to this feature. Earlier art historians' explanations that the quality of inner vitality is an indication of yogic breath control (Rowland: 35; Kramrisch 1965: 13, 15, 16; Craven: 22) lack conviction because this artistic element is used also for describing healthy livestock, as exemplified by the representation of the fat, virile bull in the Indus Valley seals and on the capital of the Aśokan pillars (Vajracharya 1999: 54.). It also appears in seventeenth century or later representation of healthy children or the cattle shown around Kṛṣṇa in Rajput miniatures. In a sense this artistic feature is the symbolic expression of amplitude and liveliness. The Sanskrit word *prāṇa* literally means "animate existence, life breath, or life." Its implication in Indian art is more closely associated with agrarian prosperity than the practice of yogic breath control as we know from Vedic texts on the aspects of monsoonal culture. People in ancient India believed that life or inner vitality descends from heaven together with the monsoonal rain. This view is clearly recorded in the celebrated *prāṇa* hymn of the *Atharvaveda:*

When *prāṇa* as a thunder cloud roars at the vegetation, they conceive, they receive embryos, then many are born.

When the monsoonal season finally arrives (*ṛtāvāgate*) *prāṇa* descends on the vegetation. Then all become happy, whatever is upon the earth.

When *prāṇa* has showered with rain upon the great earth, then the cattle are delighted: "indeed that will be great for us!" (*Atharvaveda* 11.4.3–5)

A similar concept occasionally appears in later Vedic texts as well:

When there is not a good rain, *prāṇas* go through depression since food will become scarce. But when there is a good rain, *prāṇa* become delighted since food will become abundant. (*Chāndogya Upaniṣad* 7.10.1)

Indian artists may not have been well versed in Vedic literature, but they were aware that inner vitality or *prāṇa* is an auspicious artistic element. There are at least two reasons for this continuity. First, both the Vedic authors of the Punjab and Rajput painters of Rajasthan experienced the effects of monsoonal culture. Admittedly these geographical areas are not in the main tract of the monsoonal wind. However, insufficient rainfall makes these regions thirstier for rainwater. Even the plants of Rajasthani desert wait for the few drops of monsoonal rain to bloom. Because of the great significance of the annual monsoon in the lifecycle of the Indian subcontinent, concepts of monsoonal culture survived unconsciously in the memory of the Indian people throughout history. Second, reference to these concepts can be found not only in early Vedic literature but also in much later astrological texts written around the second to the eleventh centuries A.D. Possibly, even the later texts were not directly available to the Rajput artists, but two different literary sources certainly were. The first source derives from the translation of Sanskrit texts such as the *Meghamālā* "Garland of Cloud," which advises soothsayers how to forecast the weather in traditional manner judging from the formation of the cloud, animal behavior, and the appearance of vegetation. The second source is the traditional Rajput calendar, similar to a farmer's almanac, known as *pañcāṅga.* Both of these were based on the earlier literature and astrological texts. Every year, even now, people in the countryside consult such texts and calendars for the prediction of rain and harvest. Therefore it is not surprising that the symbolism and iconography of Rajput painting reflect the continuity of the ancient belief system of monsoonal culture.

This helps us to comprehend how Indian artists saw the relationship between an artistic representation of a skinny figure and crop failure. The *Pratimāmānalakṣana,* a Sanskrit text on making images, relates that "if the image is made with a sunken belly, then there will always be destruction of crops" (Banerjea: 610). Likewise the *Viṣṇudharmottara Purāṇa* 38.18 states that an artist should not represent a woman with a flat stomach because it will cause fear of starvation, a sign of scarcity. As we noted earlier, in many other passages, the authors of these authoritative texts emphatically refer to the relationship between the artistic representation and failure of harvest (The *Viṣṇudarmottara Purāṇa* 43.14, 38.25).

Indian artists agreed with this view throughout history. Although they worked for the royal court, not for farmers, the entire society including the court was supported by agriculture. Both the agrarian society and the royal court were more afraid of drought than any other calamity. Therefore,

Figure 5. Emaciated Buddha from Sikri Pakistan, ca. 2nd century A.D. Schist, H. 31⅝ in. Lahore Museum, Lahore. Photograph by John C. Huntington. The Huntington Archive, The Ohio State University, Columbus

like the artists of ancient India, the Rajput artists always carefully avoided representing a subject that might indicate failure of harvest.

The contemporaneous Mughal artists approached art in quite a different way. Unlike Rajput artists, they saw no reason to fear representing scarcity and infertility. Thus a subject of a Mughal masterpiece could be a scene of an intense drought with leafless trees and emaciated animals and their owner. According to Sufi philosophy the *nafs* or the "soul" is almost like "the restive horse or mule that has to be kept hungry and has to undergo constant mortification and training so that, eventually, it serves the purpose of bringing the rider to his goal" (Poster: 88). The Mughal masterpiece of the emaciated horse and groom by Basawan about 1595 (India Museum, Calcutta) may be associated with this philosophy. Rajput artists must have seen many such paintings because it was a popular subject. It originated in sixteenth-century Persia (now Iran), from where it spread to Mughal India. Around the seventeenth century both Mughal artists and artists of the Deccani sultanate became fascinated with this subject. Despite such popularity, Rajput artists never found this subject appealing. The relationship between artistic representation and fertility was so obvious to them they never questioned whether depicting drought and skinny figures would really cause disaster.

The Indian artist's attempt to suggest inner vitality in human figures sharply contrasts with the approach of the Greco-Roman tradition, which described human figures with muscular tone. The artists of Gandhara in northwest part of modern Pakistan who were exposed to this western tradition created muscular images of Buddhist divinities around the second century A.D. The contemporaneous artists from Mathura, who followed the tradition of mainstream Indian art, found such treatment inappropriate and avoided emphasizing muscular structure in human figures. Rajput artists continued in the mainstream of Indian art creating firmly fleshed figures.

On two other occasions, a comparative study of Gandharan art and mainstream Indian art is helpful for understanding the symbolic significance of Rajput painting. Initially, traditional Indian artists hesitated to depict Buddha Śākymuni's emaciated form as a result of the severe practice of austerity and his nirvana. Although these two events are the main episodes of Buddha's life, the early Buddhist art from Bharhut and Sanchi carefully avoided even the symbolic reference to both these events. These episodes began to appear for the first time in the works of Gandharan artists (figs. 5, 6). The contemporary Mathuran artists did not attempt to show these scenes in their art. While the scene of nirvāṇa became popular in China and Japan, it remained a rarely depicted subject in India.

We see the dead and dying emaciated figures for a second time in Indo-Persian and Mughal art. The *Dying Inayat Khan* is another masterpiece of the Mughal school (fig. 7). This drawing was based on a real event. An attendant of the Mughal emperor Jahangir, Inayat Khan fell ill from his addiction to opium and alcohol. Jahangir wanted to see him before his death. As the emperor saw him clinging to life even in that completely wasted condition, he was amazed and ordered his artist to make a faithful representation of the scene. Jahangir refers to this incident in his autobiography in following words:

He appeared so low and weak I was astonished . . . Though painters have striven much in drawing an emaciated face, yet I have never seen anything like this. . . . As it was a very extraordinary case I desired painters to take his portrait. . . . Next day he traveled the road of non-existence (Jahangir: 44, as quoted in Beach: 107–9).

These words clearly show the difference between the Mughal approach to art and the *darśana* theory of the Rajputs. Mughal artists strove for reality and recorded real events, including a dying, emaciated drug addict. Their art was not concerned with the concept of *darśana*. Rajput artists, on the other hand were guided by the concept and made great efforts to create an auspicious world in their work, whether religious or secular. For them an auspicious sight is beautiful and worth seeing.

KING AND REGALIA

In Indian art a king is great not because he is a conqueror but because he is a rainmaker. He is rarely shown engaged in battle or killing an enemy as in other artistic traditions. Instead he is shown participating in seasonal festivals or making rain. Cakravartī, the ideal king, is capable of providing his subjects with a shower of gold coins just by touching the cloud with his stretched hand (Craven: 41). In a sense, the king himself is a symbol of fertility; he is *deva*, the god who controls the rain. In Sanskrit a synonym for "it rains" is *devaḥ varṣati* "god/king rains."

A prolonged drought brought blame on the king for being an unworthy or irresponsible ruler. Conversely, seasonal rain was considered to be the gods' blessing on the divine king. The repeated display of the royal processions (cat. nos. 35, 40, 50) and numerous regal portraits (cat. nos. 35, 40, 64) in our collection is not exclusively inspired by the spirit of recording contemporaneous events but by the auspicious nature of kingship. Because of the royal association regalia such as a fly whisk made of yak tail, a parasol, a flag or a banner, a royal throne, and elephant are worthy of having *darśana*.

As this notion merged with the concept of the auspicious couple, a royal figure and his consort are also shown involved amorously. A seventeenth-century temple statue of Nayak kings of the Vijayanagara empire depicts the Nayak king fondling the breast of his queen (Temple Museum, Srirangam). Such public display of a royal statue in a temple is possible

Figure 6. Nirvana, from Loriyan Tangi, Pakistan, ca. 2nd century a.d. Schist, ca. 17⅜ in. Indian Museum, Calcutta. Photograph by John C. Huntington. The Huntington Archive, The Ohio State University, Columbus

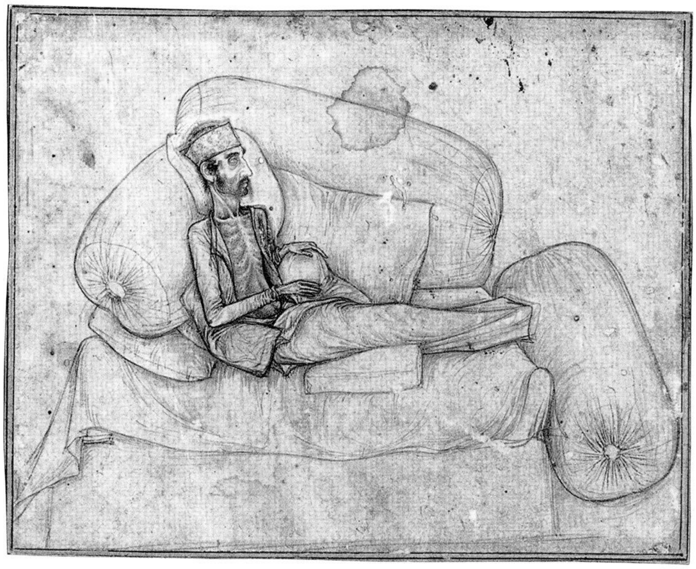

Figure 7. Attributed to Hashim (active ca. 1615–1655), *Dying Inayat Khan*, ca. 1618–1619. Museum of Fine Arts, Boston. Francis Bartlett Donation of 1912 and Picture Fund, 14.679. ©2002 Museum of Fine Arts, Boston

only in the context of traditional Indian beliefs. In Rajput paintings, due to the prevailing *purdah* system of keeping women in seclusion, the portrait of a real king and queen embracing each other is difficult to find. However, mythical royal couples wearing royal dress and headgear are frequently depicted as if they are contemporaneous Rajput kings and queens. Their romantic mood is not less intimate than that of the Nayak king and queen of Vijayanagara.

Visual Representations of Musical Modes

The theme of a loving couple also appears in the pictorial representation of musical modes, although such representation originated from a completely different concept. According to the musical and artistic traditions of medieval India, there are six fundamental musical modes known as rāgas. Each male rāga is closely associated with five secondary musical modes called rāginīs, considered to be their wives. The masculine and feminine musical modes are visually represented in paintings. Thus the feminine musical mode Lalita Rāginī (cat. no. 44) is depicted in a scene in which a princely figure is about to leave home and abandon his consort while she sleeps. Similarly, the masculine Hindola Rāga (cat. no. 92) is represented with a royal couple or Rādhā and Kṛṣṇa seated on a swing that is gently rocked by attendants. The names of the rāgas and rāginīs are often given at the border of the painting as the labels or titles of the works, but such labels or titles are not originally based on the pictorial representation of the male and female figures but on the gender of the musical modes (see Portland: 45 for a different view). Thus one can occasionally see a female figure in the painting identified as masculine musical mode or vice versa (cat. no. 49). The Sanskrit verses of a later date, which are often written on the upper section of the paintings, simply describe the iconographical features of rāgas and rāginīs as depicted; they do not explain the original relationship between paintings and musical modes. Sometimes the labels or titles contradict the statement in the verses. Rajput artists were probably unfamiliar with this complex system; the classical significance of the pictorial representation of rāgas and rāginīs had been lost. The choice of words, style, and the misuse of Sanskrit grammar indicate that the verses were composed no earlier than the ninth century. The authors of the classical Sanskrit texts on Indian dance, drama, and music show no familiarity with the nomenclature of these musical modes, which began to appear in fully developed from only around the tenth century.

Despite such ambiguity, we have some clues about how the musical modes became associated with their pictorial representations. For instance, the theme of the Rāmakarī Rāginī (cat. nos. 22, 82) is a typical theatrical scene of classical Sanskrit drama in which a man bows down to his consort in order to appease her anger. The fourth-century poet and dramatist Kālidāsa was familiar with this dramatic motif. Although the poet does not designate the motif as Rāmakarī—apparently because the nomenclature was not developed yet—he repeatedly uses the dramatic motif in his works. For example, in the second act of the *Vikramorvaśīya*, King Pururavas bows down to his queen who refuses to be appeased since she discovered that the king was having an affair with a heavenly nymph named Urvaśī. Kālidāsa also describes a painting based on this theme of courtship in his celebrated poem *Meghadūta*, "Cloud Messenger." The lovesick hero of this poem laments:

> On a stone slab, with mineral pigments, I would like to draw a figure of you, angry with me in a love quarrel; then I want to portray myself prostrated at your feet. As I proceed to do so, my vision becomes blurred with ever-increasing tears. The cruel god of fate does not tolerate our union even in a picture. (2.42)

This textual evidence indicates that the theatrical scene of the courtship was also a theme of a painting already in the fourth century. More important, this phenomenon suggests that the link between the musical modes and their visual representations could be derived from a theatrical performance where both faculties—the listening of the musical modes and the viewing the theatrical scenes—are involved simultaneously. The pictorial representation of Rāmkarī Rāginī reminded culturally trained viewers of this particular musical mode, which was played when the scene of the courtship was theatrically performed.

A strong support of our view comes from Bharata's *Nāṭyaśāstra*, the first- or second-century Indian text on dance, drama, and music. Although the author was not familiar with the nomenclature of the musical modes, he was familiar with the theatrical scene of courtship associated with Rāmakarī Rāginī. In his work he advises the stage director to play particular music when the scene of courtship was performed on the stage. I will translate the relevant section:

> She should torment him until he bows down to her feet. As he falls to her feet, she should glance at the female messenger [who is standing nearby]. Then the heroine should lift him and embrace him. Knowing that she is now interested in lovemaking, he should take her to bed. This scene should be accompanied with soft musical presentation (*sukumāra gītavidhāna*). (*Nāṭyaśāstra* 24. 286–288.)

Very likely this soft musical presentation is the early version of Rāmakarī Rāginī. Originally it was not a title of a painting but a name of particular music. Evidently such music was played in the background when the male actor, following the convention of classical drama, bowed down to the actress in the middle of the ongoing theatrical performance. It became the title of a painting only when the performance was recorded in the pictorial medium.

Likewise, the musical mode Lalita Rāginī seems to be associated with a theatrical scene in which a man abandons his consort. In the pictorial representation of this musical mode, a lover is shown sneaking out of his palace, leaving his beloved while she sleeps. This scene directly evokes an ancient theme of Sanskrit literature in which a king abandons his queen to become a wanderer. Thus the scene could change into the Buddhist legend of Great Departure if the sleeping beauty is identified as Prince Siddhārtha's queen. According to the legend, a groom who was a good friend of the prince helped him to escape from the palace. This particular element of the legend also coincides with the scene of the Lalita Rāginī because it is often depicted with a horse and a groom in the courtyard waiting for the departing prince (Barrett and Gray: 135). Furthermore, in the Buddhist story a demigod called Lalitavyūha, a hypnotist who put the harem to sleep, helped Śākyamuni to escape from the palace. Very likely the musical mode Lalita Rāginī was originally associated with the name of the demigod and considered to have hypnotic quality.

How did the dramatization of the Great Departure of Buddha Śākyamuni appear in ancient theatrical performance? A great deal can be learned about this from a Gandharan sculpture in which the episode of the Great Departure is vividly represented in a theatrical setting (on a relief from Jamalgarhi in Yusufzi, last known at the Lahore Museum) where the divine beings, including the bull symbolizing Nāndī, the benedictory verse recited at the beginning of a classical drama, are watching the episode from the balcony of the theater. Following the nomenclature of rāga and rāginī, if we attempt to associate the artistic representation of this Buddhist episode with a particular musical mode, we could easily designate the scene of the Great Departure as Lalita Rāginī. We just need to be able to listen to the musical mode while looking at the scene.

The Vilaval Rāginī (cat. no. 55) is another example that shows the antiquity of the concept of rāga and rāginī in Indic visual culture. Usually this musical mode is depicted with a scene in which a lady seated on a couch adjusts her jewels or ornaments before a maid holding a mirror. Although reference to the word Vilaval is not found in early literature, a similar scene is carved in a second-century ivory casket from India found in Begram (fig. 8). In the carving a young lady is shown seated on a square bench. A maid kneels in front of her holding a jewelry bowl. The young lady takes a tall mirror with her left hand and prepares to adjust an earring that she has taken from the bowl held by the maid. It is possible

Figure 8. Scene of the feminine toilet, 2nd century A.D. Kushana period. Ivory casket, 11⅜ x 18¼ in. from Begram, Afghanistan. Kabul Museum, Kabul. Photograph by John C. Huntington. The Huntington Archive, The Ohio State University, Columbus

Figure 9. An elephant emerging from a lotus pond, detail from the ceiling painting of Cave I, Ajanta, 5th century A.D. AAAUM, ACSAA Color Slide project, University of Michigan, Ann Arbor

that this scene was also performed together with a corresponding musical mode in a theatre. Probably in a later period, that particular musical mode became known as Vilavil Rāginī.

The relationship between artistic representation and theatrical performance is not unusual in the visual tradition of India. An oft-quoted Sanskrit verse from the *Viṣṇudharmottara Purāṇa* 43.37 recommends that artists consult texts on dance and drama. It is also true that Indian artists have often created their works by imitating theatrical performance instead of directly observing the subject in nature. Thus we have good reason to believe that some of the rāgas and rāginīs represent the scenes of the ancient drama. As this ancient concept merged with the cult of Kṛṣṇa and the theme of the amorous couple, the rāgas and rāginīs became Kṛṣṇa and Rādhā (cat. no. 92), thereby adding more layers to the already existing pile of diachronic development.

Stylistic Evolution

In order to show the relationship of the Watson collection to the earlier history of Indian paintings, we present here a brief history of the pictorial style of Indian painting.

The earliest paintings of India are found on the walls of the man-made caves of Ajanta situated in the Deccan, most belonging to the fifth or sixth century A.D. In these murals male and female figures loom over the entire paintings. The landscape is treated superficially with the background and foreground of stylized rocky hills and one or two trees. As in contemporary sculptures, the human figures are enlivened by inner vitality. The source of natural light is never defined; sometimes the male and female figures appear to be the source of light themselves (see fig. 3). Architecture and animals are often represented with reverse perspective: the corner of a building or the leg of an elephant closer to a viewer appears much smaller than those in distance (see fig. 9). Most of these artistic features of Ajanta continued in later paintings.

Following Ajanta, few paintings survived from the seventh to the tenth centuries. Notable among those are the rare surviving pieces of the ninth-century wall paintings of the Elura caves in the Deccan. These wall paintings show stylistic transitions between the Ajanta paintings and the manuscript illuminations of the eleventh century. An interesting feature of the Elura murals is the tendency is to exaggerate the eye closer to the picture plane as exemplified by the representation of Lakṣmī (Coomaraswamy 1965: 100–1, fig. 196). The artist shows lashes with the edge of the eye slightly extending beyond the contour of the faces. This tendency forecasts a mannerism that is known in Indian art history as "protruding farther eye," often depicted in a three-quarter view. Such exaggeration became a ubiquitous feature of Jaina paintings from the eleventh century onward.

After the Elura murals there are no examples of Indic paintings for almost two centuries. Only in the eleventh century did palm-leaf manuscript illuminations painted for Jainas and Buddhists begin to appear—Jaina illuminations from Gujarat and Malwa, Buddhist illuminations from Bihar, Bengal, and Nepal. A monumental quality of features distinguishes these early manuscript paintings, revealing that these illuminations are heirs to the earlier tradition of wall paintings in Ajanta and Elura. Although they are rendered in a space that is not much bigger than a large postage stamp, the artist depicts the huge elephant or a tall princely figure as successfully as if he were painting on the expansive wall of a cave. Note the continuation of the Ajanta-type stylized rocky hill on the left of the Nepalese manuscript painting depicting Sudhana in a landscape (fig. 10). Other distinguishing features that continued from Ajanta include the (1) three-body-bend pose (*tribhaṅga*),

(2) bowlike curvilinear eyebrow, (3) shade trees circumscribed by a thick dark line, and above all the (4) plasticity that is achieved by shading both sides of the object without defining the source of light. All these characteristics are seen in both early Jaina and Buddhist paintings. An early (ca. 1128) Jaina example is the illustrated manuscript cover found at the L.D. Institute of Indology, Ahmedabad, India (876/A) (Pal 1995: fig. 79) in which the continuation of Ajanta style is clearly visible mainly in the modeling of the male and female figures and moving elephants. However, the plasticity of figures is created here not only with subtle color shading but also with a curvilinear quality of the fluent lines. After the twelfth century both Jaina and Buddhist artists totally abandoned the shading technique. Furthermore, a striking difference between these two schools appeared when Jaina artists became increasingly fascinated by protruding farther eye. Although such fascination is forecast by its exaggerated proportion in the Elura paintings, the eye is depicted in the early Jaina painting without much exaggeration (Pal 1995: fig. 79). The Buddhist artists of Bihar, Bengal, and Nepal did not employ this stylistic development. Morever, in Jaina manuscript painting, the Ajanta type of a stylized rocky hill (see fig. 10) began to look like a puff of smoke (Pal 1995: fig. 59). In Buddhist paintings of Nepal, the Ajanta-style rocky hill continued relatively unchanged until the seventeenth century.

Around 1500 in India sultanate painting of a remarkable style began to appear. A superior example of the sultanate painting, as we have mentioned earlier, is the celebrated *Ni'mat-nama* manuscript illuminations. This is a book of recipes illustrated for Sultan Ghiyath ad-Din Khalji (r. 1469–1501) of Malwa. The folios of the manuscript depict the sultan, surrounded by his harem, tasting the delicacies prepared by a female Indian cook. The illustrations stylistically resemble the fifteen-century manuscript paintings from Persia such as the *Khavarnama*. The physiognomy of male and female figures, the detail of the tile work, the asymmetrical setting of the throne, the grouping of the figures, and their interaction with the sultan are similar in both manuscripts. The *Ni'mat-nama* illumination is indeed the Indian adaptation of the Persian style. However, one of the striking features of the *Ni'mat-nama* is the depiction of multiple figures in full profile. This profile style, rarely seen in Persian examples, is the most distinguishing element of Rajput paintings. Furthermore, the voluminous physical features and the bubblelike transparent *ghumghat*, the veil covering the head of the female Indian cook in the *Ni'mat-nama* (Barrett and Gray: 61) is very close to those of the figures in Indian miniatures of a slightly later date such as the *Caurapañcāśikā* illustrations (ca. 1550) (Barrett and Gray: 66). Thus the involvement of Indian artists in creating the Indo-Persian style of the *Ni'mat-nama* becomes evident. The sultanate style is a synthesis between Persian and contemporary Indian styles.

The *Caurapañcāśikā* is a Sanskrit text written by Bihlaṇa, an eleventh-century poet. A copy of the text in the N. C. Mehta Collection at the Culture Center in Ahmadabad, India bears sumptuous illuminations rendered around 1550. Art historians designated the unique style of the illuminations as *Caurapañcāśikā* style. This style has little in common with Indo-Persian style but indicates its own affinity with traditional Indian style and popular folk style. During the sixteenth century, this style spread all over north India from the Himalayan foothills to Malwa. Distinctive features of this style include the juxtaposition of contrasting color fields, two-dimensional architectural background, the depiction of a head in full profile, and the illustration of inner vitality or *prāṇa* (Beach: fig. 4). All these features persisted in the early Rajput painting.

Mughal style consists of three artistic elements derived from Persian, Indian, and European traditions. A major contribution of the Mughal school was rendering earthly reality in a naturalistic manner. Mughal artists in the height of their artistic development took a keen interest in recording con-

Figure 10. Sudhana in a rocky hill landscape, Nepalese palm leaf manuscript, ca. 11th century. Los Angeles County Museum of Art, The Nasli and Alice Heeramaneck Collection, M.70.1.1b

temporary events and making portraits with great attention to individual physiognomy, the differentiation of age, and psychological reflection. This caused a revolution in the history of Indian art. Traditional Rajput artists rarely depicted the real events of the secular world; their subject matter was otherwordly, and the paintings were created with inner vision technically known as *sādhana*. They utilized stylization, idealization, and a wealth of symbols inherited from earlier generation but did not render a work of art through careful observation of nature. Mainstream Indian artists made portraits, but they idealized them, portraying king not as he does look but as he should look. Unlike Rajput artists, Mughal artists were not content representing a two-dimensional flat architectural background, or representing water symbolically as stylized circular ripples, or representing sky by two or three flying birds. Thus within a decade of the development of Mughal painting, architectural settings became three-dimensional, representations of water much more naturalistic, sky more convincingly atmospheric, and human figures recognizably realistic. Moreover, in Mughal paintings, we often witness spatial recession, the use of light and shade for modeling, and careful handling of subtle color transition from one section to another section of the subject. Most of these qualities began to appear in Mughal paintings after contact with the European tradition of paintings through the Jesuit priests who often visited the Mughal emperors.

The assimilation of Mughal artistic elements into Rajput painting varied from court to court and time to time depending on the political and psychological condition of the Rajput leaders and artists. Artists of the Rajput court that had closer ties to the Mughal emperor readily accepted some Mughal influence in art. But Rajput rulers such as Mewars, who continued to fight Mughal domination, refused to do so for a long time. Meanwhile the Mughal penchant for realism, which reached to its peak during Jahangir's reign (1605–1627), gradually declined, and toward the end of the eighteenth century and beginning of the nineteenth century Mughal painting became more visionary or expressive than realistic. The Rajput painters' symbolic approach, which can be described as the main current of Indian art throughout history, was eventually accepted even by Mughal painters. The interaction between these two schools continued long after the period of the great Mughals (1526–1707).

DESPITE THE INTERVENING centuries, ancient Indian art and the paintings of the Watson collection often shared the same artistic approach and followed the same grammar of artistic language. This grammar was based on the theory of *darśana*, which in turn was associated with the inverted cause-and-effect belief system of the agrarian society of India. A work of art is indeed for viewing pleasure, but Indian artists believed that both religious and secular art could be beautiful only if it was devoid of inauspicious elements.

Guided by this concept, mainstream Indian artists successfully created the world beyond the phenomena of time and space. They rarely represented historical events such as great battles, killing the enemy, or scenes of heroic sacrifice that are often seen in the art of other civilizations. Indian artists were familiar with some of these subjects, but they often avoided anything that indicated human suffering.

As a general rule, a dramatic change took place in the history of Indic art when India was exposed to foreigners from other side of Hindu Kush. As a result of close contact with Persian, Greco-Roman, and Islamic cultures of the Middle East, Indian artists with tendency for sophistication did deviate occasionally from their own tradition and allow significant changes in their art. Therefore, just as in Gandharan art, so also in Indo-Persian and Mughal art, one can expect to see visual representations that do not follow the traditional belief system associated with *darśana*. The ripple effects of such a new approach to art are expected to appear occasionally in contemporary mainstream art as well. This is not, however, a one-sided influence. The sophisticated art of India also went through the process of interaction and eventually became almost indistinguishable from mainstream Indian art. Thus an observation of origin and development of artistic elements is helpful not only for understanding the evolution of Rajput art but also for the ongoing interaction between the Mughal and Rajput tradition of Indian art. Whenever applicable, we will point out the effectiveness of this new approach throughout the catalogue entries.

COLOR PLATES

1. *A Prince and Princess*. Indo-Persian style, mid 16th century. Gouache and gold on paper, 11 x 8 15/16 inches. 1972.41. Cat. no. 11

2. *A Tree Watered by Human Blood:* illustration from an unidentified manuscript. Mughal style, ca. 1575. Gouache and gold on paper, 7⅞ x 6⅜ inches. 1972.42. Cat. no. 13

3. *Zulaykha in Deep Thought*, page from a manuscript of the story of Yusuf and Zulaykha. Mughal style, ca. 1610. Gouache and gold on paper, $5\frac{5}{8}$ x $2\frac{11}{12}$ inches. 1972.46. Cat. no.16

4. *The Hoopoe*. Mughal style, ca. 1610. Gouache and gold on paper, 13⅞ x 9¼ inches. 1973.17. Cat. no. 17

5. *Portrait of a Nobleman*. Jaipur (Amber), 17th century. Gouache and gold on paper, 18 x 13⅜ inches. 1974.51. Cat. no. 88

6. *Lady and Tree*. Bikaner, late 17th century. Watercolor, gouache, and gold on paper, 10⅝ x 8 inches. 69.28.11. Cat. no. 77

7. *Rāmakarī Rāginī*. Mughal style, early 18th century. Gouache and gold on paper, 9⅜ x 6½ inches. 1974.54. Cat. no. 22

8. *A Love Scene*. Mughal style (probably Lucknow), mid 18th century. Gouache and gold on paper, 12 x 13 15/16 inches. 1975.22. Cat. no. 24

9. *The Elephant Nakhatula.* Mewar, mid 18th century. Gouache and gold on paper, 9 3/16 x 7 3/8 inches. 1977.132. Cat. no. 37

10. *Rāgaputra Kanara*. Pahari style, mid 18th century. Gouache and gold on paper, 8¼ x 6 inches. 1.1970.23. Cat. no. 107

11. Nathu Ahmad. *Toḍī Rāginī*. Bikaner, mid 18th century. Gouache and gold on paper, 7⅜ x 5⅜ inches. 1982.175. Cat. no. 83

12. *The Month of Māgha*, illustration to a verse from the *Kavipriyā* of Keśavadāsa. Marwar (Jodhpur), mid 18th century. Gouache and gold on paper, $12\frac{3}{16}$ x $8\frac{1}{4}$ inches. 1981.286. Cat. no. 63

13. *Portrait of a Nobleman*. Mughal style (probably Murshidabad), ca. 1760. Gouache and gold on paper, 13 x 10⅛ inches. 1975.21. Cat. no. 23

14. *Śrī Rāga*. Bundi or Kotah, ca. 1780. Gouache on paper, $9\frac{3}{8}$ x $6\frac{9}{16}$ inches. 1979.1719. Cat. no. 48

15. *Naṭa Rāginī*. Bundi, late 18th century. Gouache on paper, 7⅛ x 5 inches. 1979.1721. Cat. no. 49

16. *The Court of Aurangzeb*. Double-page painting from a manuscript of the *Alamgir-nama*. Mughal style, late 18th century. Watercolor and gouache on paper, 8⅝ x 5¾ inches. 69.28.3. Cat. no. 26

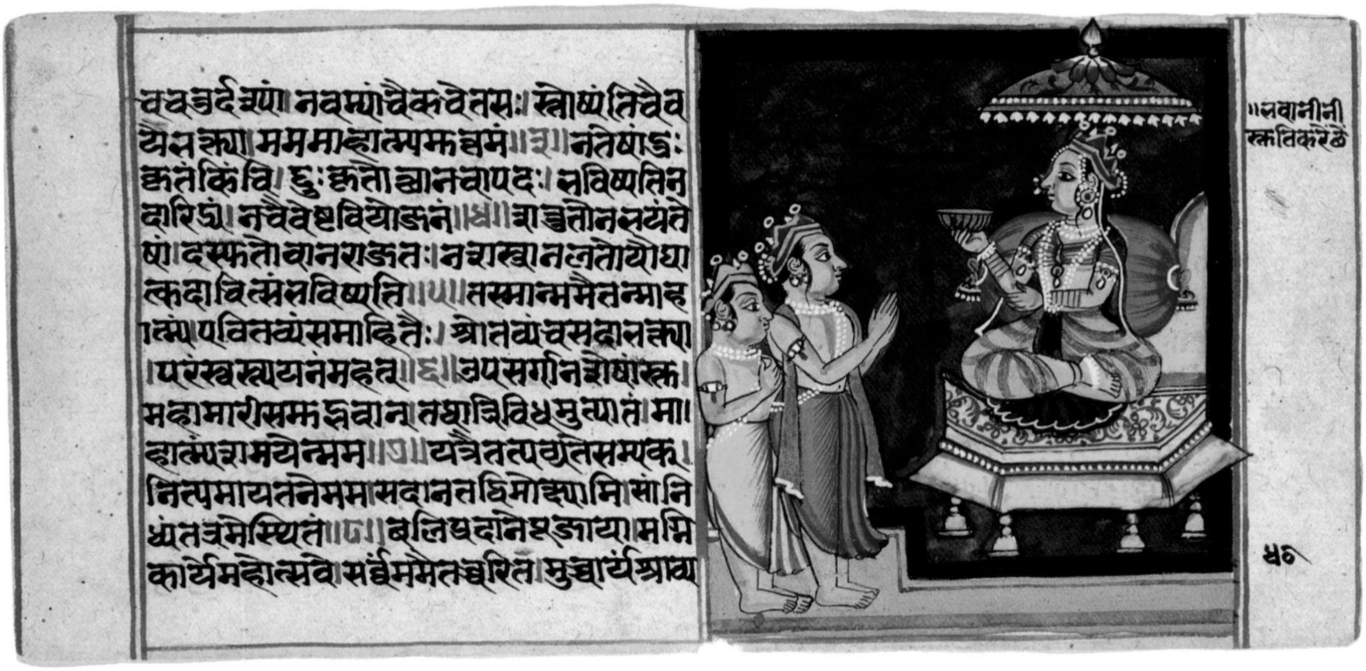

17. *The Worship of Durgā (Bhavānī)*, folio 46 from a manuscript of the *Devīmāhātmya*. Probably Sirohi, late 18th century. Gouache on paper, 4½ x 9¹³⁄₁₆ inches. 1982.166c verso. Cat. no. 68

18. *Rāma and Sītā with Raja Jagat Prakash (ca. 1770–1789) of Simur.* Pahari style, late 18th century. Watercolor, gouache, and gold on paper, 11⅜ x 9⅝ inches. 69.28.15. Cat. no. 112

19. *Vilavil Rāga*. Pahari style, late 18th century. Gouache and gold on paper, 10½ x 7¼ inches. 1984.1321. Cat. no. 116

20. *Rāma's Army*. Probably Marwar school, early 19th century. Gouache on paper, 3 5/16 x 8 inches. 1982.165. Cat. no. 66

21. *The Summer Season*. Marwar, ca. 1825. Watercolor, gouache, and gold on paper, 16⅛ x 11½ inches. 69.28.20. Cat. no. 67

22. *Megha Malhār Rāga,* from a Rāgamālā series. Jaipur, ca. 1825. Gouache and gold on paper, $11\frac{3}{8}$ x 8 inches. 1982.183. Cat. no. 96

23. *Ram Singh II (1827–1865) of Kotah in a Procession*. Kotah, mid 19th century. Gouache and gold on paper, 13⅞ x 20½ inches. 1977.136. Cat. no. 50

24. *Entertainment During the Rainy Season*. Pahari style, mid 19th century. Gouache and gold on paper, 10 x $11\frac{13}{16}$ inches. 1983.142. Cat. no. 122

CATALOGUE

I

Buddhist Manuscript Illuminations from Nepal

The early examples of South Asian paintings, most of which belong to the Gupta period, (ca. 320–600 A.D.) are found on the walls of the man-made caves at Ajanta. This ancient heritage of painting survived for a long period in several places on the subcontinent, not on the expansive walls but mainly on the tiny strips of palm-leaf manuscripts. Although the style changed considerably over time, the tradition of manuscript illumination continued in Bihar and Bengal until the twelfth century, and manuscript illumination is practiced even today in Nepal, Orissa, Gujarat, and neighboring regions.

Before paper was introduced to India in the fourteenth century, manuscripts, occasionally illustrated, were written on narrow palm leaves. The earliest illustrated manuscript belongs to the tenth century, although some of the palm-leaf manuscripts without illustrations may go back to the seventh century. Once paper was introduced, the folios of manuscripts were still designed after the elongated format of palm leaves. Artists found these leaves and wooden manuscript covers of the same design useful for depicting scenes in a horizontal format, just like in the wall paintings. Traditional Indian painters changed to a vertical format only after they came in contact with the Persian-style paintings introduced by Muslim rulers.

During the Muslim invasion and occupation of Bihar and Bengal, towards the end of twelfth century, well-known Buddhist monasteries including Vikramaśīla and Nalanda were destroyed. As a result, Buddhism, which had been struggling to survive in India in these last strongholds even before the invasions, completely disappeared from Indian plains. Thus after the twelfth century the tradition of Buddhist manuscript paintings in these regions came to an abrupt end. Fortunately a similar tradition of style survived in Nepal, which, due to the remoteness of this mountainous Himalayan country, escaped the occupation of the Muslim rulers. Although in 1349 the Muslim ruler of Bengal did plunder the Kathmandu valley, the capital of the country, the invader was not interested in ruling this isolated region and left the country within a week. Thus traditional life was not much interrupted, and the classical style of painting derived from the Ajanta style continued in this country even in the eighteenth century.

1A
Pratisarā, folio from the *Aṣṭasāhasrikā Prajñāpāramitā* manuscript [formerly an unidentified manuscript]

Nepal [formerly Eastern Indian style], 13th century
Gouache on palm leaf, 1⅝ x 16⅝ inches
1972.36

The folio of the manuscript contains five lines of early post-Gupta period Brāhmī script in black ink against the cream color surface of the palm leaf. As usual, two rectangular spaces are left empty for perforations through which goes the thread that binds the loose leaves of the manuscript together. The image described here and in cat. 2a are separated by two five-line sections of a popular Buddhist manuscript, the *Aṣṭasāhasrikā Prajñāpāramitā*. Although many copies of this text have been found, the present folio belongs to one of the few illustrated manuscripts. Unfortunately, the location or even existence of other folios of this manuscript is unknown. Because the margin of the folio is very worn, the folio number is not discernible either.

Pratisarā is one of the Buddhist goddesses presiding over "five protections," *pañcarakṣā*. Her heads are encircled with an apple-green nimbus and her body with an overlapping body halo. Such overlapping double haloes are quite popular in Nepal and Central and East Asia, but are rarely seen in India. This is one reason that makes it difficult to accept previous scholars' view that stylistically this manuscript illumination belongs to the school of eastern India. As with many other Nepalese manuscript paintings of this period, Pratisarā's face is characterized by a wide forehead, a broad space separating her brows and eyes, and the placement of her lower eyelid almost in the middle of the face. Thus we believe that this miniature is a work of a Nepalese artist. To the right of the same folio is another miniature depicting the scene of the Buddha's *parinirvāṇa* (cat. 1b), which also exhibits a Nepalese style. As usual both these images are not directly associated with the text on which they are illustrated.

The Buddhist Newars, an ethnic group of the Kathmandu valley, worship these goddesses of *pañcarakṣā* even today in order to receive protection from various calamities such as famine, flood, diseases, theft, snakebites, and fire. These goddesses apparently originated in the folk tradition and only later were incorporated into Buddhism. As their iconography developed, it became complicated. Not only do textual descriptions of the goddesses differ from artistic representations but often two different texts express slightly different views about their iconographical elements, including the various attributes that they hold in their multiple hands. However, there is no discrepancy with the respect to the color of each goddess's body and her matching principle countenance (Bhattacharyya: 78–98). Thus we can identify this goddess as Pratisarā because she has a white principal face and body. Her principal face is flanked by yellow and red faces that correspond with textual prescriptions (Chandra had mistaken the figure for a male divinity [1971: 5]). Her seven hands display (clockwise from lower left) the wish-granting gesture, a water jar, an arrow, a sword, a peacock feather, a bow, and a noose

Published: Pramod Chandra, *Indian Miniature Painting: The Collection of Earnest C. Watson and Jane Werner Watson* (Madison: Elvehjem Art Center, 1971): cat. no. 1; hereafter Chandra 1971. *Two Faces of South Asian Art: Textiles and Paintings.* Paintings from the Earnest C. and Jane Werner Watson Collection by Joan A. Raducha. (Madison: Elvehjem Museum of Art, 1984): cat. no. 2.1; hereafter Raducha.

1B

Buddha's *Parinirvāṇa,* folio from *Aṣṭasāhasrikā Prajñāpāramitā* manuscript [formerly an unidentified manuscript]

Nepal [formerly Eastern Indian style], 13th century
Gouache on palm leaf, 1⅝ x 16⅝ inches
1972.36

The followers of Buddha Śākyamuni believed that death leads to an unwanted rebirth just as birth leads to death. Like day and night, rich and poor, you and I, death and rebirth are the unavoidable duality of the world. Only because the Buddha achieved enlightenment and led an ascetic life devoid of desire was he able to break out of the circle of birth and death. For this reason his death was considered *parinirvāṇa* (total extinction), and it became one of the most popular themes of Buddhist art. The theme appeared for the first time in the Gandharan art of the second to fourth centuries A.D., and from there it spread all over Central and East Asia. Gandharan art is closely associated with the Persianized Greco-Roman tradition. Although this theme flourished in northwest India, it does not belong to the mainstream Indian artistic tradition, which did not depict death or other paintful aspects of the phenomenal world. Thus in earlier Indic art of Bharhut and Sanchi the theme of the Buddha's *parinirvāṇa* is totally absent. From the Gupta period onward, however, the theme began to appear occasionally in South Asian art; even so it never became popular as it did in Central and East Asia.

In Nepalese manuscript illuminations *parinirvāṇa* makes an occasional appearance. The paleographic and stylistic features of the present example indicate that this representation of the Buddha's *parinirvāṇa* is the thirteenth-century work of a Nepalese artist. Śākyamuni is shown here lying peacefully on the bed, resting his head on the palm of his raised right hand. His eyes are half-closed and his limbs are relaxed. By creating a peaceful atmosphere, the artist has eliminated the painful elements of death. In Gandharan sculptures and East Asian paintings this theme is represented with much more emphasis on the reality of death, with the Buddha's eyes closed and head resting on the pillow. The lamenting monks and the Buddha's other followers in the Gandharan examples make the scene even more dramatically tragic. Nepalese artists, on

IA

IB

2A

the other hand, following the mainstream tradition of South Asia, do not focus on the elements of tragedy.

Pramod Chandra, in writing on the Watson collection, considered this manuscript illumination to be stylistically associated with the Pāla school of Bihar and Bengal; however, the physiognomy of the Buddha and the paleography cause me to reject this view. In Pāla-style illumination the forehead is distinctively narrower than in Nepalese painting. In both styles faces are oval, but eyebrows in Pāla-style paintings are placed much higher than in Nepalese works. Furthermore the *uṣṇīṣa*, the cranial protuberance on the Buddha's head indicating his extraordinary knowledge, is still round in the Nepalese example as in the Gupta period Buddha's head; in Pāla manuscript illumination, however, the *uṣṇīṣa* is almost always pointed like a cone (Losty: fig. 6). Both of these features, high eyebrows and the conelike *uṣṇīṣa*, never appear in Nepalese work, thus providing valuable clues for distinguishing the styles of these two neighboring schools.

Published: Chandra 1971: cat. no. 1; Raducha: cat. no. 2.1.

2A

Vasudhārā, folio 1 from the *Āryagrahamātṛkānāmadhāraṇī*

Nepal, dated 1635

Gouache on paper, 3 x 9¼ inches

66.13.4

The material for this manuscript is paper, which had become common by this time; however, it is still designed like elongated palm leaf, with a center hold for the thread binding the manuscript together. The surface of the paper is coated with yellow pigment locally known as *haritāla*, orpiment (arsenic trisulfide). The Sanskrit text has six lines of Newari script in black ink. Although the illustrations are not painted on the manuscript itself but pasted on designated areas, the illustrations are surely contemporaneous with the manuscript. The image of Vasudhārā given in the first folio is one of the six illustrations, one per page, in a Buddhist Sanskrit manuscript known as *Āryagrahamātṛkānāmadhāraṇī*. Both the original date and author of the text are unknown, but according to the colophon the manuscript was copied at Kathmandu in 1635. This unpublished manuscript is complete in thirty-three folios. Folios 6, 17, and 18 have traces of the vermilion paste used by a reader to show reverence for the manuscript.

From previous example of the thirteenth century (1a and 1b) to this manuscript illustration of the seventeenth century (2a and 2b) the style of Nepalese painting changed. The dwarfish body proportion, decreasing linear fluency, a cruder rendering, a penchant for decorative elements such as the flame (or floral) motif above the image, and multiple ornaments are the immediately discernable elements of later period.

In the middle of a horseshoe-shaped scarlet body halo, Vasudhārā seats on the lotus pedestal with both legs folded on the seat. The right knee is raised while the other rests flat on the seat; the feet are close together. Such an attitude is known as *rājalīlāsana,* "the posture of royal ease." The yellow goddess has six hands holding various attributes. She displays, clockwise from our lower left: the wish-granting gesture, a cluster of jewels, a gesture of greeting to the Buddha, a manuscript, a sheaf of rice, and a water pot. She wears an elaborate crown and various ornaments.

Despite the fact that Vasudhārā is a well-known Buddhist deity, originally she was a goddess of rice. Even today Buddhist Newars of the Kathmandu valley worship her in the beginning of autumn when the rice paddy is ready for harvest. Fresh rice is offered to her during the ritual of her worship. The color yellow is mainly associated with her because she is, in a sense, the embodiment of fresh rice, the staple food of most of South Asia. Agrarian wealth depended upon the successful harvest of this grain. The earliest reference to Vasudhārā as a goddess of wealth and her special worship in autumn is found in the *Atharvaveda*, a well-known Vedic text composed around 1200 B.C. In Vedic literature, however, she has a slightly different name, Vasoḥ Dhārā, and seems to be regarded as the goddess of pastoral prosperity instead of rice. Originally she had nothing to do with the sectarian divisions of Indic religions, Hinduism, Buddhism, and Jainism. The Jainas of Gujarat also worshiped her. Although her Jaina iconography differs from above-mentioned Buddhist version, both of them shared her main attribute, rice. In the Jaina representation rice is, however, depicted as if it is a flowering plant like a lotus (Swali: 178).

2B

Gaṇeśa, folio 19 from the *Āryagrahamātṛkānāmadhāraṇī*

Nepal, dated 1635

Gouache on paper, 3 x 9¼ inches

66.13.4

Gaṇeśa is a well-known Indic god with an elephant's head. Although he is considered to be a Hindu deity, he is worshiped also by Jainas and Buddhists. He provides his devotees with prosperity by removing obstacles that could block the path of success.

Gaṇeśa is shown here on the nineteenth folio dancing on the back of a blue mouse, which is his animal vehicle. Characteristically almost all Indic gods are assigned animals on which they are often shown standing or seated in various poses. Although Gaṇeśa has many iconographical forms, here he has a red body and ten arms. Beginning from our lower left in clockwise fashion he exhibits a radish, the wish-granting gesture (*varada*), an arrow, a sword, and the hand-gesture of a flag (*patākā*), a battle ax, a bowl in which he is digging his trunk in search of sweets, the protection gesture (*abhaya*), a bow, the gesture of an elephant's trunk (*gaja-hasta*). He wears a golden crown and various earrings, necklaces, armlets, bracelets, a girdle, and anklets. A horseshoe-shaped red halo encircles his body.

Experts and laypersons alike often ask why Gaṇeśa has an elephant's head. The cult of Gaṇeśa derives from the Indic belief that an elephant is divine and auspicious. I will admit that nowhere in the texts is Gaṇeśa identified as an elephant. But an elephant, an auspicious animal due to its association with rain (see introductory essay), is always regarded as Gaṇeśa. The religious calendar of India also helps us to understand the original significance of Gaṇeśa and his mouse vehicle. On the fourth day of the Indic month Bhādra (August/September), Gaṇeśa is worshiped all over India. This particular day signifies the beginning of autumn and approaching harvest time. Rice is still in the field and not quite ripe. (Compare this timing with the day of worship of Vasudhārā, which is celebrated exactly two weeks later when rice is ready for harvest.) The farmers are patiently waiting to gather the crop and watchfully protecting it day and night. This is also the time of a year when the wild elephants emerged from the forest and mice from the villages. The elephants and mice can consume the rice paddy of a farmer within a day. Such calamity is known as *īti* or *vighna* in Sanskrit. A farmer could only hope to protect his rice field by begging for mercy and worshiping the elephant-headed god and his little mouse friend. Once we recognize this agrarian problem and its solution, we can better understand the significance of the worship of Gaṇeśa as the remover of the obstacles. Today, when most elephants have been eliminated from their natural habitat, it is difficult for us to imagine that they were the main challenge to the agrarian society of ancient India.

Unpublished

2B

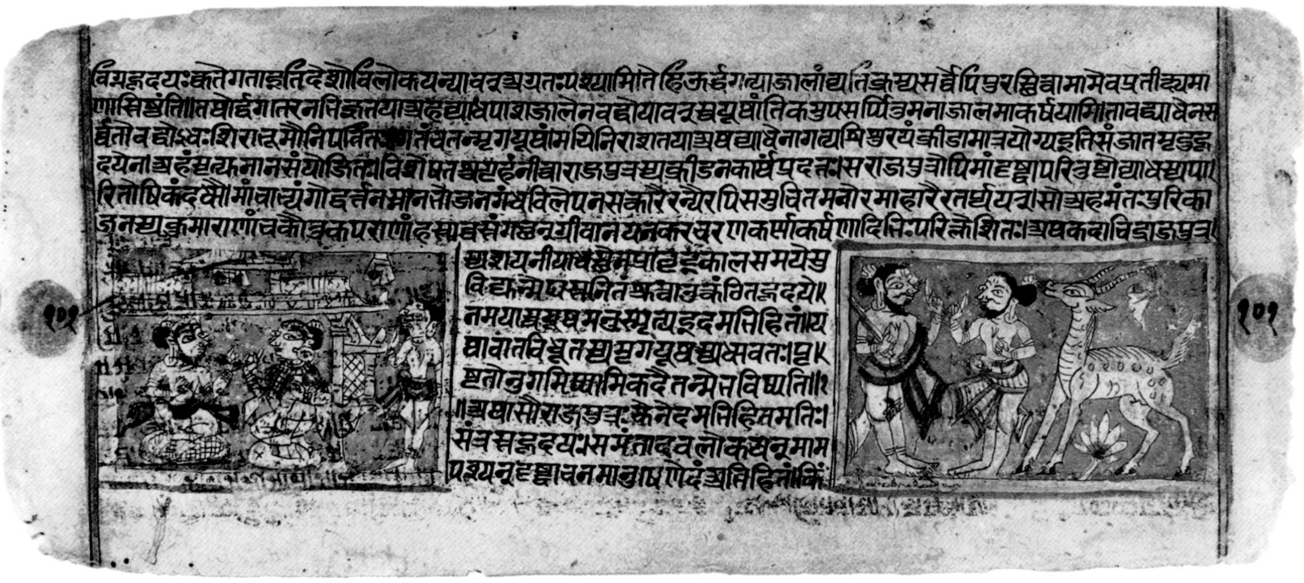

3

Jaina Manuscript Illuminations from Western India

A fascinating style of manuscript illumination developed in Gujarat and such neighboring regions as Rajasthan and Malwa. Although this style of painting was used also for secular subjects, it is commonly known as Jaina style because most of the manuscript illuminations in this style are associated with the Jaina religion. Moreover, the wealthy Jaina communities that flourished in the many cities around Gujarat, where they produced excellent textiles and traded with Arab businessmen internationally, were the main financial supporters of this artistic activity.

The purpose of commissioning manuscript illuminations was to acquire religious merit by donating the books to Jaina priests, who usually deposited them in a library known as a *Pustaka-Bhandār* (the storehouse for books). Such libraries were affiliated with Jaina shrines or monasteries, which have become famous for taking good care of their heritage for generation after generation.

Like the Buddhists, the Jainas suffered from repeated Muslim invasions and the devastation of their religious centers. For example, Gujarat, a main stronghold of the Jainas, was raided and destroyed in the early eleventh century by the Muslim invaders from Afghanistan and again in the thirteenth century by the sultan ruling from Delhi. Jainas, however, managed to survive even such difficult times. During Muslim rule they kept good diplomatic relations with the Muslim rulers and continued to prosper as successful businessmen and bankers, but they did not allow their religion and culture to be altered by outside influence. Although Buddhism disappeared from India after the twelfth century, Jainism remained one of the most powerful religions of India; however, it did not become as popular outside the subcontinent as did Buddhism.

3

A Gazelle with a Human Voice, folio from a Sanskrit storybook [formerly folio from a manuscript of an unidentified Sanskrit work]

Western Indian style, early 15th century
Gouache on paper, 4⅝ x 11⅛ inches
1972.37

The solitary folio of the missing manuscript has fourteen lines of Sanskrit text in black ink against the uncoated buff-colored surface of paper. Vertical lines on both sides of the folio designate the space for writing. The script is Devanāgarī. The number of the folio is given twice within two pinkish oval marks on the borders. The bottom corners of the folio bear two illustrations.

This secular painting provides an excellent example of stylistic similarity between the Jaina manuscript illuminations and secular painting of western India; both depict the human figures in unnatural stances, with swollen chests for both sexes, and the use the protruding further eye almost invariably human figures except for the people of foreign origin such as the Sahi king in cat. no. 5. Such an eye is used neither for animals (the gazelle here) nor for the animal-headed god (cat. no. 4).

One great contribution of India to the world is the voluminous collection of ancient folk stories embodied in the *Jātakas*. Although the *Jātakas* were compiled between the fifth and the second centuries B.C., some stories of this collection certainly originate before the sixth century B.C. Other texts such as the *Pañcatantra* (compiled between 200 and 600 A.D. and the *Hitopadeśa* (ca. 1360) also belong to the same tradition of ancient folk stories. Through traveling monks and traders, some of the ancient Indic stories migrated to the Mediterranean where the renowned storyteller Aesop translated many of them into Greek when he was active in the late sixth century B.C. at the court of Croesus of Lydia (Mukerjee: 139). Such a story is illustrated here in two rectangular panels inset into the text, and a vivid narration of the story in beautiful Sanskrit literary style is given on the same folio of the manuscript.

The text relates that a gazelle while playing in the forest with others, was unfortunately caught in the net of a hunter. Since the gazelle, popularly known as a chinkara, was cute, the hunter took it to a royal palace and presented it to a young prince. Apparently this episode is depicted at the bottom right corner of the folio where two men engage in conversation and a larger-size gazelle faces toward them. The man with the sword is perhaps a doorkeeper, and the man standing near the animal is the hunter. The next illustration on the bottom left corner shows a palace with the prince and princess inside the chamber and the hunter standing in front of the palace. According to the story the prince and the entire harem of the palace became fascinated with the animal. From the morning to evening the poor gazelle had to play with them, willingly or not. One day, during the monsoon the prince was lying in bed, and the gazelle was watching the thunderclouds raining hard with many flashes of lightning. "When will I be able to run in the forest with my friends and compete with the monsoonal wind?" said the homesick animal in a human voice. Hearing this, the prince was startled and looked around for the source of the human voice. The gazelle tells this interesting story in the first person, but the remaining story is missing. Although this is the only folio of the manuscript in the Elvehjem collection, the folio number 101, written on both sides of the text, indicates that this is a part of a much larger text.

Published: Chandra 1971: cat. no. 2; Shalini Venturelli, "Language above Time and Space," *The Christian Science Monitor* (June 28, 1982): 20.

4

4

The Transfer of the Embryo, folio from a manuscript of the *Kalpasūtra* by Bhadrabāhu

Western Indian style, late 15th century

Gouache and gold on paper, 4⅝ x 11¾ inches

1972.89

As usual the folio of the manuscript has an elongated shape. Seven lines of Devanāgarī script in the Prakrit language are written in black ink on the uncoated buff-colored surface of paper. The number of the folio is worn and difficult to decipher. Although this is a late fifteenth-century Jaina manuscript illustration, it retains such stylistic elements of early Jaina paintings as the red background of a slightly unusual shade, the bed frame with curvilinear legs resembling that of a bull, and the protruding further eye. The eyes are delineated with much more attention than any other element of the picture, whereas the trays and other container lying on the foreground are rendered rudimentarily.

According to the *Kalpasūtra*, an important religious text of the Jainas written by Bhadrabāhu, the savior god, Mahāvīra Jina, decided to be born in a priestly family and entered the womb of Devanandā, a Brahman woman. Indra, the king of the gods, did not like this idea and instructed the genie Harinaigameśa (also known as Harinegameśin) to steal the embryo of the Brahmani and transfer it into the womb of the kṣatriya (warrior caste) queen Triśalā, as she slept in her bedchamber. In the painting the goat-headed genie enters the bedchamber with the embryo in his raised hand. At the upper right corner of the folio the scene is labeled as *triśalāgarbhasaṃcararṇa* "Triśalā receiving the germ." Although the queen sleeps, her eyes were painted fully open, a conventional feature also seen in such early Indian art as the second-century Bharhut relief depicting Queen Maya's dream.

Published: Chandra 1971: cat. no. 4; Raducha: cat. no. 2.3; Gautam Vajracharya, "Tradition and Change in Rajput Painting from the Watson Collection," Elvehjem Bulletin (1994): 54, hereafter Vajracharya 1994.

5

Kālaka Preaching to the Sahi King, folio 3 from a manuscript of the *Kālakācārya-kathā*

Western Indian style, late 15th century

Gouache and gold on paper, 4⁵⁄₁₆ x 10⁵⁄₁₆ inches

1986.51

This text is in the Prakrit language in Devanāgarī script. This is the third folio of the manuscript, which is written in nine lines in black ink on buff-colored paper with the illustration on the right. Red ink is used for the vertical line on the left, the frame of the illustration, three circles, and the box around the folio number. Only this folio is in the Elvehjem collection.

The *Kālakācārya-kathā*, the story of the great Jaina teacher Kālaka and Scythian king, is a part of the important Jaina canonical work *Kalpasūtra*. The Scythian king, who is known in India as Sahi raja, is shown here in a U-shaped three-quarter profile, without the protruding further eye. Such features are used only for a foreign king, perhaps because the U-shaped physiognomy is borrowed from contemporary Persian painting where it is used to portray all figures. In a later period even the sophisticated Mughal artists, in their advanced stage of development, delineated the portrait of the foreign kings as they are depicted in the foreign works (Beach: 100).

The Sahi king wears a crown, blue-patterned robe, and a pair of high boots. In one hand he holds a sword and with the other gestures with his erect index finger intended to menace his enemy. An attendant stands behind him. At the lower register of the painting, the king, easily identified by his characteristic mustache, is shown confronting one of the two lions facing two opposite directions. The king stands with arms akimbo planting his legs on the ground triumphantly.

The king of Malwa abducted the sister of the Jaina monk Kālaka. With the help of the Sahi king, who was foreign, Kālaka was able to retrieve his sister and punish the Malwa king. The episode of the Sahi king's visit to the Jaina monk became a main theme of the Jaina manuscript paintings. Often in early manuscripts the Sahi king and his attendants are shown either standing or seated in front of the monk whose figure is always imposing due to his hierarchic proportion and center position. In the present example the Sahi king is shown in the middle of the painting inside a shrine and much bigger than the Jaina monk seated on his left. A label given at the left corner of the folio identifies the scene as *śakarāja guru*, "Śaka king and the teacher." The word *śakarāja* is the Sanskrit word for Sahi king.

Published: Chandra 1971: cat. no. 5; Vajracharya 1994: 54.

6

6

Saṃvasaraṇa of a Tīrthaṅkara, probably a folio from a manuscript of the _Kalpasūtra_

Western Indian style, late 15th century

Gouache and gold on paper, 4⅝ x 3¾

69.28.6

This is a fragment of a manuscript with a painting on the recto but no writing. Some writing is still visible on the verso. Because a thin protective paper is glued on the back currently it is not possible to decipher the writing.

The Jaina teacher Tīrthaṅkara sits on a throne attended by two standing Jaina monks, who are shown in diminutive scale. The teacher is in meditation posture with knees bent and each foot resting upon the thigh of the opposite leg. His meditative gesture is emphasized by his hands placed in his lap with palms upward. He wears a crown studded with pearls. Two elaborate side-locks of hair characteristically appear at the top of both sides of his head. The Jaina universe is indicated by four lofty gates in each direction as well as the series of circular enclosures representing the protective walls. No mountain is shown, contrary to Chandra's description (Chandra 1971: 10). Instead, just like in the Buddhist thanka painting, the gates, the walls, and the main deity are depicted in a mandalic perspective, which shows a bird's-eye view and side view simultaneously, disregarding the artistic theory of consistent viewpoint.

Beyond the enclosures, against the red background of the painting, are various auspicious animals such as lions, elephants, bulls, and horses. These animals were considered auspicious mainly because they are associated with rainwater and fertility. According to ancient Indic tradition, all these animals appear in the formation of rain cloud. Technically they are known as *jaladharajāla,* "patterns of a rain cloud." In Indian art they were represented the first time around the abacus of a pillar erected by the Buddhist king Aśoka in the third century B.C. (Vajracharya 1999: 69–75). Although the original symbolism of the animals was gradually forgotten after Buddhist and Jaina artists borrowed the images, their auspiciousness remained intact throughout Indian art history.

In Jaina literature *saṃvasaraṇa* indicates a religious gathering or an assembly. In Jaina painting the word is used for the circular representation in which Tīrthaṅkara is shown seated in the center preaching to the assembly, symbolically the entire Jaina universe. In Jaina architecture, the same word also implies a temple or an assembly hall of cosmic significance. Thus in concept, Jaina *saṃvasaraṇa* is no different from the Buddhist and Hindu mandala, a ritual geometric design representing a free-standing architectural structure or a palace symbolizing the universe. Such diverse meanings of *saṃvasaraṇa* and the word itself derive from the Vedic Sanskrit word *saṃvatsarīṇa,* which originally denotes a transitional time when the dry summer ends and the rainy season begins (Vajracharya 1997: 4–20). At this particular time the monks of all Indic religions gather in a place for rainy season retreat. During such a retreat a famous teacher shares his knowledge with his many disciples from around the world. Thus the retreat became synonymous with universal gathering. This seems to be the main reason that in Jaina art and architecture the word *saṃvasaraṇa* means a universal gathering or cosmic assembly. The eve of the rainy season retreat of the *Digambara,* "sky clad," Jaina monks is still closely associated with the original word *saṃvatsarīṇa*. Today, the eve is known as *Saṃvatsarī*.

Published: Chandra 1971: cat. no. 6; Raducha: cat. no. 2.4.

Hindu Manuscript Illuminations from Orissa

Orissa lies along the eastern coast of India. The sharply defined natural boundaries created by mountains, rivers, and ocean helped the Hindu rulers of this region protect their land from the Muslim invasions from Bengal and the Deccan. Orissa retained its autonomy until the sixteenth century, although it temporarily lost its freedom to the Delhi sultanate on two occasions. Only after Akbar annexed it to the Mughal empire in 1572 did Hindu rule end. Because of this political situation the traditional style of painting did not disappear as quickly as it did in Bihar and Bengal but was prolonged into the seventeenth and eighteenth centuries. Indeed, the tradition of palm-leaf manuscript painting continues even today.

Unlike north India and Nepal, in Orissa the outlines of the paintings were not made with regular line drawings but with incisions made with the point of a stylus. Then charcoal or other pigment was rubbed into the lines. Very likely the Buddhist artists of India and Nepal used a similar stylus when they made sand mandalas. Tibetan artists still use such a stylus even today.

The style of the traditional paintings of Orissa is very conservative. Even after the style was exposed to sultanate and Mughal styles of painting, it did not show much change. Age-old stylistic features such as physiognomies marked with an upward glance, a pointed nose, and a swollen chest, and Orissan architecture encompassing the scene persisted throughout the history. Because of this enduring conservatism, dating manuscript illumination of Orissa is difficult.

7

Attributed to Raghunatha Prusti

The Goddess Durgā Fighting with the Buffalo Demon [formerly Devi Slaying the Buffalo-demon]

Orissan style, 18th or 19th century

Ink on palm leaves, triple folios sewn together, 4⅞ x 7 7/16 inches

1973.16

The *śikhara* type of Orissan shrine that envelops the scene is arranged symmetrically. Flying birds and peacocks perch on the architecture; bearded devotees and female attendants waving fly whisks are also placed on either side of the goddess to emphasize the symmetry of the composition. Other remarkable stylistic features include the weightlessness of the puppetlike standing figures and physiognomies marked by pointed noses, diminutive mouths and chins, and tilted body positions. According to Williams and Das's recent study, this picture is the work of a nineteenth-century artist Raghunatha Prusti, who was also responsible for several other works (Williams and Das: 131–59.) Their view is mainly based on a stylistic and paleographic analysis.

This drawing is based on the Hindu story of the goddess Durgā, who subdued the formidable demon Mahiṣāsura. According to the story, Durgā, equipped with weapons given by various divinities, went to the battlefield on her lion vehicle. Although she easily chopped off the head of the demon who came to fight with her in the form of a gigantic water buffalo, the real demon remained unharmed and emerged from the decapitated body of the buffalo. In the drawing the severed head of the buffalo lies on the ground, but the demon has emerged from the corpse of the animal. Durgā stands triumphantly. Placing her right foot on the back of the lion, she tramples the beheaded buffalo with her left foot. She has four arms. With her raised upper arms she holds the wheel and the conch; with her principal arms she grabs a double-ended trident and stabs the chest of the demon before he can take the sword from his sheath. The dynamic movement and the aggressive body posture of the victorious goddess lend dramatic quality to the scene that takes place in the hills, indicated by the stylized circular rocks depicted under the feet of the lion.

Published: Chandra 1971: cat. no. 8; Raducha: cat. no. 2.19; Joanna Williams and J. P. Das, "Raghunatha Prusti: An Oriya Artist," *Artibus Asiae* 48. 1–2 (1987): 131–59, pl. 38.

8

Episodes of Viṣṇu's myth: folio from an unknown manuscript

Orissan style, 18th or 19th century

Polychrome on palm leaf, 1½ x 14 inches

66.13.3

This palm leaf manuscript is a copy of an unknown Sanskrit text written in Orissan script. It has thirty-four folios with sixty-seven illustrated pages, sometimes one, other times two, three or four per page. There are no folio numbers; the text is in a single column. The ink is black, and the original buff-colored surfaces of the palm leaves have darkened through time. The illustrations are colored by black, red, and blue inks.

This painting is stylistically characterized by typical physiognomy and physical features of Orissan painting such as pointed nose, upward glance, and swollen chest and hips of both sexes. The wirelike dark lines displayed without any attempt to cover them with color is another distinctive feature of the Orissan manuscript illumination. Preference for linear rendering over the painterly treatment is ubiquitously seen in Orissan art. Such treatment indeed stems from the Orissan technique of incision with the point of stylus for drawing a picture.

The Hindu deity Viṣṇu periodically incarnated himself on the earth to protect the people from demonic force. Of his ten incarnations, Kṛṣṇa was, undoubtedly, the most important. Therefore, both Kṛṣṇa and Viṣṇu are described having a

7

8

dark complexion, which is regularly translated in Indic painting as blue.

Placed almost in the middle of the elongated folio of the manuscript, Viṣṇu rides on the shoulder of the big bird Garuḍa, who is depicted here in human form. In his four hands, Viṣṇu holds a club, a conch shell, a wheel, and a lotus. Because of the diminutive nature of the painting, in our example these attributes are not clearly visible. His club looks like a lotus bud and the wheel resembles a stylized flower with multiple symmetrical petals.

The big bird Garuḍa is shown here in flying posture with his both hands stretched out and one leg bent, the other extended far behind, thus creating the sense of aerodynamic quality. He has a black beard and mustache. Despite the difference in space and time his pointed nose immediately reminds us of the famous eighth-century wall painting of Elura where the bird is shown carrying Viṣṇu's spouse Lakṣmī (see introductory essay). Usually the bird has two wings even though his body is rendered anthropomorphically. The wings are missing here, but the artist has successfully created Garuḍa and his master hovering in the atmosphere weightlessly by using the flying posture. Such treatment of a wingless aerodynamic flying figure can be traced back to the Gupta period (ca. 320–647). The swinging garlands of Viṣṇu emphasize the flight.

In front of Viṣṇu and Garuḍa stands a divine figure in red color with four heads and multiple hands. Although his attributes are not delineated, the figure probably represents the creator god Brahma who seems to be admiring Viṣṇu's role of protection.

Immediately behind the figures of Viṣṇu and Garuḍa lies the cosmic ocean with a mountainlike tide, rapidly approaching the viewer and about to collapse after reaching the shore. The artist, who was indeed quite familiar with this natural phenomenon of the Orissan seashore, convincingly represents the oceanic creatures swinging together with the rhythm of tides with great delight in rendering them in linear style.

In this cosmic ocean Viṣṇu, attended by his consort Lakṣmī, reclines peacefully on the floating bed consisting of the soft body of the multiheaded serpent Ananta. This scene is based on a popular Hindu myth, which relates that at the end of the creation, the entire universe including the atmosphere will be covered with water. Thus there will be no distinction between the celestial ocean (the rain cloud) and the terrestrial ocean. In this compact cosmic ocean Viṣṇu will sleep until the beginning of the next creation of the new universe. This is not, however, a one-time event, but a periodical event which has been reoccurring every eon. This periodical event is also associated with the annual Hindu calendar, because Hindus believe that a Hindu year is a micro representation of the cosmic time. The four months of the rainy seasons are considered to be a period when the entire universe is covered with deluge. The Hindu calendar also informs us that Viṣṇu sleeps in the beginning of the rainy season and wakes up four months later when the rainy season is officially over.

Indo-Persian Style

In 1192 the Muslim invader Muhammad of Ghor established his sultanate in Delhi where he built, within a decade of his victory, the magnificent mosque Quwwat ul-Islam. This is the earliest surviving Islamic art in India. The early Muslim rulers of India may have commissioned paintings, but no Indian example of Islamic painting prior to the fourteenth century has been found. Only in the fifteenth and the first half of the sixteenth century did some recognizable examples of Islamic painting begin to appear, mainly in Malwa, Delhi, and Bengal.

Just as in building superstructures, so also in painting, Muslim rulers hired local artists to paint in accordance with their taste, which they developed before they came to India. Thus Islamic paintings of India are stylistically affiliated with various schools that flourished in contemporaneous Persia; yet the traces of the innate characteristics of the local artists remain visible in their works. Because these works consist of both Persian and Indian features, they are designated as Indo-Persian. Persian features include decorative elements such as flowering vines and grasses, varieties of arabesques, a stylized cloud pattern with pointed tails, and a typical physiognomy marked by U-shaped profile, joined eyebrow, and slightly tilted diminutive eyes. Likewise, Indian features are characterized by the display of bright contrasting colors, bushy round trees encircled by a dark line, a penchant for full profile, and a distinctive Indian physiognomy such as big eyes.

9
Ta'ir Being Put to Death, folio from an illustrated manuscript of the *Shah-nama*

Indo-Persian style, Malwa, early 16th century
Gouache and gold on paper, 8⅞ x 6⅛ inches
1972.40

The manuscript is in a vertical format, which contrasts with the elongated horizontal format of the Jaina and Buddhist manuscripts. As mentioned in the introductory essay, this newly introduced format also affected the format of Indian painting. Above the painting it has Arabic script in four columns in golden-brown separated by two vertical lines in same color. The fourth column on the right extends noticeably far below thus partially overlapping the painting. Such a treatment frequently appears in Indo-Persian and Mughal painting.

Perhaps the most exciting aspect of this painting is such distinct stylistic features as the stylized cloud patterns with pointed ends like tails, the flowering tufts of grass, and the rolling hilltops marked with dots. All these features clearly reveal its close stylistic association with the celebrated *Ni'mat-nama,* an illustrated manuscript on cookery that was commissioned by Sultan Ghiyath ad-Din Khalji of Mandu (r. 1469–1501) but completed only in the reign of his son Nasir ad-Din (Beach: 10). The significance of the *Ni'mat-nama* style lies in the synthetic approach of the artists, who rendered the illustrations in the contemporary Iranian style with Indian accents. In the present example the use of vibrant color and more importantly the green tree lacking separate branches clearly indicates the involvement of native artists. This forecasts the emergence of the syncratic style of the Mughal school. This valuable painting in the Watson collection is one of the very few survivors of this style.

The capital punishment takes place under a huge tree at the bottom of a rolling hill. The aged king with gray hair is seated on a square throne equipped with a yellow bolster and a blue cushion. He is attired in a blue robe and black boots and wears a crown of Persian origin. He watches the execution attentively and points a long spear toward the criminal. As the executioner cuts off the head of the criminal with a huge saw, blood drips from his neck. The saw is shown at such an angle that the executioner would be cutting the head rather than the neck. The observers of this gory event include a bodyguard on the left, a group of courtiers on the right, and a ferocious wolf hiding under the shade of a tree with some patches of light. The mysterious beast is rendered in such a way that it is visible only with some imagination. Thus the tiny red flowers with white dot almost in the middle turn into the sparkling red eyes of the wolf, the leaves and stems into his nose and whiskers, and the shady area into the contour of the animal's frontally projected face. Such a representation of a painterly riddle was a fashion in contemporaneous Persian paintings as well.

9

Besides the monarch, all the observers and the executioner are formally dressed for the event. Their fancy headgear and robes are rendered in pink, red, blue, orange, black, and white. The criminal wears only a white lower garment. His bare torso emphasizes the muscular structure of his body. In front of the throne on the ground is a golden tray with pitchers.

Published: Chandra 1971: cat. no. 10.

10

10

A Man with a Camel

Indo-Persian style, mid 16th century

Gouache and gold on paper, 4⅛ x 5⅞ inches

1974.48

Stylistically the composition of the painting features a newly introduced artistic motif, which is comprised of a rolling hill and a group of people watching an event from the other side of the hill. This is a popular motif in Persian, Indo-Persian, and Mughal works (see Beach: 30, 31 for illustrations). Pre-Islamic India was not familiar with this motif. It began to appear in Rajput painting with some stylistic variation (cat. nos. 47, 87) only after India was exposed to Islamic art.

A well-dressed nobleman, who wears an elaborate cap decorated with plumage, attempts to control a running camel by grabbing its left hind leg. Two other noblemen stand immediately behind him. The camel is about to step into a stream, which runs diagonally downhill. Stylized circular ripples indicate the water of the stream. Across the river are rolling hills behind which groups of people watch the event. Their concern with the event is expressed by their bodily and facial juxtaposition. There is a border formed of tufts of flowering grasses and floral design. Apparently this is a narrative scene.

Published: Chandra 1971: cat. no. 11.

11

A Prince and Princess

Indo-Persian style, mid 16th century

Gouache and gold on paper, 5¼ x 5⅛ inches

1972.41; see color plate 1

In this palace chamber scene, the bearded prince sits on a bluish green seat and leans against on orange bolster. He wears a pointed crown, which resembles that of the ruler depicted in the late fifteenth century *Khabarnama* manuscript of Iran (Beach: 13). His white *jama* has four yellowish brown buttons and a matching belt. A pitcher on a tray and a basket with a pointed cover are in front of him. Two huge candles burn on his left. The drama is heightened by the entrance of a tall, youthful princess dressed in an orange and light blue *jama*. The princess draws back the billowing silky curtain as she enters the chamber. An old woman prostrates herself at the princess's feet. The prince watches serenely.

As Chandra noted, the color scheme of this painting closely resembles that of illustration given in the Indo-Persian manuscript *Chandayan* in the Prince of Wales Museum of Western India in Bombay. This color scheme is the main reason for attributing the present painting as Indo-Persian (Chandra 1971: 16).

Published: Chandra 1971: cat. no. 12.

11

Mughal

The Mughal period is extraordinarily significant in the history of Indian painting. Within a short time, particularly from 1556 to 1627, the Mughal school developed and introduced so many new ideas and stylistic features that it affected both the mainstream Indian and the preexisting Indo-Islamic heritage of pictorial art of the subcontinent. The impact of Mughal style is often clearly discernable in the works of Rajput artists, although they incorporated only those artistic elements that harmonize with their traditional belief system.

Babur (r. 1526–1530), the founder of the Mughal dynasty, was a Central Asian prince who had blood ties with both Turks and Mongols. Although a highly cultured person who wrote his own memoir, he did not engage in artistic activities. After his death his son Humayun (r. 1530–1540; 1555–1556) inherited the kingdom and ruled peacefully for a decade. When in 1540, the able Afghan Sher Shah from Bengal invaded the Mughal kingdom, Humayun was unprepared. The Afghan ruler seized control of the Mughal kingdom, and Humayun fled to the court of the Safavid Shah Tahmasp of Iran, where he spent fifteen years in exile. This was an unfortunate event for the political history of the Mughal dynasty, but not for the history of Mughal painting. In the court of Shah Tahmasp, Humayun met two great painters, Mir Sayyid Ali and Abd as-Samad. In 1555 when Humayun returned to India and reclaimed his patrimony with the help of the Iranian king, he brought these two artists with him, planning to establish an atelier. But within a year of regaining his kingdom, Humayan fell down a staircase and died of serious injuries. The crown prince Akbar (r. 1556–1605) was about thirteen, (Beach: 13) but even at this young age he proved himself a brilliant and able ruler. Within a decade he had expanded the empire; he understood that without the support of the people, who were mostly Hindus, even a mighty king could not rule successfully. In order to win Hindu support he abolished the *jijya*, a tax on non-Muslims, and established matrimonial relationships with Rajput dynasties. Some Rajputs, mainly the Mewars, remained strong opponents to the Mughal emperor in battles and also to his policy of bringing Hindus and Muslims closer through marriage.

Even in this turbulent period of history Akbar found time to guide the newly established Mughal atelier. He encouraged the artists to develop an eclectic style by improving native Indian styles under the guidance of the Persian masters who were brought to the Mughal court by his father. Local artists who were previously working in Jaina, *Caurapaṇcāśikā*, and other styles were hired in the Mughal atelier. With imperial encouragement they were able to create a magnificent Mughal style that was very different from both Persian and contemporary Indian styles.

Around 1580, through Jesuit missions, the Mughal school also came into contact with contemporary European style. The Mughal artists adopted some of the European elements into their works harmoniously. The early Mughal style of Akbar's time is characterized by the plunging viewpoint (a carryover from the Persian style), vibrant colors such as bright red, yellow, and orange (reminiscent of the color scheme of the early Indian manuscript illuminations although not the same), spatial recession and the effective use of light and shade (borrowed from European works), energetic movement with some exaggeration (a quality not seen in the Persian, Indian, or European traditions), and the expression of heroism, which represents the enthusiasm for adventure and bravery of Akbari period. This expression contrasts with the erotic and sensuous expression prevalent in Rajput painting.

Akbar's son Jahangir (r. 1605–1627), who inherited the Mughal empire and the imperial atelier, was a great connoisseur of art. Once he boasted that by just examining the style of the painting he could tell exactly who had painted it. He encouraged the artists to paint more naturalistically and demanded greater refinement in the quality of color and line. The vibrant colors of Akbar's time were now replaced by subtle colors, energetic movement by a formal and ceremonious manner, and the sentiment of heroism with spirituality. The Mughal artists began to capture not only the time but also the personality and psychology of the subject very successfully in such a masterpiece as the *Dying Inayat Khan* created during Jahangir's reign (see introductory essay).

Jahangir's son Shah Jahan (1627–1658), who built the Taj Mahal, the seventh wonder of the world, was more interested in architecture than painting. Although the Mughal atelier remained active during his reign, Mughal painting began to wane stylistically. The emphasis on naturalism and psychological effect, so much appreciated in Jahangir's time, gradually declined. Irrational elements began to appear, and even the phenomenon of spatial recession was sometimes misunderstood (Beach: 133–36).

Shah Jahan's son, Aurangzeb (1658–1707), who emerged victorious in a series of battles with his siblings, imprisoned his own father and ascended the throne with a strong determination to establish Islamic rule and orthodoxy all over the subcontinent. He spent most of his life extending the territory of his empire into the Deccan. His policy toward the Hindus was just the opposite of Akbar's. He persecuted Hindu religious centers and spent time reading the Koran. As an orthodox believer, he led an abstemious life, which may explain his lack of interest in art (Beach: 172). Thus the great Mughal school, so lovingly nourished by his grandfather and great-grandfather, struggled to survive during Aurangzeb's reign. The artists of the Mughal atelier sought jobs elsewhere, including Rajasthan, Bihar, Bengal, and Deccan. Although in the second quarter of the eighteenth century, during the reign of Aurangzeb's great-grandson Muhammad Shah (1719–1748) the spirit of Mughal painting was briefly revived, the heyday of the great achievement of the Mughal school was gone forever.

The interaction between Mughal and Rajput painting, which began with the origin of the Mughal school, persisted even in the later period. Thus even in the eighteenth century Mughal painting remained influential in the development of Rajput painting. Similarly the tradition of Rajput painting continuously played an important role in the history of Mughal painting. Some Mughal painting of the later period, particularly of mid-eighteenth century, appears similar to Rajput painting not only because the Mughal school of painting was highly influenced by the spirit of the Rajput tradition but also because by this time some paintings of the Rajput school were very much Mughalized.

12

12

The Birth of a Prince

Mughal style, 16th century

Gouache and gold on paper, 9 x 6⅜ inches

1972.43

The birth of a prince, a popular subject of the Mughal schools, was treated by various Mughal artists in different periods. Both in the classical and in the Mughal periods, it was customary among the Mughal and Hindu rulers to give a generous *baksis* or tip, to the messenger who first brought the news of the childbirth to the sovereign. This miniature records that custom. The Mughal emperor stretches out his hand toward the courtier as if giving him something precious that is not visible in the picture. The empress rests on a bed with a canopy and a curtain inside a one-story building. Close to her feet a nurse in a white gown carefully holds the newborn. Four other female figures, including the nurse, wear *chaghtai,* Turkish headdresses. Because no male is allowed at a birth, the mustachoed Mughal emperor sits on the throne in the terrace behind the birth room. The emperor is attended by *chowrie* bearer and two courtiers who seem to be congratulating him on the birth of a prince. The Mughal sovereign sits on the throne in the classical royal posture known as *lalitāsana*, in which his right leg rests on his left knee.

A noteworthy feature in this miniature is the emperor's archaic turban with its crisscrossed design and protruding *kula*, or a small staff fastened inside the cloth of the turban. Such turbans were derived from the fashion of the early Safavid period of Persia and prevailed in India during Humayun's time (r. 1530–1540, 1555–1556). Akbar, who was born in 1542, wore such a turban only when he was a teenager. After he ascended the throne in 1556, Akbar is never represented in Mughal painting wearing such an archaic turban. Hence the middle-aged Mughal king celebrating the birth of a prince must be Humayun and the newborn, Akbar. We have no paintings from Humayun's time, except possibly some pages from the dispersed Fitzwilliam Album deposited mainly in the Fitzwilliam Museum at Cambridge. A folio from the album depicts *Prince Akbar Hunting a Nilgai*. According to Beach, the hunting scene is based on a real event that occurred on July 20, 1555 when Prince Akbar was thirteen (Beach: 20). His argument is mainly based on the description of the event given in the *Akbar-nama* and on the Humayun-period turban worn by the young prince. If this reasoning is correct, the present miniature would be even older than *Prince Akbar Hunting a Nilgai,* because Akbar is shown here not as a teenager but as a newborn. Often in Mughal painting, even for depicting a historical event that happened several decades or centuries before, contemporaneous fashion is shown. Therefore this painting appears to be rendered soon after Akbar was born when the turban of Humayun's time was still prevalent. Although this may be considered, it cannot be confirmed by a comparative study of the style, because no dated and/or inscribed painting firmly attributable to Humayun's time has been found. Besides, as Chandra notes, the Watson example "is extensively retouched and repainted, notably the sky, the parapet and terrace, and the red canopy and the curtains of the bed" (Chandra 1971: 20).

Published: Chandra 1971: cat. no. 14.

13

A Tree Watered by Human Blood, illustration from an unidentified manuscript

Mughal style, ca. 1575

Gouache and gold on paper, 7 x 5⅝ inches

1972.42; see color plate 2

This painting was extracted from a folio of a manuscript. Any text that might have been written on the borders of the folio has been completely removed. Therefor it is not possible to identify the name of the manuscript or the scene depicted in the painting precisely. However, we can discern several stylistic elements of early Mughal paintings. Of them perhaps the most remarkable is the descending point of view, as if experienced by a bird diving toward ground. In Indian art history such a view is also known as a plunging view. In the present example the descent begins from the top of the tree and the summit of the hill and rests momentarily in the middle ground where the main episode of the drama, involving the decapitation of the man, takes place. Then the view plunges further to the foreground. This effect of a constantly moving viewpoint is created with the combination of a bird's-eye view (the representation of the corpse lying flat) and a side view (the horses and riders). Another early Mughal feature is the artist's fascination with such bright colors as orange, red, and green. Because Akbar, the great Mughal king, hired for his atelier many Indian artists who had previously rendered traditional paintings with vibrant colors, early Mughal paintings resemble Jaina and *Caurapañcāśikā*-style painting in color scheme. Within a few decades, however, the Mughal artists of the Jahangiri period (1605–1627) began to use muted colors. Evidently this painting was rendered long before the later period. Moreover, the cloudlike rolling hills, hand gestures, and distinctively recognizable representation of the protagonist without using hierarchic proportion, a later development of in Mughal painting, indicate that this painting is contemporaneous with the works of the Akbari atelier.

This miniature shows an unidentified mythical event occurring under a tree that bears human heads as its fruits. Very likely this is the well-known Wakwak tree of Arabian legends. Amidst the excited crowd, the protagonist standing near the tree directs a servant to water the tree with human blood collected from the dead man, who lies on the ground. The dark-skinned servant pours the blood from a big bowl into the roots of the tree. The intensity of the scene is heightened by the lament of the lady who raises both her hands in distress and by the vigorous gestures of the audience, particularly the horse-riders shown in the foreground. Some put their forefingers to their mouths, while others throw up their hands in amazement at the sight.

13

Published: Chandra 1971: cat. no. 13.

14A
A Scene of a Bed Chamber, recto from an unidentified manuscript folio

Popular Mughal style, ca. 1605
Gouache on paper, 6 x 6½ inches
1972.45

This fragment of a folio in a horizontal format belongs to an unknown manuscript. Both sides of the folio are illustrated; the recto side depicts the scene of a chamber against the background of a huge scarlet curtain that covers most of the picture. The curtain is embellished with a yellow border and tiny black pompoms. In the foreground a handsome young nobleman garbed in an orange *dhoti*, a purple scarf, and a white turban reclines on a luxurious bed, furnished with a blue pillow, a dark green coverlet, and yellow bed-ruffles. Three female companions attend him; two sit on the ground close to the footboard of the bedstead and seem to be conversing. The figure of the third female companion is partially preserved and can be seen close to the headboard.

Because there is no superscript on the recto, it is not clear how this scene of the chamber is related to the other painting on the verso. However, the facial features of the protagonist in both paintings are similar enough that we can safely assume that both paintings are related to same story.

Published: Chandra 1971: cat. no. 16.

14B
A Divine Child, verso from an unidentified manuscript folio

Popular Mughal style, ca. 1605
Gouache on paper, 6 x 6½ inches
1972.45

On the verso seven lines of Devanāgarī script in Prakrit language are written in black and red ink on the buff-colored surface of paper. The border of the folio containing the folio number is missing. The horizontal emphasis on textual and pictorial format is still visible. Both recto and verso paintings are rendered in popular Mughal style, which differs from the imperial style of the Mughal court in several aspects including the color scheme, perspective, and the degree of naturalism. Already in 1960 Chandra had recognized the popular Mughal style. In his often-cited article, "Ustad Salivahana and the Development of Popular Mughal Style," Chandra demonstrated that Ustad Salivahana was one of the main artists responsible for developing the popular Mughal style (Chandra 1960: 25–46). He argued that both these paintings are probably the work of the same eminent artist. I want to reexamine this proposition, for these two paintings differ stylistically from Ustad Salivahana's work. For example the artist uses vertical format together with the Akbari style of plunging view and subtle shading, but in our paintings the scenes are shown horizontally almost in the *Caurapaṇcāśikā* style and most of the time the figures are rendered linearly. Furthermore, the type of female figures of this painting differs from that of the work attributed to Salivahana. Thus we have good reason to believe that although the artist of these painting rendered his work in popular Mughal style he was not Ustad Salivahana.

The verso side of the folio shows the nobleman bending down to lift a child from a bamboo grove on the bank of a river. This time he wears a red *dhoti*, a white scarf, and a similar turban. Between the child and the man is a small *surahi* (ewer), which indicates that he was there to fetch water from the river. The dark brown water of the river runs horizontally in the foreground, and the narrow strip of the pink sandy shore dissects the entire picture. The blue sky beyond the dark green hill of the bamboo grove is executed more naturalistically than the river and gives coherence to the horizontal format of the painting.

According to the Prakrit verses given in the superscript, the child found on the bank of the Ganga river was not an ordinary child. The splendor radiating from his body was as bright as a solar beam. He was so handsome that poets had difficulty finding any appropriate simile. He is described in the text as a divine child (*devakumāra*). People called him Naḍavīra (the bamboo hero), because he was found in the bamboo grove. The entire city, including the king and sages, was delighted to receive him.

This story is very close to the myth of the Hindu god Skanda/Kumāra, who was also found in a bamboo grove.

14A

14B

Chandra, however, identified the scenes of the paintings as the episodes of the romantic story of Mādhavanala and Kāmakandalā (Chandra 1971: 22). Several authors have narrated this romantic story (Majumdar, 1-5), but they do not mention the episode of finding a divine child in a bamboo grove as a part of the story. Therefore it is difficult to accept Chandra's identification.

Published: Chandra 1971: cat. no. 16.

15

15

A Woman Visiting an Ascetic

Mughal style, ca. 1605–1610

Gouache and gold on paper, 5¾ x 3¾ inches

1974.49

Chandra links this painting stylistically with the illuminations of the well-known manuscript *Anwar-i-Suhaili* in the British Museum. The manuscript, dated 1604–1610, contains significant works signed by such renowned artists as Aqa Riza, Abu'l Hasan, Bishan Das, and Mohan. All these works are rendered in their individual styles (Wilkinson: 1–5). Chandra does not identify in his brief statement any particular artist and style with which this painting is associated. However, the style of this painting differs from many of the paintings in the manuscript, especially from the style of Aqa Riza, who came to India from Herat to work for Jahangir, and brought fresh contact with the Safavid court style and remained aloof of Indian stylistic elements. But this miniature is by a Mughal artist who adopts the Indian artistic approach with the full profile of the woman, voluminous rendering of her body, the combination of bright yellow and orange colors, and multiple use of black tassels as ornaments. All these features are derived from *Caurapaṇcāśikā* style. Thus this painting somewhat resembles Bishan Das's and Mohan's eclectic works found in the *Anwar-i-Suhaili* which suggests that this is a work of Jahangir's time and agrees with Chandra's dating. As he pointed out, later hands have retouched the painting.

In an isolated place with steep rocky hills a young woman visits an aged ascetic. The woman is clad in blouse, trousers, and tunic with jagged edges, known as *cākdār jama*. A diaphanous veil covers her head and shoulders. Holding a golden tray with a box on it, she stands respectfully in front of the ascetic. She is shown here in full profile and with demure and humble facial expression. The aged ascetic sits under a flowering tree on the right. He has white hair and beard and wears a cloak decorated with golden flowers. He looks downward with the slightly tilted head. Two golden trays lie on the ground before him.

As in many other Mughal paintings, the artist treats the background rudimentarily with stylized pink rocky hills under the blue sky partially covered by puffy white clouds. A similar stylized rocky hill, bluish in color, also appears in the foreground dotted with two small plants, one in blossom. Between these hills lies an expansive grassy land that is rendered here with bluish green color.

Published: Chandra 1971: cat. no. 19; Raducha: cat. no. 2.88.

16

Zulaykha in Deep Thought, page from a manuscript of the story of Yusuf and Zulaykha

Mughal style, ca. 1610

Gouache and gold on paper, 4½ x 2¾ inches

1972.46; see color plate 3

Manuscript of Yusuf and Zulaykha by Mawlana Abdul Rahman (1414–1492)

Mughal style, ca. 1610

Red and black ink, 5⅝ x 2⅜ inches

1972.47.1–55

The illustrated page is in vertical format. The recto of the folio has one line of writing above the illustration and two lines at the bottom. The verso has two columns of writing, each consisting of thirteen lines including one diagonal line on each side. The writing is in black ink; there is no folio number. In addition to the illustrated page, the Elvehjem has what appears to be a complete manuscript of fifty-five unnumbered folios in a vertical format. It is written in beautiful Arabic script in black and red ink on buff-colored paper. The edges of the folios are gilded, and vertical lines of gold ink mark the center margins of the double columns. The language recorded may be Persian. Although the Watsons collected two illustrated pages with this manuscript, both duly recorded in the 1971 catalogue, the Elvehjem now has only this single illustration.

The vertical format gave the artist an opportunity to describe the scene in multiple viewpoints. Persian artists in India introduced such a format around the second half of the sixteenth century. Prior to this Indian artists almost always executed their works in a horizontal format. Often they found

16 recto

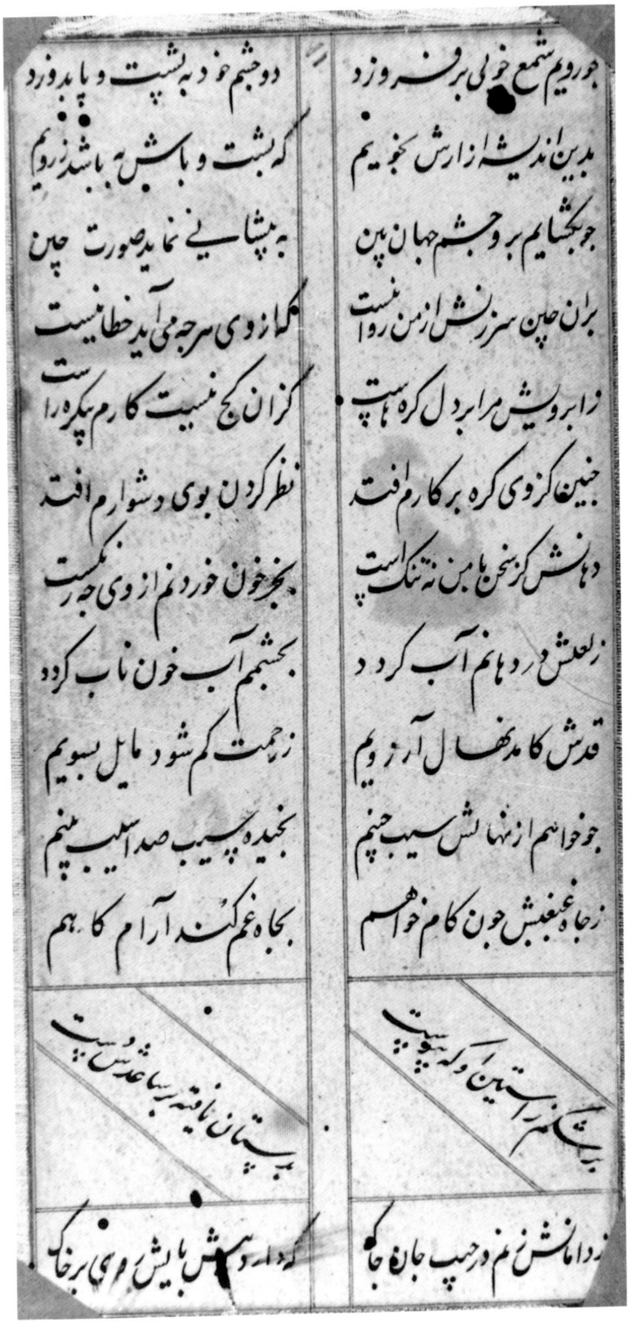

16 verso

this format useful for describing the story in continuous narration either on the wall or on a narrow palm leaf. Due to the rapid development of Mughal art, within few decades, the vertical format with multiple viewpoints became outdated in the art of the Mughal atelier of Akbar (1556–1605) and Jahangir (1605–1627). But it continued in popular Mughal art even in the later period. The present miniature is an early seventeenth-century example of such popular Mughal style. The artist who painted this miniature is familiar with the Rajput style as evidenced by the color scheme, for example, the juxtaposition of large areas of contrasting palettes: blue, yellow, brick red, and white. The scheme may appear different from that of the Rajput style only because the color-fields are decorated here with flowering plants.

This miniature is an illustrated folio of a manuscript story of Yusuf and Zulaykha, an instance of the folktale type called Joseph and Potiphar's wife (Rogers: 86–87), by the well-known Persian poet Mawlana Abdul Rahman (1414–1492). The queen Zulaykha fell in love with a slave, Yusuf, who was endowed with attributes of a superhuman. This story is allegorically interpreted as love between God and human beings, a concept that existed in India independently long before the story was written but became more popular after this Islamic story was introduced in India.

In the miniature the lovesick Zulaykha leans against a green bolster inside a pavilion. Placing both hands on her raised knee, she gazes pensively toward the ground. She wears a golden crown embellished with a plume. An attendant stands respectfully in front of her in the courtyard. Three other attendants are shown just behind the blue wall of the palace inside the courtyard that has a yellow ground dotted with flowers. She holds a tray on her left hand and a *surahi* (ewer) with her right. Another maid (in the middle) wearing a pink dress and a light blue *orhani* also holds a ewer and tray and carries a green towel on her left shoulder. Yet another expresses surprise with the convention of placing her middle finger on her lower lip. In the foreground a tall doorkeeper stands at the gate of the palace. Alert, he carries a long staff.

Published: Chandra 1971: cat. no. 18; Raducha: cat. no. 2.89.

17

The Hoopoe

Mughal style, ca. 1610

Gouache and gold on paper, 10⅞ x 7⅜ inches

1973.17; see color plate 4

The colorful bird, perched on a stone on a stylized bluish gray rocky hill, has a long and slender beak, a fanlike crest, and black-and-white striped wings and a tail. The flowering bushes emerging from the rocks and a huge maple tree with the curvilinear trunk and branches growing above the hill against the gold sky enhance the natural beauty of the wilderness. At the top and bottom of the miniature are blue stripes embellished with a golden arabesquelike motif. Although this decorative motif frequently appears in Mughal paintings, apparently it is derived from an auspicious Jaina symbol consisting of two fish and vegetation.

The detailed brushwork used in depicting the bird indicates that the artist was rendering it through actual observation of the bird. As we know from the visual and textual sources, the emperor Jahangir (r. 1605–1627) inspired such a naturalistic approach. However the tendency to render the work of art naturalistically with actual observation seems to be prevalent in Mughal artistic tradition from inception. This view is based on *Tezkereh al Vakiat*, a diary record of Jauhar who was the private servant of the Mughal emperor Humayun (r. 1530–1540; 1555–1556). He describes an event that happened during Humayun's flight from India in the following words:

> The king undressed and ordered his clothes to be washed, and in the meanwhile he wore his dressing gown; while thus sitting, a beautiful bird flew into the tent, the doors of which were immediately closed, and the bird caught; his Majesty then took a pair of scissors and cut some of the feathers off the animal; he then sent for a painter, and had a picture taken of the bird, and afterwards ordered it to be released (Jauhar: 43, as quoted in Beach: 15).

This statement clearly shows Mughal interest in naturalism, which is intended to be achieved by actual observation. Such intention is difficult to find in Rajput art. However, it is interesting to note that in Mughal paintings including in the present example, the stylized rock formation derived from the Persian tradition was seldom treated naturalistically. This reminds us of a similar phenomenon in the classical period when the artists of the Ajanta caves (first century B.C. to sixth century A.D.) strived for naturalism, as it was known to their contemporary world, but never tried to change the stylization of the cubic rock formation into a realistic representation (see introductory essay).

17

Published: Chandra 1971: cat. no. 20; Jane Werner Watson, "Down the Lotus-Petal Path," *The Connoisseur* (September 1972): 38, hereafter Watson; Nergis Dalal, "A Sacred Trust," *The Christian Science Monitor* (April 24, 1980): 20.

18

18

A Prince Restraining an Elephant

Mughal style, ca. 1615

Gouache and gold on paper, 7 x 10 inches

1972.44

Like the kings and artists of classical India, Mughal princes and painters were fascinated with that majestic beast, the elephant. Subduing or restraining the creature had been a favorite theme of Indian artists for many centuries as exemplified by a third century A.D. Amāravatī sculpture (see Craven: 78 for illustration). That sculpture shows a maddened elephant tossing people aside with its powerful trunk in the middle of the market. Persian artists were not acquainted with this typical Indian theme mainly because Persia is not a natural habitat of the elephants and her artists were completely unfamiliar with these animals. Thus neither the Persian nor the Indo-Persian artists took much interest in this theme. But from the beginning of the Akbari school of Mughal painting this theme made a vigorous reappearance. This present painting showing an unidentified prince taming the elephant is an excellent example of the Mughal artist's interest in this theme.

The prince appears to be in fairly good control of the enormous elephant. He holds an elephant goad with his right hand and raises the other to signal the horseman ahead of the elephant who helps to control the running animal. The rapid movement of the elephant is captured by showing its huge body moving diagonally with its tail erect and trunk curled safely inward and two feet off the ground. The lofty steps of the beast indicate its enormous physical strength and deny the law of gravity. Immediately behind the elephant a foot-soldier carries a long staff; another foot-soldier runs ahead of the elephant. The foreground is covered with bluish green grass. Apparently the yellow middle ground represents atmosphere, whereas the white and blue band at the top suggests the sky.

An interesting pictorial element that began to appear in Jahangir's rule (1605–1627) is the carefully designed patches of smudge on the *jama* around the armpits of male figures to indicate perspiration. A few decades later this element began to appear in some Rajput paintings, particularly of the Bundi schools as an clear sign of Mughal influence (see Barrett and Gray: 147 for illustration.)

Published: Chandra 1971: cat. no. 15; Raducha: cat. no. 2.71.

19
Capturing Wild Elephants

Mughal style, late 17th century
Gouache and gold on paper, 10¼ x 6¾ inches
69.28.2

Mughal and Rajput rulers of India were fascinated not only with taming elephants but also with the more dangerous adventure of capturing wild elephants in a jungle. In the present example the artist exhibits his familiarity with the behavior of wild elephants by showing the adults frolicking in a lake and along its bank with baby elephants. During the hot summer season, elephants spend most of their time in a lake or a marsh. Knowing this animal behavior, hunters usually look for elephants in such places. The artist has also recorded the fact that in times of danger the leader always faces the troublemaker in an attempt to protect his herd. Here the leading wild elephant is shown in the middle of the picture fighting with a tamed elephant (with two riders and a bright orange carpet on its back) which is attempting to bring the wild one under control as guided by its human masters. In accordance with the tactics of the game, a snare is placed in the open area. As soon as the feet of the wild elephant become tangled in the snare, the hunters will pull the rope that tightens the snare. In the painting one foot of the wild elephant is depicted entangled in the noose of the snare. The artist seems to be describing an episode that he has observed. A large, dark green tree with a mauve trunk stands in the background where there is another elephant, three horsemen armed with spears, and a man standing between two rocks.

Published: Chandra 1971: cat. no. 23.

19

20

20

Aurangzeb Crossing a Lake in a Boat

Mughal style, late 17th century

Gouache and gold on paper, 7¼ x 11⅞ inches

1974.52

This painting differs stylistically from earlier Mughal works. The emphasis on spatial recession and a fuzzy distant horizon is the immediately noticeable difference. Those features had begun to appear sparingly and tentatively in Jahangir's time (1605–1627).

The great Mughal emperor Aurangzeb (r. 1658–1707) was eighty-nine years old when he died in 1707. Here he is depicted at an advanced age with a completely gray beard. He looks feeble and detached from what is happening around him. He bends his head to read a book, perhaps the Koran, which he holds with his both hands. He is seated in front of the boat on a golden throne equipped with a parasol on a light purple carpet. He wears a yellowish brown *jama* and a matching royal turban embellished with a white plume. The radiant nimbus that usually appears around the head of the divine monarch is conspicuously missing. Just behind him stands a courtier on whose gloved hand is perched a hawk, which may suggest that this is a hunting expedition. Three courtiers stand on the boat joining their hands to express their respect and humility before the emperor. Several colorfully dressed men vigorously ply the oars. At the back of the boat is a man overseeing the rowers and another man holding a musket. In the background are more boats, elephants, horse-riders, and foot-soldiers outside a walled city, all shown in spatial recession.

Unlike earlier Mughal emperors, Aurangzeb, who adopted an abstemious way of life and believed in iconoclasm, was not interested in sponsoring art. Lacking imperial patronage, the Mughal artistic tradition began to wither, and toward the end of his reign many artists left the atelier to seek employment elsewhere. Thus it is hardly surprising that only a few excellent paintings of this period are known; this miniature is one. Unfortunately, it is in a deteriorating condition, and restoration work has been done on some sections.

Published: Chandra 1971: cat. no. 30; Raducha: cat. no. 2.77.

21
Portrait of Shah Jahan

Mughal style, 18th century

Watercolor, gouache, and gold on paper, 7⅝ x 4⅛ inches

69.28.1

This formal portrait of Shah Jahan (r. 1627–1658) shows him in full profile against a blue-green background. Facing toward his left, he stands erect with dignity. He wears a burgundy-colored turban embellished with bluish plume, and his head is encircled with the golden ring of the nimbus. His beard, except for his mustache, is entirely gray, suggesting the advanced age of the emperor. With his left hand he holds a black fly whisk and with his right hand grabs the hilt of a sword, encased in a purple sheath, with its blade pointed upward and diagonally resting on his right shoulder. His diaphanous *jama* reveals chartreuse trousers that contrast with his purple shoes. A dragger is tucked fashionably in his sash.

The fly whisk, or *chowrie*, is a prominent royal symbol made of a bushy tail of the bovine (*bos grunniens*), a denizen of the Himalayas. In classical Indian art a royal figure is usually shown attended by a retainer waving or holding a fly whisk. Originally it was more practical than symbolic. Therefore it is understandable that in the mainstream Indian iconography a *chowrie* is always held by a retainer, not by a king, who indeed never had to wave a fly whisk himself. Representation of a royal figure attended by a *chowrie*-bearer continued even in eighteenth-century Rajput painting. However, in early Mughal and Deccani painting the royal attendants often waved a silky cloth instead of a fly whisk. As a result of Indianization, during the later Mughal period it began to appear as a part of regalia. Apparently the function and practicality of the fly whisk was forgotten, and it was remembered only as a royal symbol. Since a monarch is often shown holding regalia such as a scepter or a sword, the Mughal artist responsible for the present example saw no objection in depicting the emperor holding the *chowrie* as a royal symbol.

When we compare this portrait with other representations of Shah Jahan, we see that the artist has attempted to make Shah Jahan's facial features be recognizable. One of the emperor's such facial features is the gliding transition from the forehead to the nose with a slight depression immediately below the eyebrow. The crescent shape of the beard is another distinctive feature. Despite the fact that these features bear similarities with the physiognomy of other portraits of the emperor, we can not presume that this is a contemporaneous portrait of the emperor. Perhaps Chandra was correct when he suggested that the stiffness of the posture and line that can be detected in this work indicates eighteenth-century Mughal painting. Very likely this is a cruder copy of the seventeenth century original portrait of the emperor. The

21

naturalistic fluency of Jahangir's time was, however, decreasing already in Shah Jahn's time, and it was gradually replaced by stiffness and formality (Rogers: 108).

Published: Chandra 1971: cat. no. 28; Walter M. Spink, *Krishnamandala, A Devotional Theme in Indian Art* (Ann Arbor, Mich.: Center for South and Southeast Asian Studies, The University of Michigan, Special Publications, no. 2, 1971), 6, fig. 12; Raducha: cat. no. 2.61.

22

22
Rāmakarī Rāginī

Mughal style, early 18th century

Gouache and gold on paper, 7½ x 4½ inches

1974.54; see color plate 7

This miniature is based on a notion that one can enjoy a musical mode not only by listening but also by looking at the visual representation of the mode. A series of paintings representing such musical modes is known as a *rāgamālā*, "garland of musical modes." Such representation in Mughal paintings is comparatively rare because it is derived from ancient Indian artistic traditions that survived primarily in the Rajput repertoire. For this reason this Mughal painting exemplifies the merging process of the Mughal and Rajput traditions. In the lower center of the margin, a two-syllable short inscription in Devanāgarī script describes the painting as *desi*, "native," which perhaps is given here to suggest that this theme is indigenous.

Here a well-dressed young man is about to prostrate himself at the feet of his beloved to apologize for the grave mistake that he has committed. She draws away from him to prevent it from happening, perhaps because it was considered impolite to accept such apologetic greeting from a husband or a lover. Her attendant standing close to her expresses conventional astonishment by putting her finger on her lower lip. A man bowing down to a woman publicly is, indeed, an unusual scene in Islamic or traditional Indian society. In a private life, however, it is totally different story. The *Kāmasūtra*, an ancient Sanskrit text on lovemaking, prescribes doing so in a courtship ritual.

As I suggested in the introductory essay, the Rāmakarī Rāginī represents the scene of such courtship ritual of a classical theater, which was always performed with background music. The Rāmakarī Rāginī is the name of such music. This nomenclature is, however, a latter development not found in early texts. The earliest textual reference to Rāmakarī Rāginī comes in the eleventh-century text called the *Saṃgītārṇava,* whereas the earliest visual representation is found in the sixteenth-century illuminated manuscript, *Devīmāhātmya*. We still do not know exactly why this scene is called Rāmakarī. Some inscriptions given in Rajput painting refer to this rāginī as Rāmagahri;, "associated with Rāmagahr (a town)." Thus it is possible that it is named after a locality whose inhabitants specialized in representing this scene or performing the background music or even acting the theatrical scene. The identification of the locale is, however, difficult for there are several towns in India with this name.

Published: Chandra 1971: cat. no. 32.

23
Portrait of a Nobleman

Mughal style (probably Murshidabad), ca. 1760

Gouache and gold on paper, 13 x 10⅛ inches

1975.21; see color plate 13

Because of the heavy shading of the figures, particularly around the neck and nose, and the peculiar design of the turban and *jama*, this painting can be attributed to Murshidabad, the capital of Bengal, which flourished during the eighteenth century. Although it is rendered in the spirit of the Mughal tradition, the plunging view of early Mughal style has been replaced here by an insect's-eye view, which offers a view level with the nobleman and allows us to see the underside of the canopy instead of the upper part. However, such a view appeared occasionally even in the early seventeenth-century Mughal paintings. The color white and other softer palettes dominate the scene, in accordance with the popular color scheme of the eighteenth century.

A white canopy, held aloft on poles, is set in a garden terrace fenced off by a scarlet railing. The terrace is surrounded by red and white flowering plants. It is a sunny day, as indicated by the solar disc endowed with facial features, a conceit that appeared first in the seventeenth-century Rajput paintings, then afterwards in Mughal paintings. Under the canopy a bearded nobleman dressed in a white turban, a transparent *jama,* and striped orange trousers reclines against the bolster on a white carpet with a border of alternating yellow and purple squares. An attendant clad in a chartreuse *jama* and dark green turban stands behind him and waves a fly whisk. Several food-trays, a spitoon, and such weapons as a dagger, a sword, and a shield lie to the right side of the nobleman. Holding a flower in his left hand, he seems to be enjoying the music performed by a female singer flanked by two female musicians, one tuning a *tanpura* (a stringed instrument), the other playing a drum.

Published: Chandra 1971: cat. no. 37.

23

24

24
A Love Scene
Mughal style (probably Lucknow), mid 18th century
Gouache and gold on paper, 7 x 8 15/16 inches
1975.22; see color plate 8

Indo-Islamic artists, including Mughal painters, did not originally depict love scenes. Rajput artists, in contrast, from the beginning of their tradition were obsessed with this subject. Such a scene of the intimacy of a loving couple is derived from ancient Indian tradition going back to the first century B.C. or even earlier. It began to appear in Mughal painting during Jahangir's time (1605–1627) and became increasingly popular in later periods as a result of the ongoing integration of Mughal and Rajput art.

In this painting an amorous couple sits, surrounded by orange bolsters and cushions, on a beautiful carpet with a border of green foliage. Trays of wine bottles, fruits, and *pan* (a savory delicacy made of betel leaf and spices) lie in front of them. In the background is an elaborate building tastefully decorated with niches, lotiform pilasters, and hanging carpets.

The painting focuses on the romantic couple. The young man wears a white transparent *jama*, necklaces, bracelets, and bright orange turban and trousers. The woman is clad in a blue sari with flower pattern and an orange *coli* that has been pulled up, exposing her bosom. His passionate gestures and her shyness suggest their honeymoon night. Although he embraces her intimately, she demurely turns away. The burning candles and bluish gray walls indicate evening hours.

Published: Chandra 1971: cat. no. 38.

25
Honhar
Musicians on a Terrace
Mughal style, mid 18th century
Gouache and gold on paper, 8 7/8 x 6 5/8 inches
1975.23

According to Chandra's reading of the Persian inscription on the verso of the painting, it states that Roshanabadi is an inmate of the harem of Muhammad Shah, that the artist who rendered this painting is Honhar, and that the price of the painting is Rs. 325.

We can date this painting on stylistic grounds to the mid-eighteenth century, approximately when the Mughal emperor Muhammad Shah ruled, 1719–1748. Thus the master of the harem, named in the inscription Muhammad Shah, may well be the Mughal emperor. If this is correct then Honhar, the artist responsible for this painting, must not be the famous painter with same name who was active about a century before in the atelier of Shah Jahan (r. 1627–1658). Although the inscription does not attempt to associate the painter either with Shah Jahan or with the famous painter, Chandra comments: "This Honhar, if the inscription is reliable and not a later addition, is obviously a different person than his famous namesake who belonged to the atelier of Shah Jahan." I believe the inscription is genuine and does not intend to invoke the seventeenth-century artist of the same name.

A royal figure or a dignitary listening to or performing music is a popular subject among Mughal and Rajput artists. In this Mughal example, the lady Roshanbadi, in the middle of the painting shown in hierarchical proportion, kneels near a corner of a bed on a white terrace. She holds a *tanpura* with her right hand and the tip of the *hookah* pipe with her left. She is well dressed and lavishly adorned with pearl necklaces, earrings, and armlets. She faces female musicians, one play-

25

26

ing a *tabla,* the other apparently singing a song, as her animated hand gesture suggests. A female retainer leans against the frame of the bed, drowsing.

The terrace is flanked by two separate groves emerging from the shadow of the moonlit night. One on the left consists of flowering plants and plantains, the other on the right, several tall trees with tiny birds perched on them. Most of the upper half of the painting represents the nocturnal blue sky with the full moon represented by dark blue lunar disk encircled by golden moonlight. This phenomenon could be described as the lunar eclipse, but in fact is a conventional way of depicting a moonlit night. The idealized flower garden and the running fountain in the foreground had become, by this time, common property of both Mughal and Rajput painters.

Published: Chandra 1971: cat. no. 39.

26

The Court of Aurangzeb, double-page painting from a manuscript of the *Alamgir-nama* (a history of the reign of Aurangzeb written by Mirza Muhammad Kazam)

Mughal style, late 18th century

Watercolor and gouache on paper, 8⅝ x 5¾ inches

69.28.3; see color plate 16

Above the illustration are two lines of Persian writing in Arabic script and two lines beneath. They are written in black ink against the creamy surface of good quality paper. This late Mughal-style painting stylistically repeats several earlier traits such as the grouping of the courtiers arranged in layers in order to avoid too much overlapping and the radiant halo around the head of the monarch. Although both features had began to appear in Jahangir's time (r. 1605–1627), this work distinctively represents a later period. Noticeable elements of the later period are the idealization of human figures, heavy shading, and greater emphasis on decorative elements.

This late eighteenth century double-page painting nostalgically depicts the court of the Mughal emperor Aurangzeb, also known as Alamgir I (r. 1658–1707). The emperor is shown on the right page seated on the historic peacock throne, which had been in 1739 taken by the Persian invader Nadir Shah to his country. The artist must have had access to an earlier painting showing every detail of the throne, including the pair of colorful peacocks perched on the roof. The crowned head of the bearded emperor is embellished with a radiant golden halo set up against the apple-green background. Dressed in the imperial garb, the monarch is about to give a *jigha*, the feathered turban ornament, to the nobleman dressed in a pink *jama* and a red turban as a reward. Holding a tray, he stands nervously yet attentively in front of the emperor. In addition to him, many other courtiers stand courteously at either side of the monarch on the floor furnished with blue carpet with a flower motif. On the left page are a groom with well-caparisoned horses, doorkeepers holding staffs, a musician with *vīṇā*, dancers, servants taking the gift inside the tent, and elephant with riders, one of whom appears to be vassal king attending the ceremony. His retainer is holding a parasol above him as a symbol of kingship.

Published: Chandra 1971: cat. no. 50; Raducha: cat. no. 2.80.

Rajasthan and Rajput Art

Rajasthan is geographically located in the northwestern part of India. It includes both sides of the Aravalli range and a large part of the Thar Desert. During the medieval period many small kingdoms were established here; sometimes there were more than ten kingdoms. Historically this region is also known as Rajaputana because it was ruled by Rajputs, the Hindu warriors. As I explained in the introductory essay, the Rajputs played an important role during the Mughal period of Indian history and developed a rich culture and a magnificent artistic tradition, which rivaled the contemporaneous imperial art of the Mughals. This Rajput culture and art spread beyond the geographical boundary and interacted with cultural and artistic heritage of neighboring regions such as Gujarat and Malwa. Thus we examine here the miniatures of the collection from different cultural centers of Rajasthan including the neighboring regions.

GUJARAT

Gujarat, lying south of Rajasthan in the western part of India, is a major center of Jainism and, to some extent, also of Hinduism. Jainism is as significant as Buddhism to the religious history of the Indian subcontinent. However, even after the artistic tradition of the Buddhists disappeared from the subcontinent except in Nepal and Sri Lanka, that of the Jainas and Hindus continued to flourish in Gujarat and the neighboring regions. Although, from the eleventh century on to the Maratha control during the eighteenth century, Gujarat was ruled by various Islamic rulers including the Mughals, the religious, cultural, and artistic spirits of both Jainas and Hindus remained intact in this region.

Just as with the Buddhist manuscript illuminations of the eleventh or twelfth centuries from Nepal, the Jaina manuscript paintings of the same period are distantly related to the classical mural paintings of Ajanta and Elura. Early Gujarati paintings of around 1610 are stylistically associated with traditional Jaina manuscript illuminations and demonstrate transitional features linking them to the Rajput-style paintings of a later period. Thus the study of Gujarati paintings is often valuable for understanding the relationship between classical and Rajput painting.

27

27

The Goddess Pṛthvī Lauds Kṛṣṇa, folio from a manuscript of the *Bhāgavata Purāṇa* (a Sanskrit text dedicated to Viṣṇu)

Gujarat, early 17th century

Gouache on paper, 7⅜ x 12½ inches

1975.46

Immediately above the illustration are eight lines of Sanskrit writing in Devanāgarī script and fifteen lines on the verso. The text is written in black ink on buff-colored paper with the numbers of the Sanskrit verses in red. The folio number 226 on the left border indicates that it is a part of a large manuscript. Following archaic system, the scribe writes the number of folio not in decimal system but in syllables. According to such system the long vowel *ā* stands for 200 and *tha* for 20, and *ja* for 6. Even by the third century A.D. this system was archaic, and a new system was in use. But people in India do not discard earlier tradition deliberately although often it does go through metamorphosis.

As described in the Sanskrit text of the *Bhāgavata Purāṇa* given on the upper section of this folio, the earth goddess Pṛthvī, standing between two stylized trees, greets Kṛṣṇa and praises him for killing the notorious demon king Narakāsura. The slain king's son, the crown prince of the demons, was, however, a devotee of Kṛṣṇa. In order to express his loyalty to the god, the prince dismounts from his elephant, walks down the hill, and prostrates himself before Kṛṣṇa. Behind Kṛṣṇa stands an attendant with a bowl in his hand.

Against an apple-green background, bright orange is used to accent the tree trunks, the costumes of Kṛṣṇa and the earth goddess, and the carpet on the back of the elephant. Although the elephant's bluish gray body and the dark green branches are rendered with some degree of naturalistic color, as usual the artist uses contrasting colors such as green and orange. Pink is used for the dress of the prince and his attendant and even for a branch of the tree.

Published: Chandra 1971: cat. no. 83; Raducha: cat. no. 2.35; Vajracharya 1994: 44.

28

Kṛṣṇa and his Companions Playing, folio from a series illustrating the *Bhāgavata Purāṇa* (a Sanskrit text dedicated to Viṣṇu)

Gujarat, mid 17th century

Gouache on paper, 8½ x 7¼ inches

1977.125

Set against a blue background is the colorful clothing of the figures. The plant with huge orange flowers and green leaves is placed almost in middle of the picture. Similar flowering plants decorate the background. Such floral decorations are a main feature of Gujarati paintings. Big pupils of a sparkling dark color placed close to the nose are another characteristic of the style. As in many other Rajput style paintings hair is treated rudimentarily with black pigment above the forehead and earlobe. Only when Rajput artists are influenced by Mughal and Deccani painting do they render the hair naturalistically. But this artist invokes Indian artistic tradition by employing the same physiognomy for all figures, differentiated only by gender (see introductory essay).

This painting consists of two scenes, both related to Kṛṣṇa. In the upper section Kṛṣṇa and Rādhā sit in a swing, attended by a group of young women, some who rock the swing. While Kṛṣṇa wears an orange *dhoti* and a wide variety of ornaments including a triple-lobed crown, Rādhā is attired in a pink sari, a dark green blouse, an orange *dupattā* and necklace, bracelets, and earrings. Their female companions also wear bright-colored dresses.

Rādhā and Kṛṣṇa are depicted again in the lower section playing a game. The gestures and movements of the members of two rival teams indicate an exciting competition. Rādhā and her two female companions vigorously challenge Kṛṣṇa's team of males. Both teams hold long-handled sticks that resemble hockey sticks. Two balls are on the ground; one is stuck between the sticks of the team leaders.

Published: Chandra 1971: cat. no. 85; Raducha: cat. no. 2.37.

MEWAR

In the political, cultural, and artistic traditions of Rajasthan, Mewar is eminent among the Rajput kingdoms. It is bordered by Malwa in the east, Gujarat in the south, the Aravalli range in the west, and Ajmer, Bundi, and Kota in the north and northeast. The original capital of Mewar was Chitor. After the violent attack of the Mughal imperial forces in 1568, Udai Singh (1537–1572), the ruler of Mewar, built a new capital Udaipur, named after himself, closer to the Aravalli range which often provided safety to the Rajput from invasions.

Akbar (r. 1556–1605), the most illustrious Mughal emperor, had a master plan to subdue the Rajput and bring them into imperial service, either by force or by intermarriage. Although he succeeded in many instances, he did not with the Sisodiya dynasty of Mewar. Generation after generation, the kings of Mewar, even after they lost their original capital, fought the Mughals. In 1576 Rana Pratap (r. 1572–1597), the successor of Udai Singh, even lost the second capital, Udaipur, to the Mughals for a period and retreated to the town of Chawand. Although this is a small town situated south of Chitor, it is a familiar site for the history of Indian painting because a valu-

28

able set of *rāgamālā* paintings was executed here in 1605 by an artist named Nisaradi. The significance of the set lies in its stylistic features, which exhibit a transitional phase from sixteenth-century *Caurapañcāśikā* style to later Mewar style, and its relationship to contemporary Mughal paintings and those of other neighboring schools of art.

Despite the remarkable effort made by the Mewar rulers, in 1614 the kingdom suddenly collapsed. Amar Singh (r. 1597–1621) had no choice but admit to the superiority of the Mughal imperial power. His heir, Prince Karan Singh (r. 1621–1628), extended a friendly hand to the Mughal emperor Jahangir (r. 1605–1627) and attended his court as a gesture of accepting Mughal overlordship. Realizing the symbolic significance of this event, Jahangir, as we know from his memoirs, received him warmly and provided him with many valuable gifts. Due to the imperial favor, like other Rajput kingdoms such as Bundi and Ajmer, Mewar also began to enjoy prosperity. During the reigns of Karan Singh and his son Jagat Singh I (r. 1628–1652) several impressive constructions including the well-known Jagmandir palace were built. The Mewar kings lived comfortably for several generations. Many sets of paintings commissioned during this prosperous time including the *rāgamālā*, *Gītagovinda,* and *Rāmāyaṇa* have been found. The earliest Mewar painting in the Watson collection is catalogue number 29, Rādhā Conversing with a Confidante. This valuable painting is so stylistically similar to the *rāgamālā* series dated 1628 and other works of the famous artist Sahabdi (also known as Sahibdin) that the painting can be attributed to him without any doubt. (Compare Ebeling: 127). This early Mewar artistic tradition continued in the eighteenth century without any intentional dramatic changes and survived even in to the nineteenth century, but its early artistic spirit began to decline rapidly. Meanwhile the Nathdwara school of painting, which flourished around the well-known temple of Śrīnātha, carried on the technical way of executing a painting on cloth, which goes back to classical period. Here we can expect the survival of early iconographical and stylistic elements to be still recognizable.

As a result of the close association with the Mughal court, some aspects of Mughal cultural and artistic approaches were incorporated into the Mewar tradition. But the traditional view and idealism of the Mewar artists remained unaffected. The Mewar artists continued creating idealized works of art and did not admire the realistic approach of the Mughal artists. Following the concept of *darśana*, which I explained in detail in the introductory essay, Mewar artists continued to render their works symbolically. Some artistic elements such as the radiant nimbus, shading, the plunging point of view, two or three simultaneous scenes within a picture, and a noticeably decreased size of female breasts were indeed borrowed from Mughal art, but they had very little effect on the main spirit of the Mewar artistic tradition.

29

Attributed to Sahabdi (also known as Sahibdin, active around the second quarter of the seventeenth century)

Rādhā Conversing with a Confidante

Mewar, ca. 1625

Watercolor, gouache, and gold on paper, 8¼ x 6¾ inches

69.28.8

This miniature displays several stylistic features of the Mewar school. One is the almond-shaped eyes with tiny irises touching the upper lids in the middle section. Compare these eyes with those of the figures shown in the Gujarati painting, cat. no. 28, where much bigger irises are located closer to the tear ducts. Another Mewar feature is the diminutive head with the straight vertical flow of wet-looking hair at the back of the head resembling the head of the golf club. The style of rendering the vegetation, including the rare appearance of a tree, with fanlike circular foliage is typical of the Mewar school. The style of this painting is very similar to the *rāgamālā* series painted by Sahabdi in 1628 at Udaipur, the *Bhāgavata Purāṇa* of 1648, and the *Rāmāyaṇa* of 1648–1650 and can be attributed to him without any doubt (Chandra 1971: 56).

Indian literature often describes the anguish of separation with much exaggeration. According to the poetic convention closely associated with such exaggerated statement the moonlight does not have a cooling effect on separated lovers, instead it gives them a burning feeling. The Devanāgarī script given on the upper section of the painting says that Rādhā was much worried because she found out that Kṛṣṇa was having fun with other pretty girls. She was surprised to learn that even in such an unbearable state of separation Kṛṣṇa enjoyed not only moonlit nights but also the cool breeze of

॥राधीकासषीप्रतैकहै छै: हसषी: सोधन छै त असत्री कीसनरामुषरिबात सांनलतीहो
सी: तीणी असत्रां देमलया चलप्र बतरो बायबेदन नहीकरतोहोसी: चंद्रमा: चंदन
पीओनेनदीहांही पुरण वासीरो: ते नलांसीरजि छै: मनोहर सुंदरमु षथिकीसीबात सांन
लतां परमसंतोष लागतोहोसी:
29

30

31

the Himalayas and the fragrance of sandalwood. This poetic convention is illustrated in this painting through the technique of simultaneous narration, in which a viewer can see two different episodes taking place at the same time. This technique is different from continuous narration in which sequential episodes of the story are depicted within a picture. Thus on the upper left corner Rādhā and her friend talk inside a building. Another girl is about to enter the room, perhaps with more information about Kṛṣṇa, who in the main image flirts with several girls in the middle of a forest full of exotic shrubs and trees of brilliant colors shown against a red background. The full moon appears as a disc in the upper right corner just above the slanting horizon. Such treatment of the horizon indicates a transitional phase, because in an earlier stage of development, as exemplified by *Caurapañcāśikā*-style paintings (Craven: 218, Chaitanya vol. 3: figs. 11, 13), the horizon was suggested either by a convex line or a diagonal line that cut off an upper corner.

Published: Chandra 1971: cat. no. 87; Raducha: cat. no. 2.36.

30
Kṛṣṇa Surprises the *Gopīs* at a Game of *Caupar*, illustration of the *Rasikapriyā* of Keśavadāsa (written in the late sixteenth century)

Mewar, mid 17th century

Gouache and gold on paper, 7½ x 7 inches

1977.127

This illustrated folio of Brajabhāṣā text has four lines of Devanāgarī superscript in black ink against the uncoated buff-colored surface of paper. There is no folio number.

In the portico of a house two groups of ladies wearing bright saris and contrasting blouses engage in a lively game of *caupar* punctuated by vigorous hand gestures. On the left Kṛṣṇa, serene and composed, appears in Mugal *jama* and turban. Startled by his unexpected arrival, one lady embraces the pillar of the portico with an expression of surprise and sudden shock, a gesture first seen in the Chawand *Rāgamālā* dated 1605 (Barrett and Gray: 132). The artist has successfully arrested the moment.

The roof of the building is embellished with a bulbus white dome and a pink *chatri* (a kiosk with an umbrellalike dome) at the corner of a flat roof. The walls of the building are painted in two different colors—bright yellow juxtaposed to red—a stylistic element reminiscent of such a rendering in early Rajput miniature paintings. The artist intends to render the architecture in three dimensions by projecting the portico away from the rest of the building. Such attempts are not seen in early Rajput paintings where the architecture is always flat and symbolic.

Published: Chandra 1971: cat. no. 88; Raducha: cat. no. 2.38.

31
A King and an Angel, folio probably from a series illustrating the *Bhāgavata Purāṇa* (a Sanskrit text dedicated to Viṣṇu)

Mewar, ca. 1675–1700

Gouache and gold on paper, 7⅝ x 14 7/16 inches

1977.128

We have been unable to identify the scene depicted in this painting. The continuous narration is obvious, since a royal person with a golden crown and a dagger stuck in the sash around his waist is shown conversing with a winged angel, or *apsarā*, three times: once in a grove seated on a deck and inside each of the pavilions located on the tops of two different mountain peaks. In the lower left corner of the painting, the monarch is shown again, conversing with a younger prince. At the foot of the mountain a Brahman extinguishes a fire, and a noble couple seated on a platform adore a sacred cow.

The color combination is perhaps the most noticeable element of the painting. The rocky yellow mountain against the dark background and the flat foothills sharply defined with a red coloring are depicted in such an intense tonality that they are obviously far from the reality of nature; they are, however, aesthetically stimulating. Furthermore, the trees surrounding the grove create a supernatural space beyond the natural phenomena such as one might expect to see only in a pleasant dream.

Published: Chandra 1971: cat. no. 90; Vajracharya 1994: 50.

32

32
Kṛṣṇa Embracing Rādhā by the Riverside
Mewar, early 18th century
Gouache and gold on paper, 3⅝ x 3½ inches
1989.8

On the bank of a river—very likely the Yamunā river since its water is dark— Kṛṣṇa and Rādhā look at each other lovingly. He holds her hand gently and rests his other hand on her shoulder with great affection. Kṛṣṇa wears elaborate headgear decorated with peacock feathers and a yellow undergarment, *pītāmbara*, on top of which he wears a brown skirt matching the color of Rādhā's sari. In the middle of the river is a golden pavilion encircled by white and pink lotuses, some in full bloom, others about to blossom. Near the river dam some cowherds attempt to cross the river with cattle, but the current of the water is so strong that some of the animals will be drowned. The waves of water are shown with curvilinear brushstrokes.

Across the river two girls, wearing multicolored saris, chat and gesture animatedly. In accordance with Rajput tradition their hair is rendered rudimentarily rather than naturalistically. Note that all female figures share same physiognomy. In the background is a thick forest with a flowering plantain tree in the middle. Above the forest is a narrow strip of horizon with pink and golden clouds. This tiny painting is within a rectangular frame, but the pinnacle of the pavilion breaks through the frame and to magnify the scale of the architecture. The unnatural growth of lotus in the running water of the river is a common scene in Indian art. A viewer can see such auspicious phenomenon not only in Rajput painting but also in the second and first century B.C. stone reliefs from Bharhut and Sanchi (see introductory essay for detail).

Published: Chandra 1971: cat. no. 91; Watson, 39; Vajracharya 1994: 49.

33
The Tīrthaṅkara Nemīnātha,
folio 78 from a manuscript of the *Nemipurāṇa*
(a text describing the life and deeds of Nemīnātha)
Probably Mewar, early 18th century
Gouache and gold on paper, 4⅝ x 4⅛ inches
1972.49

This illustrated folio has fifteen lines in Devanāgarī superscript written mainly in black with some words and verse numbers in red on white surface of the paper. In the middle of the text is a flowering plant. This is a scene of pūjā, a ritual of worship. It shows the stone statue of the Jaina god Tīrthaṅkara Nemīnātha and his worshipers. The epithet of the god *tīrthaṅkara* literally means "the ford-maker," the ford being a place where the river of worldly phenomena is shallow enough to wade across. In Jaina literature Nemīnātha is also known as Ariṣṭanemi. Here the dark blue Tīrthaṅkara meditates in cross-legged position under a tree, on a ruby-red throne covered with a golden parasol. A label in Hindi, given above the illumination, describes the god as *nemanāthajī nailavamta rupu chai*, "Neminatha has blue appearance." His chest is

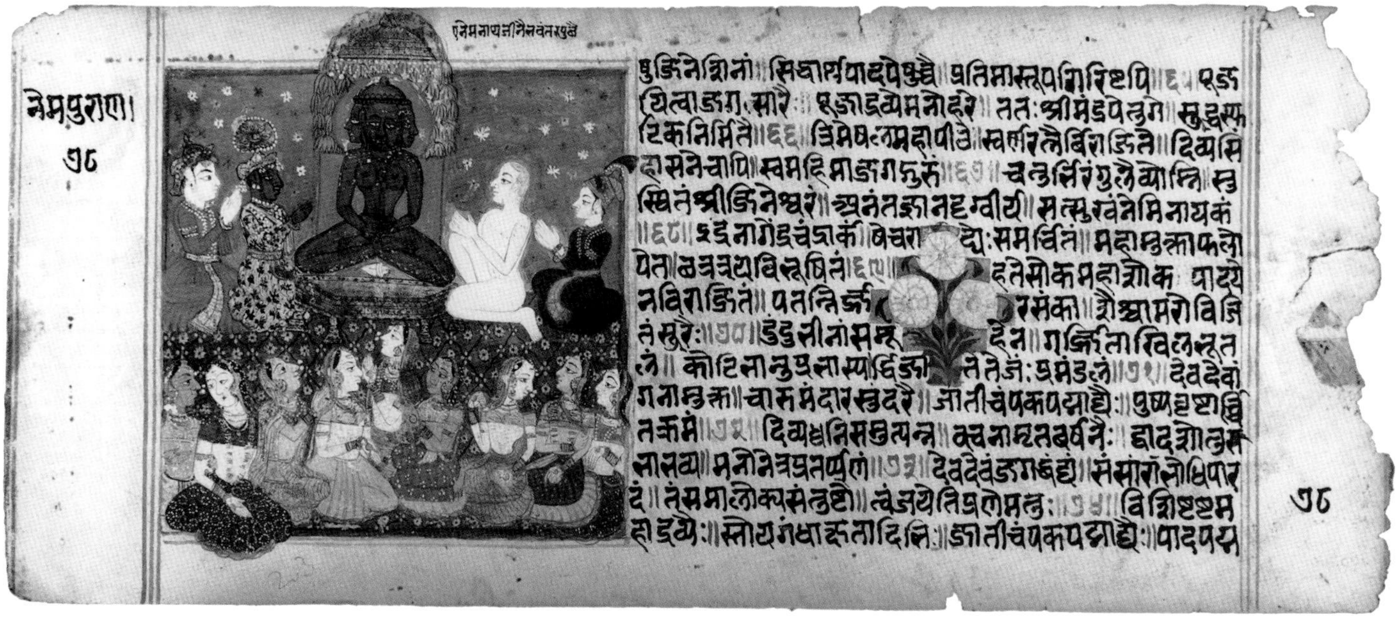

33

adorned with the auspicious symbol *śrīvatsa*. The divine image is enlivened by *prāṇa*, the inner vitality or life breath, shown as a slightly swollen chest, a prominent symbolic and stylistic feature throughout the history of Indian art (see introductory essay for detail). The Jaina god has three heads and elongated earlobes. In front of him is a tiny conch-shell, which seems to be his attribute.

In the foreground nine noble ladies sit on a beautiful flowered carpet, for worship. On the left of the Tīrthaṅkara, a naked Jaina monk and a princely figure in Mughal dress both join their hands in adoration to the god. The Jaina monk is shown here in a particular kneeling position of devotees with one knee on the ground and the other raised. This posture is often seen both in classical and also in prehistoric Indian art of the Indus valley civilization. In Rajput painting, this posture became rare perhaps because it was replaced by the Muslim position of kneeling for prayer.

On the right of the Tīrthaṅkara, two well-dressed men, one with dark and the other with a fair complexion, show their devotion to the god with the same hand gesture. They are the Hindu gods Kṛṣṇa and his brother Balarāma respectively. According to Jaina literature, the Hindu gods are the devotees of the Tīrthaṅkara Neminātha. At the request of Balarāma, the Tīrthaṅkara predicted that Kṛṣṇa would be a great king of the world but would be killed accidentally by a hunter with a poisonous arrow, and he would be born as a Tīrthaṅkara in his next life (Jaina and Kothia: 205–6). This story illustrates Jaina ambition to incorporate the Kṛṣṇa cult in to the Jaina tradition: thus Kṛṣṇa and Balarāma are depicted as the devotees of the Jaina god. Such representations of the Hindu gods are found also in the classical period stone sculptures (Raducha: 75). The Sanskrit manuscript on this folio describes the elaborate worship of the Jaina deity performed by Vedic god Indra, the sun and moon, and serpent kings.

Published: Chandra 1971: cat. no. 92; Raducha: cat. no. 2.6; Vajracharya 1994: 55.

34

34

Maharana Jagat Singh II (1734–1751) **of Mewar at the Festival of Holi**

Mewar, ca. 1740

Gouache and gold on paper, 16 13/16 x 10 11/16 inches

1977.129

The Rajput painter uses traditional multiple viewpoints and reverse perspective in depicting the architecture and figures. Thus viewers can see the rooftop and the inner section of the canopy simultaneously, and the section of the building closer to the viewer becomes much smaller than the rear section.

The Mewar king Maharana Jagat Singh II celebrates the festival of Holi, a vernal celebration, which is taking place around the palace by the hillside. The king sits on a low bench on the rooftop of the main building of the palace. The golden ring of the halo surrounding his head and shoulders draws attention to him. One of his retainers holds a mirror in front of him, a formal act of the ceremony associated with the festival. While looking at the mirror, the well-dressed, bearded monarch ritually touches the *pūjā* tray held by an attendant. Although this is a solemn ceremony, the king holds the pipe of the hookah between his lips.

Sanskrit literature and inscriptions inform us that an ancient Indian palace compound included multiple courtyards, stables for horses and elephants, and most important a building several stories high as the main residence for a monarch. The tall building was usually located in the middle of the compound. A more remarkable feature of palace architecture was, however, a network of courtyards that were accessible only through gates and the interlocked courtyards for safety reasons. A palace was also the center for cultural activities and some annual festivals. On these special occasions, *rājāṅgaṇa* (the front courtyard of the palace) was accessible to the general public also. Such a palace tradition continued in India even in the eighteenth century.

Down in the courtyard dancers, elephants, and horses with their riders including soldiers carrying royal paraphernalia wait for the monarch to join the procession that will begin just after the mirror-viewing ceremony is over. For the procession, very likely the king will ride the royal elephant, which is presently confined in the stable located in a corner of the second layer of the courtyard.

Published: Chandra 1971: cat. no. 93; Raducha: cat. no. 2.81.

35

Maharana Jagat Singh II (1734–1751) **of Mewar in Procession**

Mewar, ca. 1740

Gouache and gold on paper, 8⅝ x 8⅞ inches

1977.130

In the kinetic quality seen in the length of the stride of the foot-soldiers and the rapidly moving elephants, almost shaking the earth, this work admirably differs from other Mewar painting, which seldom captures movement.

Maharana Jagat Singh II represents a typical eighteenth-century Mewar ruler. Partially supported by the Mughals, the Mewar rulers of this time led voluptuous lives exactly as expected by the designers of the Mughal master plan for the Rajput future. Jagat Singh was more interested in elephants than taking care of his kingdom, which was in danger because of the rise of the Maratha power in the neighboring regions. The maharana's most favorite elephant was Soondur Gaj, "beautiful elephant," and the king was proud to own this majestic animal. In a letter he describes the elephant as capable of doing a thousand tricks (Tod I: 336, 338).

35

Soondur Gaj may be the royal elephant that is represented much larger than four other elephants here. Usually a mahout drives the elephant, and the king, flanked by attendants, sits in the howdah. But here the Mewar king, with nimbus, drives the elephant himself, which indicates his great interest in the animal. The middle-aged monarch, in orange *jama* decorated with golden leaves, converses with the courtier riding a smaller elephant, which is slightly ahead of the royal elephant. The courtier turns back towards the king and shows his respect with folded hands. The king holds a goad with his right hand and with his left gestures to the courtier. Immediately behind the royal elephant an attendant on the back of another elephant holds a huge parasol, a significant royal emblem. The fly whisks are other regalia carried by two elephant riders flanking the royal elephant. Furthermore, on the ground six more attendants on foot carry such regalia as a quiver, a bow and arrow, and a staff. Other regalia are wrapped within a cloth patterned like a peacock feather. This is not, however, a scene of a royal celebration such as coronation or wedding but a hunting expedition, indicated by a hawk perched on the hand of retainer on the front row and two hounds controlled by a groom shown almost in the middle of the foreground.

Published: Chandra 1971: cat. no. 94.

36

36

Autumnal Delight,
folio from a series illustrating the *Satsai* of Bihari

Mewar, mid 18th century

Gouache and gold on paper, 8¾ x 7⁷⁄₁₆ inches

1977.131

This miniature is a folio from a well-known series illustrating the *Satsai* of Bihari, a collection of about 700 verses written in the early seventeenth century (Chandra 1971: 62). The black ink superscript in Devanāgarī on yellow surface gives the verse number 425 from the text. Both the verse and the illustration are associated with autumn. The Hindi verse poetically describes autumn as arriving in the disguise of a beautiful young lady. The seasonal pink lotuses are her feet, the wagtail bird, *khañjana* (that appears around this time of the year) are her eyes, and the autumn moon is no other than her countenance. There is no reference to the dawn or to the woman who "has decorated her feet" as Raducha suggested (Raducha: 102). Works from this large series are now scattered in many museums and personal collections all over the world.

A two-story, white building with a flat roof stands in vivid contrast to the yellowish brown background; in front is a lotus pond with three white ducks. The second floor of the building has a red wall, whereas the ground floor has a bluish green wall, demonstrating the Rajput artists' ongoing interest in juxtaposing two contrasting color-fields. Inside the upper room, the blue Kṛṣṇa attired in his regular dress—a yellow *dhoti* and a golden crown decorated with the plume of a peacock—converses with a woman, perhaps a *gopī*, a Hindi word for a milkmaid. She wears a beautiful orange sari with a deep purple pleated middle section that is displayed in a semicircular pattern on the ground as she sits stepping on it. Such a circular pattern of the sari indicates later developments often seen in the eighteenth-century paintings. In early seventeenth century Mewar painting, following *Caurapañcāśikā* style, the middle section of the sari is always shown in a triangular pattern (Beach: fig. F).

Kṛṣṇa and the *gopī* are not alone; downstairs in the portico, two other *gopī* girls talk. Another woman, who walks by the lotus pond, has been identified by previous authors as Rādhā (Chandra 1971: 62) by the golden dress she wears (Raducha: 102). I see no reason to identify her as Rādhā, because a golden sari is not Rādhā's identifying attribute, nor is she otherwise shown to be distinct. All the women wear almost the same ornaments and have such similar faces that only the color of their saris distinguishes them. It is common for a mainstream school of Indian art to use the same type of physiognomy in all the work of the school (and is used to distinguish one school from another), but seldom practiced by the Mughal artists.

Published: Chandra 1971: cat. no. 96; Raducha: cat. no. 2.46.

37
The Elephant Nakhatula

Mewar, mid 18th century

Gouache and gold on paper, 7⅞ x 6⅛ inches

1977.132; see color plate 9

37

According to the Devanāgarī inscriptions given on the upper margin and on the verso, this painting represents the Mewar king, Maharana Raj Singh (1754–1761) riding his favorite elephant Nakhatula. The bearded young monarch, wearing an orange turban and a black and yellow patterned *jama,* sits astride the elephant holding one goad in each hand. The elephant's massive, dark blue body is depicted against a bluish green background merging gradually into grassy green landscape in the foreground.

The diagonal line of the elephant's body and the stretched-out legs suggests the animal's rapid movement. This treatment reminds us of the famous elephant of the Ajanta ceiling painting where the animal jumps out of a lotus pond in almost exactly the same manner (see introductory essay). Just as in the Ajanta painting, here too, the source of light is not fixed, but the artist, following the ancient artistic tradition, has created the massive volume of the elephant by shading both sides of the figure, especially around his legs.

Published: Chandra 1971: cat. no. 98.

38

A Tīrthaṅkara Renouncing the World

Rajasthani style, perhaps Mewar, late 18th century

Gouache and gold on paper, 3¾ x 7½ inches

1972.52

Indo-Persians and Mughal artists did not use the technique of continuous narration, but Indian artists including Rajput painters remained fascinated with it. In this continuous narration, the scene gradually moves from right to left, unlike most Indian work. Such narration is first seen in the first century B.C. Buddhist stone sculptures. Despite the time and sectarian difference, this Jaina painting shows undeniable artistic affinity to the well-known Sanchi relief depicting Buddha Śākyamuni's departure (Dehejia: 52–53). The theme of the departure, the elongated horizontal format, and the technique of continuous narration in both works are similar enough to suggest that some aspects of the ancient artistic tradition survived even into the eighteenth century. In the early Buddhist example the narration moves from the palace on the left to the forest on the right.

This scene seems to be associated with Tīrthaṅkara Neminātha's great departure from the palace and the beginning of a new, ascetic life in the forest. The palace compound partially enclosed with a pink wall is on the right. It consists of several white edifices from where palace ladies watch the departure of the prince who is already in the palanquin. The great departure is depicted here as a royal procession moving from the royal palace to the isolated forest on the left.

In Jaina literature, this palanquin is designated as Uttarakuru, a name derived from an ancient prosperous kingdom between the Indus and Gangetic river systems. The golden palanquin is rendered here with its curvilinear shape creating the sense of resilience and comfort. The prince, still wearing the scarlet royal headgear and princely robe, sits inside the vehicle. Three or four well-dressed men carry the palanquin and several groups of musicians, flag holders, *chowrie* bearers

38 recto

(adjacent to the prince), and many other pedestrians, cavaliers, elephant riders, including the gods Surya and Indra participate in the procession. A tiny figure of Surya, the sun god, is located in the middle ground at the left quadrant. He can be identified by his radiating solar halo and white horse-drawn chariot. Likewise, Indra, the king of the gods, mounted on his elephant Airavata is depicted just above the white horse. The *Neminātha Mahākāvya* explains that when the prince left for the forest all the deities and demigods of heaven and the atmosphere came to the earth and followed him to the forest.

The main event takes place under a big tree, shown close to the left margin of the painting. The tree and the rocky hills represent a hermitage. The prince sits in a lotus posture on top of the stylized rocky hill and has placed the princely robe and headgear on the ground. The prince, now a naked Jaina ascetic, is ritually removing the hair from his head. A well-dressed man with dark complexion stands next to the ascetic and apparently assists him in the ritual. A Jaina monk, following the monastic rule, does not shave his hair but pulls out the hair in order to avoid killing head lice. A baldheaded middle-aged man adores the ascetic by prostrating himself on the ground. Many other dignitaries pay homage to him through hand gestures. The entire scene is depicted against the yellowish green background representing the grassland with rolling hills. A strip of blue sky above the grassland creates the distant horizon.

Published: Chandra 1971: cat. no. 215.

38 verso

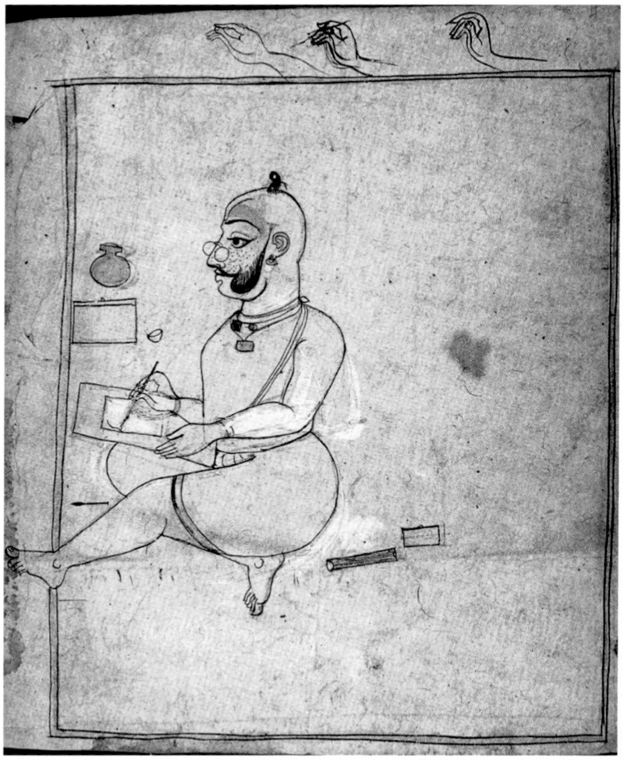

39

lace with charm boxes, and a simple *dhoti*. He has peculiar sideburns resembling a plume. In traditional fashion he is seated on the ground with his left leg stretched out and his right placed under his thigh. He holds the board on his thigh with his left hand and starts a sketch, holding the brush between the thumb and middle fingers of his right hand. The naturalistic depiction of the hand of an artist holding a brush seems to be the main concern of this artist. In the upper section of the sketch, beyond the double line border, are studies of such working hands. Furthermore, the artist was not happy with his earlier representation of the hand, traces of which are still visible, although he has replaced it with a new version. Around him are a typical Indian round-bottom water pot and artists' tools such as a brush and a small container, perhaps for pigment and brush cases.

Published: Chandra 1971: cat. no. 101.

39
An Artist at Work

Mewar, ca. 1800

Ink and wash on paper, 7⅛ x 6⅛ inches

1977.135

This sketch shows us how an Indian artist saw his work in progress. With the board in his lap, he could feel comfortable handling his work and inspecting it as if it were a tiny *āmalaka* placed on the palm, an expression often mentioned in ancient Sanskrit texts. This seems to be a reason why multiple viewpoints became the norm of Indian painting. Note also the fact that Indian art critics believed that the universe is a macro painting and the painting is the micro universe (see introductory essay). Indian fascination for miniature painting may be also associated with this concept.

Very likely this sketch is a self-portrait in which the artist is painting a miniature. The topknot protruding from his bald head indicates he is a Brahman. He wears eyeglasses, a neck-

40
Maharana Sambhu Singh (1861–1874) in Procession

Mewar, ca. 1875

Watercolor, gouache, and gold on paper, 10½ x 14½ inches

69.28.13

This elaborate royal procession moves from left to right with stately splendor. It is silhouetted against the green background with a strip of the high horizon where the yellowish green rolling hills meet the blue sky.

The young monarch Sambhu Singh, with radiant nimbus, sits in a beautiful golden howdah. He wears a pink *jama*, a royal turban lavishly adorned with pearls, and pearl necklaces. Immediately behind him is a retainer and in front of him a mahout with an elephant goad in hand. Both the retainer and mahout are bearded, wear a white *jama* and a red turban, and wave a voluminous, white fly whisk.

The huge royal elephant is also decorated with golden ornaments, including a tiny golden statue of a lion on its head. Its body is rendered here in black pigment, perhaps to identify him with the mythical elephant Añjana, "Black Pigment," used to paint the eyelashes, collyrium. However, much of its body is covered with a trapping decorated with yellow and scarlet geometric patterns. Beside the elephant are colorfully dressed soldiers and retainers carrying regalia including a para-

40

sol. The elephant appears to be floating slightly above the surface, making visible the feet of the retinue walking on the other side of the elephant. Following the ancient tradition, Rajput artists believed that an elephant, like the dark rain cloud, descends from the heaven in the form of rain. This view is indicated both by the floating position of the elephant and also by the Hindi inscription on the top margin:

Mahārājādhirāja mahārānā śrīsambhusanghaji savāri mā hāthi bādalasanagar pache rāvata sumana sanghaji

(Maharajadhirja maharana sri Sambhu Singh on the elephant Badalasanagar "Cloud Ornament." Behind him is Ravata Sumana Singh.)

This identification of the procession elephant with the cloud is significant. Such concept is also found in ancient Buddhist and Hindu texts (see introductory essay for detail).

Published: Chandra 1971: cat. no. 106; Raducha: cat. no. 2.76.

41

41
Śrī Nāthajī in Goloka

Mewar, Nathdwara, mid 19th century
Tempera on linen, 52 x 40½ inches
69.28.18

According to the followers of the Vallabha cult, this painting represents Kṛṣṇa as Śrī Nāthajī. Such painting is rendered by the artists of the Nathdwara temple in Mewar. Usually the painting is placed behind the main image of a shrine because of which it is called as *pechwai* or *picchava,* which literally means "backdrop." Technically, it resembles Tibetan or Nepalese thanka painting. As the tradition of thanka painting originated in India, the similarity between *pechwai* and thanka painting may indicate the same origin.

In the middle of this painting a lotus-eyed blue Kṛṣṇa stands with right hand on hip, and like a Buddhist god of the classical period, holds in his right hand the stem of a full-blown lotus. He raises his left hand toward the sky in the typical gesture of lifting the mythical mountain Govardhana in order to shelter the cattle and cowherds from a torrential rain discharged by the rain god Indra. The mountain is never shown; instead a wind-blown silky shawl goes through his hand. His feet are turned out, and as always in *pechwai* painting he is depicted in frontal position, correlating with the classical Indic tradition of representing a main deity in a sculpture or a painting. In typical Ṛajput paintings Kṛṣṇa is almost always shown in full profile. The iconography of this god is surely much earlier than the Vallabha cult itself. The god is shown within a rectangular frame indicating his shrine.

The milkmaids adore Śrī Nāthajī and raise their hands just as he does. Behind them mango trees are interspersed with plants. Immediately above the trees several divinities in aerial chariots together with their spouses make a shower of flowers over the shrine. Some divinities are identifiable as Indra, Śiva, Viṣṇu, and Kārtikeya because their animal vehicles —an elephant, a bull, the bird Garuḍa, and a peacock—are respectively shown in front of their chariots. Such representation of divinities, together with their animals hovering over the heads of the main figures dates back to the Gupta period, as exemplified by a stone relief depicting recumbent Viṣṇu on a wall of the Daśāvatāra temple in Deogarh (Craven: 120). In addition some *pechwai*, although not this example, include different episodes of Kṛṣṇa's story given in small rectangular compartments around the border of the painting (Leach: fig. 93). This interesting stylistic feature also helps us to see the further link of *pechwai* to early Indic works. Such an arrangement of compartments appeared in the sixth-century Aurangabad cave sculptures (Harle: 130) and continued in Tibetan and Nepalese thanka paintings. This feature is missing in this example because the border is occupied here by the figures of cows.

Below the figures of Kṛṣṇa and milkmaids is a narrow horizontal panel depicting a group of devotees worshiping the tiny image of Śrī Nāthajī. In addition, several cowherds with their cattle and three young ladies carrying milk jars on their heads, move toward the shrine. Immediately below the panel several dappled cows are flanked by two cowherds. The multiple representation of cows indicates that this is Goloka (the world of cattle) where Kṛṣṇa resides. A detailed study of *pechwai* paintings may reveal many important links between classical paintings and Rajput paintings.

Published: Chandra 1971: cat. no. 109; Raducha: cat. no. 2.33.

BUNDI AND KOTAH

The state of Bundi was bordered by Jaipur to the north and by Mewar to the west. Originally the rulers of Bundi were the vassals of the Mewar kings. According to legend, in the fourteenth century Bundi was founded by a chieftain of the Hara clan. In the sixteenth century when the Mughal emperor expanded his empire, Rao Surjan (r. 1554–1585) ruled Bundi. Recognizing the superiority of the Mughal military power, the Bundi ruler handed over the great fortress of Ranthambor (Ratnastambhapura, city of the jewel pillars) to Akbar and submitted to his imperial power. In return the emperor appointed him the governor of Varanasi, where he built a palace. Hence, the earliest examples of Bundi-style paintings are found in the well-known *rāgamālā* series painted in 1591 at Chunar near Varanasi. This series was probably commissioned by a member of the royal family of Bundi when they were doing gubernatorial service in for that region. This *rāgamālā* series combines the stylistic elements from the early Mughal school with local features. Rādhā Afraid (cat. no. 42), although rendered a few decades later in the seventeenth century, in many ways resembles the Chunar *Rāgamālā*. The plunging

42

view, the three dimensionality of the architecture, colorful tiles, and pointed cypress trees are obviously derived from the Mughal school, but the full profile, flowering mango trees, and overlapping plantains are elements of Rajput inspiration.

Despite the fact that Bundi was a small principality, it was not free from political turmoil. Mainly political tensions resulted from rivalries among members of royal families. The Mughal court had great interest in such rivalry. Just after Satrusal (r. 1631–1658) inherited the kingdom of Bundi from his father, his brother Madho Singh (r. 1631–1648), with the help of Shah Jahan, succeeded in separating off the region of Kotah from Bundi and founded a new principality. In its beginning stages the style of Kotah did not differ that of Bundi. But within a few decades Kotah developed a new style befitting the environment of its tropical hilly jungle, with an unprecedented interest in depicting the scene of hunting with beasts hiding behind rocky hills and leafy vegetation and hunters shooting the game from the pavilion in moonlit night. Kotah style continued even into the nineteenth century. Catalogue number 51 is a sketch for such painting.

42

Rādhā Afraid, miniature from a series illustrating the *Rasikapriyā* of Keśavadāsa

Bundi, late 17th century

Watercolor, gouache, and gold on paper, 10¼ x 6⅞ inches

69.28.9

The verse number 276 of the *Rasikapriyā* is the subject of this illustration. The verse is given in Devanāgarī script on yellow surface at the upper section of the painting. The superscript comprises three horizontal lines. As described in these lines, the miniature illustrates the sudden arrival of the thunderstorm of the monsoon, a characteristic of Indian weather of this time when an extremely hot and dry season is abruptly interrupted by a cool monsoonal thunderstorm and rain.

The three-dimensional approaches to rendering the architecture, the colorful tiles outside the pavilion, the dense vegetation, and the scarlet borders of these paintings are prominent stylistic features of Bundi miniatures. The dark-blue clouds, emerging from the horizon and issuing serpentine flashes of lightning, are shown rapidly spreading and covering the entire sky. The cloud patterns shown on the left just above the two-storied white pavilion resemble the head and trunks of elephants. In ancient India such cloud formations were designated as *jaladharajālas,* "water-cloud patterns," and they were studied carefully in order to predict rain (Vajracharya, forthcoming).

The pavilion is located in the middle of a garden dense with vegetation including banana plants and mango trees, with fresh leaves turning pink. On the ground floor of the structure Rādhā, frightened by the lightening, embraces Kṛṣṇa.

Immediately below the cornice on the left wall is the serpentine lightening, which almost enters the pavilion. According to ancient customs of Indian life, a woman is not supposed to be first to approach. Kṛṣṇa, therefore, was surprised and thrilled by this incident which is the main subject of this illustration. The yellow carpet on the ground floor and the mauve and white paint of the wall brightens the room. The upper floor is furnished with an orange carpet and a yellowish brown bed with a blue pillow. It is easy to agree with Chandra that this is "an exceptionally fine painting [that] captures the colors and mood of a monsoon thunderstorm with urgency and immediacy" (Chandra 1971: 66).

Published: Chandra 1971: cat. no. 110; Watson, 39; Raducha: cat. no. 2.40.

43
Dhanaśrī Rāginī

Bundi, end of the 17th century or early 18th century

Gouache and gold on paper, 7⅝ x 4½ inches

1973.35

Just outside the house in the carpeted courtyard, leaning against a cushion, a young lady paints a portrait of her lover. She wears multiple pearl necklaces and a bright yellow sari. Her green complexion seems to be her iconographical feature. She is identified in the Devanāgarī superscript as "Ghanasari Rāganī" which seems to be closer to her original correct name. Only because of the similarities of GHA and DHA in Indian scripts, Ghanasari (Sanskrit Ghanaśrī) and Dhanasari (Sanskrit Dhanaśrī) are often used interchangeably. We see same script-related phenomena also in Buddhist name such as Sumegha or Sumedha, a Brahman boy destined to be the Buddha in his future life.

According to a verse cited by Waldschmidt (264) from the *Saṅgītadāmodara* (a Sanskrit text on musical modes), "Dhanaśrī is a charming young woman, with a body dark [*śyāma*] like the blade of *durvā* grass, who–holding a picture panel in one of her hands is about to paint the (far-off) lover, while her breasts are being washed by drops of tears falling down (from her eyes)." This description accords well with our painting. Her complexion "dark like the blade of *durvā* grass" may even provide us with a clue to investigate her real name. The Sanskrit word *śyāma* is used here as a synonym for dark. However, in Sanskrit literature *śyāma* also means dark green or dark blue. It is used not only for describing the color of the cloud, as in Kṛṣṇa's epithet *ghanaśyāma* "dark blue, like a cloud" but also for the color of a bean as in *mudga-śyāma*, "dark green, like *mudga* bean." In Sanskrit-English dictionaries this bean is identified as *Phaseolus mungo*. The Hindi (and English) word for this bean is *mung* and its color is dark green. Note also the fact that Kṛṣṇa is not always blue; sometime he is shown dark green as exemplified by some early Akbari paintings. Indian painting, from the fifth century onward, often depicts people either green, as in the Ajanta murals, or both green and blue,

43

44

45

as in medieval painting, to indicate their dark complexion. Furthermore such a complexion is constantly compared in literature with a dark cloud. If we keep this artistic and literary phenomena of "either blue or green" in mind, it becomes clear that the identification of a dark green rāginī as Ghanaśrī "Cloud Luster" may be more significant than her other name, Dhanaśrī. Very likely her green body indicates her cloudlike dark complexion. Her iconography is very different in the paintings of the Punjab hills where she is depicted playing with hares. There she is not always green either (Poster: 266–67).

Published: Chandra 1971: cat. no. 113.

44
Lalita Rāginī

Probably Bundi, 18th century

Gouache and gold on paper, 7⅞ x 4½ inches

1979.1718

This painting is attributed to the school of Bundi because of the pair of flying birds, the rising sun, the three-dimensional architectural setting with its distinctive *chatri*, the colorful courtyard tiles with the six-pointed star pattern, and the noticeable black outline of the eyes. Some of these features appeared even in the Chunar *Rāgamālā* (dated 1591), which is the earliest example of the Bundi school. Chandra believes that due to lack of brilliant coloring and refined detail, "the painting may belong to Uniara where a variant of the Bundi style developed in the late eighteenth century" (Chandra 1971: 69). However, I would argue that the Uniara style in general is not much different from the Bundi style in terms of briliancy in color and detailed refinement.

The theme of the painting is derived from the ancient motif of Indic literature in which a young prince, in order to lead an ascetic life, secretly abandons his palace while his beloved is still sleeping. Some earlier versions of the subject such as in the Khajanchi collections (Barrett and Gray: 135) even include a stallion and a groom waiting for the prince in the palace courtyard. This scene is so similar to the departure of Siddhārtha Gautama and Mahāvīra Jina, the founders of Buddhism and Jainism respectively, that the theme cannot be the invention of the Rajput artists. Although in the context of Rajput painting the scene of the sleeping princess represents Lalita Rāginī, when this theme is used for the spiritual leaders it easily becomes a part of the story of the great teachers. (See the introductory essay for details.)

In Indic art sleeping female figures are almost always are shown fully dressed and ornamented as they are here. Attracted by the sleeping beauty, the prince can not help glancing back over his right shoulder at his beloved one more time. This gesture shows the deep emotion of the prince to his beloved whom he is about to abandon forever.

Published: Chandra 1971: cat. no. 114.

45
Vasanta Rāga

Probably Uniara, ca. 1725

Gouache and gold on paper, 9⅜ x 6$\frac{1}{16}$ inches

1985.322

A stylistic feature that deserves special attention is the crescentlike half-nimbus depicted in front of Kṛṣṇa's face. Such a partial halo is a characteristic of the late eighteenth century Uniara school. The subtle wrinkle lines drawn immediately below the lower eyelids of the female figures are another feature of the school. The colorful brahmany ducks swimming in the water full of blossoming lotus flowers are, however, omnipresent in Bundi, Kotah, and Uniara styles.

This is a pictorial representation of the melody of spring, Vasanta Rāga. Kṛṣṇa, performing the spring dance, holds in his right hand a *vīṇā* (a lutelike instrument) and in his left a flower vase with a spout. He flexes his knees in time with the symphony of cymbals, a drum, and a trumpet, played by female musicians dancing with him at the foot of wooded hill near a lotus pond.

The entire middle ground is covered by the slope of the hill, which is shown as pinkish red to orange red to indicate perhaps the romantic red chalk hill *gairikācala*, often enthusiastically described in Sanskrit literature. The hill is full of many kinds of vegetation including a plantain tree and flowering shrubs. Springtime is also suggested by the sunny blue sky in the background.

Published: Chandra 1971: cat. no. 115; Elvehjem Bulletin (1987): 63.

46

An Illustrated Folio of the *Bhagavadgītā*

Bundi or Kotah, 1725–1750

Gouache and gold on paper, 9⅛ x 5½ inches

1989.10

The *Bhagavadgītā* is a prominent Hindu text in Sanskrit, an early version of which may have existed even before the Christian era. In this text, Kṛṣṇa teaches his philosophy of life and death to the warrior prince Arjuna. Although the text has not much to do with the love story of Kṛṣṇa and Rādhā, their courtship is the main theme of both illustrations given in this manuscript. These paintings, therefore, provide us additional examples of discrepancy between the text and the theme of the manuscript illuminations.

Although we have considered this work as one illustrated folio of a manuscript, this folio has three sections that are skillfully folded so that they appear to be three independent folios of the manuscript. The Devanāgarī script containing the Sanskrit verses of the Hindu text is flanked by two horizontal illustrations found in the upper and lower section. The script is on buff-colored paper mainly in black ink, but the numbers of the verses, as usual, are in red. The folio number is 157.

In the upper illustration Rādhā and Kṛṣṇa sit in front of an arched bower flanked by two female attendants. Keeping the traditional color scheme, the artist has painted the space inside the arch in bright orange, which contrasts both with the green vegetation of the bower and with the yellow margin lavishly decorated with dark green floral patterns. The jewel-like quality of the painting is further enhanced by Kṛṣṇa's yellow *dhoti* and his blue complexion. Rādhā and her female companion wear yellow saris with reddish stripes that contribute to the variegation. A bluish gray river runs horizontally in the foreground.

The lower illustration depicts the circular dance called *rāsamaṇḍala* in which Kṛṣṇa, the divine lover, has multiplied himself so that he can dance with every milkmaid. In the painting his multiple figures alternate with the milkmaids who dance vigorously with him. Several female musicians play trumpets and cymbals. The vigor of the dance echoes in the meandering foliage and floral patterns that decorate the bright yellow margins of the both illustrations.

Published: Chandra 1971: cat. no. 116.

47

The Auspicious Sight of Rādhā

Probably Bundi, ca. 1750–1775

Gouache and gold on paper, 9 13/16 x 6 1/16 inches

1986.53

Kṛṣṇa's head is encircled with a lunar halo which differs from the radiating nimbus, or solar halo, that we see in Mewar painting (cat. nos. 34, 35). In Rajput paintings Kṛṣṇa is often depicted wearing a yellow *dhoti* (*pītāmbara*); here he wears a type of Mughal dress but its color is still yellow. Lush vegetation with plantain trees is a feature of the Bundi school, and elongated eyes with half-covered pupils also help us to identify this painting with that school.

Rādhā was bathing nude in a lotus-pond near a hill, in an isolated place, where no one was expected to come. Suddenly Rādhā and her female companion heard a horse and rider coming through the dense grove of plantain trees on the other side of the hill. It was Kṛṣṇa on a white horse. Rādhā hastily came out of the water, but it was too late to put on the clothes that she had left on the bank of the pond. Her friends held up a sari to block the view, and she sat there shyly hoping that Kṛṣṇa would go away. Kṛṣṇa found the situation amusing, so he halted. The artist has shown this episode so well that it does not require a label to explain the event.

Published: Chandra 1971: cat. no. 117.

भ·गी· च॥२॥ममयोनिर्महद्ब्रह्मतस्मिन्गर्भं अ·
२५७ दधाम्यहं॥संभवःसर्वभूतानांततोभ २४
वतिभारत॥३॥सर्वयोनिषुकौंतेय
मूर्तयःसंभवंतिया॥तासांब्रह्ममह रामः
द्योनिरहंबीजप्रदःपिता॥४॥सत्वं २५७

46

47

48

48
Śrī Rāga

Bundi or Kotah, ca. 1780

Gouache on paper, 9⅜ x 6$\frac{9}{16}$ inches

1979.1719; see color plate 14

A fresh green tree on the left partially blocks the sunset suggested by the deep orange horizon and light blue sky above. As the evening approaches, two birds fly. Such depictions of birds flying in pairs in the distant atmosphere are a prominent feature of the Bundi school.

The enthroned princely figure is perhaps an anthropomorphic representation of Śrī Rāga, the king of love songs. He leans against a large, dark red bolster. It is a classical Indian type of throne flanked by two *makaras* (mythical creatures like crocodiles). This archaic element makes this throne very different from contemporaneous Rajput or Mughal thrones. Only because the artist borrowed it from earlier copy such archaic element survived in Rajput painting. The colorful parasol over the throne has the *āmalaka* type of fluted round forms used as the crowning member of the superstructure of northern-style Hindu temples.

The princely figure is accompanied by an attendant who wears a yellow transparent *jama* and yellowish green trousers and holds a fly whisk and a shield and a sword. In front of the throne are two male figures, one singing, another playing the *vīṇā*. The latter's age is indicated by his white beard. Apparently he is the teacher of the young singer, for in India, even today, a teacher often participates in his student's performance as a musician.

Published: Chandra 1971: cat. no. 118; Vajracharya 1994: 56.

49

49
Naṭa Rāginī

Bundi, late 18th century

Gouache on paper, 7⅛ x 5 inches

1979.1721; see color plate 15

This painting is iconographically valuable because in it the Naṭa Rāginī is depicted as female, not male. Medieval texts on musical modes prescribe that this musical mode, although called a rāginī and not a rāga, be depicted as a male figure. The standard representation of Naṭa Rāginī is a male figure riding a horse with elephant-hide armor striking down enemies (for example, Poster: 161, 221). The title word *naṭa,* which means "a male dancer" or "an actor," is further confusing, as neither the standard depiction nor this painting incorporates any element of dance or acting. Although such visual elements as the elephant's hide suggest a narrative background, the story is missing. Very likely, as in the case of Rāmakarī Rāginī, this is also a theatrical scene, and originally Naṭa Rāginī was not the title of the painting but the name of the background music played behind the stage (see introductory essay).

The sky is filled with turbulent clouds, dark bluish and white gradually turning into a golden orange horizon. The sun, about to set and partially visible behind the tree on top of the grassy hill, is rendered as a face—a feature that repeatedly appears in Bundi paintings. The artist emphasizes the foliage of the tree, the pair of birds perched on it, and the peacock on the ground, by making them disproportionately large. The slope of the hill is not visible because it is covered by a purple, abstract color-field. Such a color-field, usually red, is a stylistic feature reminiscent of Rajput paintings of the sixteenth and seventeenth centuries.

The main event of the painting is the equestrian heroine Naṭa Rāginī engaged in a fight with her enemy. Wearing an armored coat, she brandishes her sword menacingly while her adversary on foot approaches her bravely, holding a sword and a shield. Another brave adversary lies gravely wounded and fallen on the grassy foreground. He is about to die although he is still holding the broken sword and the shield. Two crowlike scavengers await his death.

Published: Chandra 1971: cat. no. 120.

50

51

50

Ram Singh II (1827–1865) of Kotah in a Procession

Kotah, mid 19th century

Gouache and gold on paper, 12⅛ x 19³⁄₁₆ inches

1977.136; see color plate 23

Monumentality is an admirable quality that frequently appears in Rajput miniature paintings. Here the artist has successfully imparted such artistic quality through the device of the architecture, the figure of the elephant, and the crowded scene.

This painting provides a glimpse of the nineteenth-century life of a Rajput king. Ram Singh II (1827–1865), the king of Kotah, sits on a majestic elephant that emerges above the orderly crowd of the ostentatious royal procession. The godlike king, whose head is encircled with a radiant halo, is delineated in the middle of the painting in hierarchic proportion. Holding a sword, he sits comfortably on the howdah decorated with a vine-and-floral pattern. He is flanked by a mahout and a bodyguard, both fanning him with large, white fly whisks. According to Chandra, the latter represents a prince (Chandra 1971: 75).

The bearded king wears a golden crown and a matching robe. The elephant is caparisoned with its head and tail covered with a brilliantly colored quilt with multiple borders around a foliage and floral design on the mauve ground. An unusual attraction of the procession is the girl dancing inside the cage supported by the elephant's tusks. On the ground, musicians, including a female singer, face the dancer, singing and playing musical instruments. A band attired in French military dress leads the procession, followed by hundreds of foot-soldiers distinguishable by their uniforms as European and Rajput. By this time the Rajput kings were becoming much influenced by the European type of military training. Often they hired Europeans to teach their system of soldiery, a phenomena this painting clearly reflects. The troops carrying guns with fixed bayonets and wearing blue hats, dark green jackets, and white trousers are a European-trained military unit. Immediately behind the unit soldiers with red turbans and orange jackets carry royal insignia and seem to be marching out of step with others, thus indicating the features of the traditional Rajput army. They are followed by another unit wearing flat red hats, blue *jamas*, and yellow trousers and carrying rifles with bayonets. Others, dressed in a wide variety of fashions, either hold regal paraphernalia or carry a palanquin covered with red silk with a small lattice window in the middle.

The procession is actually in front of a palatial building, which has windows screened with variegated purdah. The women of the palace can not watch from these windows because they are wide open and too close to the street and public. Therefore they and children run toward the edge of the flat roof to watch the procession. Nonetheless, a few can be seen in the windows of the upper story. This scene reminds us of the fascination of classical Sanskrit poets such as Aśvaghoṣa and Kālidāsa for describing incidents that happen when women in the middle of dressing, decorating themselves, or feeding babies run hurriedly to watch a procession going through the front yard of the royal palace.

Published: Chandra 1971: cat. no. 123; Watson: 40; Raducha: cat. no. 2.75.

51

A Tiger Hunt

Kotah, dated 1868

Ink and gouache on paper, 14¹¹⁄₁₆ x 20¾ inches

1979.1726

This preliminary study of a tiger hunt bears an inscription at the upper margin and the names of the figures in the areas where they will be depicted in the final version. According to the Devanāgarī inscription in a local language, possibly Hindi, this event took place in the spring of 1868 during the reign of Satrusal II (1865–1888), a rare example of a dated sketch, possibly made on the spot.

This sketch exemplifies the vivacity of the Kotah artists of the nineteenth century when the spirit of Rajput painting in many other places was in decline. The tiger hunt, a theme extremely popular with artists, sharply contrasts with the approach of the classical tradition where the subject of hunting is difficult to find (see introductory essay). Many examples of this subject are available in the Mughal school of painting, but it remained unpopular among Rajput schools other than Bundi and Kotah. The distinctive elements of Kotah style that we can recognize in this painting are the cloudlike formation of rocky hills, the stylized foliage, and the jumping posture of tigers.

A river rushing through a gorge separates the rocky hills,

on which a hunt is in progress. Frightened by the loud noises of barking dogs and beaters playing trumpets and drums, the tigers come out of the bushes. Then they are driven to the narrow space of the riverbank that abruptly ends in the turn of river due to the vertical gorge. Apparently this is a traditional strategy of the tiger hunt. In the water are several boats; the largest is labeled as the boat of his majesty Satrusal and the palace staff (*srīdarbar*), a word that Chandra mistook as the title of the king (Chandra 1971: 78). Although the artist has not drawn the figures of the important people yet, he has shown his skill of organization in placing the vital elements of the picture such as the boats, the turn of the river, and the figures of the beaters and tigers in the right places. One can easily imagine that the royal figure, who is indicated now only by name, will be shown in the final version aiming a gun at the tiger driven by the beater on the other side of the river.

Published: Chandra 1971: cat. no. 127.

MALWA

Malwa, located in central India, borders on Mewar and Gujarat. In classical times this region was known as Avanti and its capital was at Ujjayinī (modern Ujjain), a prominent cultural center of ancient India. At the beginning of the fifteenth century, Maṇḍu (the Maṇḍapa Durga of ancient times) became the capital of the Islamic rulers of Malwa. This fortified city standing on the hilltop was significant not only from a strategic point of view but also from an art historical perspective. Excellent Jaina manuscript paintings were produced here in traditional style. Toward the end of the fifteenth century or at the beginning of the sixteenth century the well-known *Ni'mat-nama* (Book of Delicacy) manuscript was illuminated here in a remarkable syncretic style that resulted from the modification of Persian style due to the involvement of native artists trained in traditional Jaina paintings. The *Ni'mat-nama* is an illustrated cookbook commissioned by Sultan Ghiyath ad-Din Khalji (r. 1469–1501), an eccentric Islamic ruler of Malwa who was more interested in voluptuous thought than in politics. He ruled peacefully, collected beautiful women in his harem from Rajput daughters to Turki slaves, and enthroned his elder son Nasir ad-Din in 1500, while he was still alive. The Book of Delicacy was completed only after his abdication. The significance of this illustrated manuscript lies in the fact that the new trend towards a syncretic style predicts the upcoming Mughal school (see cat. no. 9 for the Ni'mat-nama-style painting). Some scholars (Archer 1958: 4) think that the well-known early Rajput paintings such as *Laur Chanda*, *Caurapañcāśikā*, and *Bhairavī Rāginī* were also rendered in Malwa. Although that is possible, there is no substantial textual or stylistic evidence to prove this theory.

Typical Malwa-school paintings began to appear in the second quarter of the seventeenth century (Beach: 121) when the *Rasikapriyā* (dated 1634) was commissioned. A couple of decades later, in 1652, a series of paintings based on a Sanskrit text, *Amaruśataka* (the hundred love lyrics of Amaru), was painted at a place called Nasratgadh (Barrett and Gray: 149). This place seems to be same as Narsyanga Sahar where a dispersed *rāgamālā* series was rendered by an artist known as Madhau Dās. Both these manuscripts share the characteristics of the Malwa school, including a penchant for a black ground, the juxtaposition of color-fields, and delicate-looking, slender female figures wearing colorful saris that are either horizontally striped or decorated with a flower pattern. Most Malwa paintings in the Watson collection display these features.

52

Vasanta Rāga from a *Rāgamālā* series

Malwa, 1675–1699

Gouache on paper, 5⅜ x 5⅜ inches

1979.1729

Just above the painting, a two-line Devanāgarī inscription is written in black ink on the light yellow paper. The inscription in Sanskrit describes Vasanta Rāga, the musical mode of spring.

Although the Sanskrit verse refers to this musical mode as a rāga, the label in the upper right corner identifies the musical mode as Vasanta Rāginī "female musical mode." Such internal contradictions are often found when we carefully examine the inscriptions and the labels on the paintings. The Sanskrit verse can be translated loosely in following words: "His coiffure is adorned with the peacock's feather. He lures the cuckoo bird to hop from the tree and perch on his hand. He ... wanders happily [around the forest] like an elephant in rut. He is Vasanta Rāga."

Vasanta Rāga is personified in this painting as a male figure of blue complexion holding a sword in his right hand and a cuckoo bird in his left hand. Both the male and female figures are accentuated here by the red panel sharply contrasting with the adjoining color-field (in this case dark blue), a stylistic element that we encounter in earlier Rajput style paintings (Pal 1978: figs. 3, 4), but rarely in Mughal paintings.

In India a cuckoo bird symbolizes spring, because its song announces the arrival of the season. The male figure is accompanied by a fair lady carrying a *vīṇā* and a flower in her hands. Both of them are barefoot; yet they are sumptuously dressed. Although he is described in the Sanskrit verse as having a coiffure adorned with peacock's feather, he is actually shown here wearing a pointed golden crown, a necklace, a garland of white flowers, and a yellow *dhoti* with a flower design and double anklets, one of which is decorated with a black tassel, thus resembling that of the lady. Her decoration includes more tassels attached to the bracelets, tied to the end of her hair, and dangling on her hip. She wears a blue sari with a white-pleated middle section. Apparently they are heading toward a nearby grove inhabited by a pair of peacocks and other birds. In the context of classical Indic art, a god of knowledge that includes musical skill is iconographically described as a holder of a sword symbolizing the sharpness of his wisdom. Therefore the sword in his hand helps to define the rāga not as a warrior but as personified music sharing the iconographical feature of the heavenly musician Vidyādhara or Gandharva. After all, spring is the time of music and flowers.

Another stylistic feature is the flowering-vine motif shown here at the bottom of the painting. Although by this time this motif had begun to look like an arabesque often seen in Islamic art, its Indic origin goes back to the second century B.C. sculptures of Bharhut, where this motif is shown sometimes coming out of a water pot, other times from the mouth of the mythical creature *makara*.

Published: Chandra 1971: cat. no. 130.

52

53

53
Āśavarī Rāginī

Malwa, ca. 1675–1699

Gouache on paper, $5\frac{3}{8}$ x $5\frac{3}{8}$ inches

1979.1730

This is another folio of the same *rāgamālā* series as cat. no. 52. Thus we see same language, script, paper, and format used for the inscription. In this example, however, the inscription describes the iconography of a feminine musical mode, Āśavarī Rāginī. In the miniature she is anthropomorphically represented as a young woman of dark brown complexion holding a cobra with her left hand. She is in the deep tropical forest, as indicated by a tiger in its den, monkeys on the rocks and trees, and cobras wound around the trunk of a huge tree. The designation of this particular rāginī is derived from a tribal name, for Āśavarī means a Śavara woman. The Sanskrit inscription describing her iconogaraphical features can be loosely translated as follows:

> On the sandalwood hill, a Śavara girl of vibrant dark blue complexion covers herself with peacock feathers and wears a beautiful necklace made of elephant pearls. [In ancient India people believed that the protuberance on an elephant's head contains such pearls.] And she makes her bracelet out of the snake that she picked up from the sandalwood tree.

The depiction of the Śavara woman in the painting closely resembles this description of the verse, except that her complexion is dark brown instead of dark blue.

A beast resting in a lair of a stylized rocky hill is an ancient motif. In the wall paintings of the Ajanta caves, a jungle is often evoked using this motif. However, in Ajanta the beast is always a lion. This ancient motif also includes monkeys at play among the rocky hills and stylized trees much as delineated here in the background.

Published: Chandra 1971: cat. no. 131; Watson: 41; Vajracharya 1994: 47.

54
Kedāra Rāginī

Malwa, late 17th century

Gouache and gold on paper, $6\frac{13}{16}$ x 6 inches

1986.54

The juxtaposition of the contrasting upper red and lower blue color-fields and the black strip of the dark horizon, the ribbed dome of the shrine, and the figures' dreamy eyes with a scarcely visible pupil all indicate that this is a seventeenth-century Malwa miniature.

The iconography of Kedāra Rāginī is complicated because the description of the musical mode given in various texts differs widely, and the illustrations do not agree with any textual description. Sometime the musical mode is represented as a bearded male ascetic (Lee: 19). The present example bears some resemblance to the representation of the rāginī published in Walter Kaufmann's work (Kaufmann: 87), where the musical mode is identified as a female rāginī from inscriptional evidence. According to another inscription given above an illustration the heroine Kedāra "has smeared ash all over her body, which is reduced to a skeleton. . . . In this yogic garb, her body is terrifying and looks like a male body. . . . Lovesickness is killing Kedara" (Leach: 213). In accord with this concept, the skinny figure seated under the tree in the Watson illustration is the female ascetic. Her body does not display any feminine quality, but her hairless face may indicate her femininity. Compare her face with the male ascetic engaged in worshiping Śiva's emblem in the shrine on the right. Such gender confusion often appears in rāga and rāginī paintings.

This entire picture represents a *tapovana,* a hermitage. From Sanskrit literature we know that a pious king visits the hermitage often, because he cares for the welfare of the hermit. The royal figure standing in front of the ascetic describes such a custom. It is considered bad manners for a monarch to drive a chariot or ride a horse all the way to the hermitage. In order to show respect to the ascetic, he dismounts far away from the area and proceeds on foot, as the white horse equipped with a saddle in the foreground indicates. Note that the king left his bow on the saddle.

Published: Chandra 1971: cat. no. 132.

54

55
Vilaval Rāginī

Malwa, late 17th century

Watercolor, gouache, and gold on paper, 7¼ x 5 inches

69.28.7

Vilavil Rāginī is portrayed as a lady adorning herself while looking in a mirror held by a maid. In accordance with such iconographical features the rāginī is here adjusting her earring. She sits on the coach under a canopy. On the ground are several cosmetic boxes similar to those in earlier Nepalese sculptures representing Śiva and Pārvatī. Two maids, one holding a round mirror, stand in front of her. All female figures wear the horizontally striped skirts so typical in Malwa painting. Other frequently shown Malwa features are architectural elements such as the fluted domes of the *chatri* and the high podium consisting of trifoliate niches. Such decoration of niches with fancy bottles and cups is a ubiquitous feature in Rajput paintings, a custom introduced by Islamic rulers; thus one can not expect to see it in classical Indic art.

Published: Chandra 1971: cat. no. 133.

55

56

56

Vilaval Rāginī

Malwa, ca. 1700

Watercolor, gouache, and gold on paper, 8½ x 5½ inches

1981.280

The subject of this painting is same as cat. no. 55. As we explained in the introductory essay, this subject was known to the artists of the classical period, the earliest surviving example being an ivory carving of the second century A.D. This is a scene of *śṛṅgāra*, a youthful activity associated with passion and desire. Such a scene was considered to be auspicious and worth seeing in artistic representation. Furthermore, like Rāmakarī Rāginī, this rāginī probably also originated from the ancient Indian theatrical tradition, although the title Vilaval seems to be Rajput invention of the late mediaeval period. Despite the gap in time, the iconography of this subject changed very little. Perhaps the most noticeable difference is the type of the mirror. The second century example shows the lady holding a mirror made of polished metal, for the glass mirror was not invented yet. But in the present example the artist replaces the archaic mirror with the new type of rectangular glass mirror in which the lady is reflected. The Malwa stylistic elements such as the horizontally striped skirt and the fluted dome remained intact.

Published: Chandra 1971: cat. no. 134; Raducha: cat. no 2.97.

57

57

Guṇakali Rāginī

Probably Malwa, early 18th century

Gouache and gold on paper, 9½ x 5¾ inches

1981.282

On the verso of this painting is a bilingual inscription in Brajabhāṣā and Sanskrit describing the iconography of Guṇakali Rāginī. The script is Devanāgarī, which is written on buff-colored paper with red and black ink. The folio number 21 is also given on the verso.

This painting is not a typical Malwa style but an unfamiliar style where pictorial elements are treated linearly; thus the miniature looks like a drawing rather than a painting when it is reproduced in black-and-white photographs. The yellow margin with arabesque in green is the only reason that this miniature can be attributed to Malwa school.

Guṇakali Rāginī is iconographically displayed as a woman sitting on a carpet, holding a flower, and facing a flowering tree. The artist, however, seems to be much more interested in rendering a landscape than a detailed figure. Under the blue sky a typical Indian temple, designed to resemble a mythical mountain peak and designated *śikhara*, stands in the distance shaded with trees. The grassland adjoining the temple extends all the way to the middle ground where there is more vegetation, including a row of plantains with large linear leaves. A conventional lotus pond inhabited by aquatic birds embellishes the foreground.

Published: Chandra 1971: cat. no. 136.

58

58

Vairāṭī Rāginī

Probably Malwa, probably early 18th century

Gouache and gold on paper, 9½ x 5¾ in.

1986.55

This is another folio of the same manuscript as cat. no. 57. In both examples, the inscription on the verso is written in same script, languages, and format. The number of this folio, which is given on the verso, is 61.

The present example depicts a lady dressed in a yellow sari. Her diminutive figure is silhouetted against the expansive red background immediately below the blue sky. In her vigorous performance, she bends her right leg and extends her left away from the axis. Almost in the imitation of a flying bird, she stretches her arms up and down creating a diagonal line across her shoulders. These dance movements are performed to the beat of cymbals played by a female musician who is clad in a pink sari and stands under a tree on the lower left of the painting. A tall flowering branch of a vine that extends far above the tree creates an arch above the dancer. More trees on the other side of the painting emphasize the symmetry with the arch in the middle. Chandra observed that the "bright yellow margins with arabesques in green" are a recognizable feature of Malwa painting (Chandra 1971: 85)

Published: Chandra 1971: cat. no. 137.

MARWAR (JODHPUR)

Marwar (the land of death), a state lying at the edge of Rajasthan desert, is famous not for agricultural prosperity but for the commercial skill of wealthy businessmen known as Marwaris. Most are the members of local communities bonded both commercially and religiously as devoted followers of Jainism. Catalogue number 60 is commissioned by such a Jaina community.

The state was renamed Jodhpur when Raja Rao Jodha, a descendant of Kannauj royal family, in 1459 founded the capital city of Jodhpur. In 1561 Emperor Akbar forced Jodhpur to submit to the Mughal empire and later on to engage in marriage alliances with the Mughal princes. With this relationship the Rajput rulers of Marwar/ Jodhpur became important members of the Mughal court inner circle. It is not, therefore, surprising that Mughal stylistic elements were introduced into the Marwar school of paintings. What is surprising is that even after the high society of Jodhpur began to admire the Mughal way of living, traditional painting—untouched by the style of the Mughal atelier—continued in Marwar as exemplified by the lucky discovery of a *rāgamālā* series that was rendered in 1623, painted in the small town of Pali.

The archaic quality and simplicity of the *rāgamālā* reminds us of the independent approach of the well-known *Caurapañcāśikā* style which was popular in Mewar, Malwa, and neighboring regions around the mid sixteenth century. The wide-open eye with the tiny pupil gazing upward, a feature associated with a charioteer in catalogue number 59 appears to be derived from this Pali *rāgamālā* style. The same feature also appears in the early Mewar paintings (compare to cat. no. 30 for example). This similarity, however, seems to indicate the existence of an earlier source from which both derived, particularly because in the Marwar school one can expect to see not only the features of Jaina and Mughal paintings but also the continuity of much earlier stylistic and iconographic elements as exemplified by catalogue numbers 60, 61, and 62.

59

59
Chariot Drawn by a Pair of Bulls

Probably Marwar (Jodhpur), ca. 1650–1675
Gouache on paper, 5¾ x 5¾ inches
1981.283

Due to the dark, rich color scheme, Chandra tentatively attributed this miniature to Marwar school; however, he noticed that the physiognomy of the human figures, especially the petal-shaped eye with tiny pupils in the center, is characteristic of the Mewar school of the mid-seventeenth century (Chandra 1971: 86). Because of the active interaction among the neighboring schools of paintings, exact stylistic identity is often almost impossible. Against the deep indigo background a pair of bulls pulls a shrinelike chariot with a golden roof embellished with three pinnacles. In Indian architecture some temples are known as *ratha* (chariot) because they were originally designed after chariots and vice versa. The walls of the chariot and the frame of the windows are red; the undercarriage and the wheels are painted chocolate. A lady dressed in light blue *coli* elegantly holds the border of the veil with her right hand. She is seated by the window through which she has stretched her left hand outside the chariot. The charioteer, dressed in a yellow *jama* and pink turban, holds a whip in his right hand and a rein in his left. As mentioned in the introductory essay, the wide-open eye with the tiny pupil gazing upward seems to be a Marwar feature associated with an earlier work known as the Pali *Rāgamālā* (Beach: 127).

Published: Chandra 1971: cat. no. 138.

60

60
A King and Courtier Conversing with Holy Men

Probably Marwar (Jodhpur), ca. 1650–1675

Gouache and gold on paper, 4¼ x 4¾ inches

1989.11

This painting demonstrates the continuity of several stylistic features of the classical tradition—red background, continuous narration, royal sitting position, and hierarchical proportion. Perhaps the most striking classsical feature is the skinny figure of the ascetic and his matted hair. As we know from the *Viṣṇudharmottara Purāṇa* (24. 3–4), a representation of a robust body is not recommended for an ascetic. Therefore, he is almost always represented with an emaciated yet energetic type of body.

Against the red background often seen in the eleventh and twelfth century palm-leaf manuscript illuminations, two episodes of a religious event are illustrated in two horizontal rows. The illustration of the holy man reciting makes it very likely this is associated with the rainy season retreat during which holy men recite religious verses and stories. On the top row a princely figure, well dressed in Mughal attire, leans against the bolster in a classical position befitting a monarch, hence called *rājalīlāsana* (the position of royal ease). He converses with a Brahman and a nobleman. The Brahman wears a sacred thread, a necklace, a brown turban, and a yellow *dhoti*, whereas the nobleman is dressed in green *jama* and white-striped turban. They may be discussing the organization of the religious recitation by a holy man, which is actually taking place below. The holy man is shown as an ascetic seated on the ground in the lotus position; he holds a folio of a manuscript in his left hand and puts his other hand behind his back on the ground to balance his body. He is skinny and aged with a dark complexion indicated by the light blue color. His matted hair is tied with yellow ribbon and black string in order to form a topknot flanked by two flaps of hair-locks. The princely figure, dressed in yellow *jama*, listens to the holy man and expresses his support by joining the index fingers and thumbs of both hands. Behind him stand the Brahman and a nobleman. Due to the use of hierarchical proportion, the standing figures are not much taller than the seated figure of the prince and ascetic.

Published: Chandra 1971: cat. no. 139.

61
A Lady at Her Toilet

Probably Marwar (Jodhpur), ca. 1650–1675

Gouache on paper, 6½ x 6⅛ inches

1981.284

This miniature painting is somewhat deteriorated. To the left of the extant fragment of the painting is a scene of a bathroom that is rendered against the blue color-field. Two domes are shown above the scene to indicate the bath is indoors. In the middle of the room a nude young lady of a fair complexion stands on a golden stool in contrapposto. She has just finished her bath. Her long hair is still dripping water, from which a bird drinks. Before she dresses, apparently she will apply some cosmetics, which she is about to pick up from a tray carried by a female attendant, who stands in front of her in classical *svastika* posture—standing on her left leg with the right ankle crossing the left. A pair of copper-red water jars on the ground suggest the bath. The right side of the painting is rendered against the yellowish brown background. Most of this side is ruined except for a female figure clad in a skirt with horizontal stripes. Her expressive eyes and hand gestures indicate that she is conversing with a person now completely missing.

61

62 recto

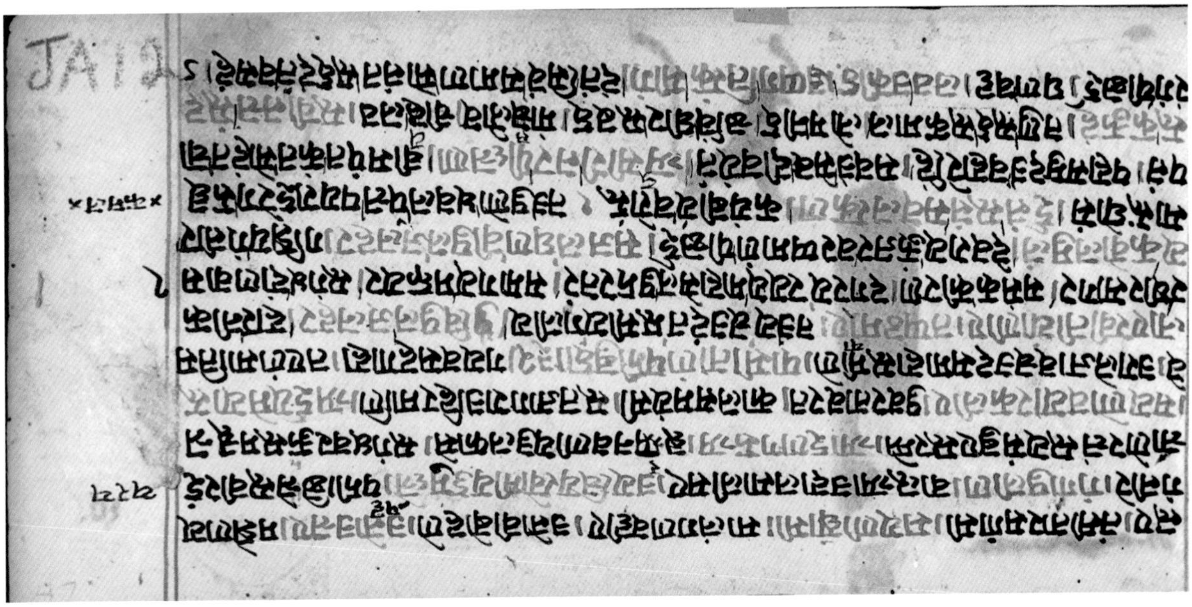
62 verso

The motif of the bird drinking the droplets of water fallen from the hair of a bathing beauty is borrowed from the classical tradition. Exactly the same motif is depicted in the first and second century sculptures from Mathura (Pal 1978: 21). Evidently the ancient tradition of classical art was not completely forgotten by Rajput artists. More important, just as in earlier time, a main theme of the painting is to create an auspicious ambiance by depicting the scenes of *śṛṅgāra*, youthful activities. The locale of this painting is presumed to be Marwar because its color scheme is related to the painting of that region (see Chandra 1971: 89).

Published: Chandra 1971: cat. no. 140.

62
Triśalā's Dream, a folio from *Kalpasūtra* manuscript

Probably Marwar (Jodhpur), ca. 1650–1675
Gouache on paper, 4½ x 7⅞ inches
1972.50

The Prakrit language text in Devanāgarī script is given on the verso. As usual it is written mainly in black ink on buff-colored paper and red ink is sparingly used for the verse number. This is the only folio in the Watson collection, which is numbered 10.

This manuscript painting is particularly significant for the study of symbols that are considered auspicious by Jainas, Buddhists, and Hindus. Some symbols, such as the elephant, the bull, and the lion, are found on the third-century B.C. capitals of Aśokan pillars erected in order to promote Buddhism, but have no direct a relationship to Buddhism, Jainism, or any other religion. Originally they were considered auspicious mainly because of their association with the imagery of water and the rain-cloud. As we explained in the introductory essay, an aspect of Indian art is the expression of a monsoonal culture. Therefore such motifs as the flower, the lotus pond, the lotus goddess Lakṣmī, the full water vase, the water-boat, the heavenly mansion—also visualized in the formations of the clouds—and the smokeless fire that represents lightning are all auspicious. One might see them in reality, in an artistic representation, or in a dream.

According to the Jaina story Queen Triśalā saw them in an auspicious dream when she was about to conceive Mahāvīra, the founder of the Jaina religion. She reclines on the bed in her chamber, which is represented within the large rectangular area to the left. This scene is identified with a label on the upper left corner, *triśalāsūti*, "Triśalā's Conception." The fourteen auspicious objects that she saw in the dream are depicted in smaller panels, organized in three registers. In the first register are an elephant, a bull, a lion, the goddess of wealth, a pair of garlands, and the moon; in the second register are the sun, a banner, a full vase, and a lotus pond; and in the third register is a ship, a heavenly mansion, a heap of jewels, and a smokeless fire. The other label given on the right corner identifies the objects as *caudasa nyāsai*, "fourteen symbols."

Published: Chandra 1971: cat. no. 141; Raducha: cat. no. 2.7.

63

63
The Month of Māgha, illustration to a verse from the *Kavipriyā* of Keśavadāsa

Marwar (Jodhpur), mid 18th century

Gouache and gold on paper, 11¼ x 6¾ inches

1981.286; see color plate 12

The five-line Devanāgarī superscript in Brajabhāṣā language is beautifully written with white ink that stands out against the black background. As Chandra has noted, the superscript is quoted from Keśavadāsa's work describing the spring season.

The Māgha month (February / March) of the Indian calendar is considered the first month of the spring season, which is celebrated with great enthusiasm throughout the continent. According to an ancient traditional custom, the spring season officially began on the fifth day of the Māgha month when it was celebrated not only by the common people but by the members of the royal family in the palace. When this old custom was incorporated into the legend of Kṛṣṇa, it became an essential aspect of his cult. This seems to be a reason that the artist of this magnificent painting describes the arrival of the spring showing Kṛṣṇa dancing with milkmaids in the distant background.

The foreground displays the symmetrically arranged formal garden with multicolored flowers. The border of the garden is paved with pink marble that divides the white courtyard from the garden. A middle-aged monarch, probably representing the contemporary king of Marwar, stands in the courtyard receiving the bowl of flowers offered by the ladies of the palace approaching from the doorway. The ladies wear colorful printed and flowered saris and cover their head and shoulders with veils of contrasting colors. The artist has taken more care in rendering the royal figure, who wears an elaborate golden turban embellished with jewels and a feather. The distinctive long whiskers and the sideburns seem to be personal features of the king. His shoulders are covered with a light yellow shawl worn on top of the pleated pink *jama* that reaches to his knees, partially covering the pleated orange undergarment. His ornaments include earrings, necklaces, and bracelets. He also wears a silky yellow *patka*, (girdle) and carries his royal insignias such as the shield and swords dangling below his waist.

The architectural background is also colorful. The flat yellow roof is decorated with foliage. One of *chatris* has a bluish red dome with a light blue border and white columns; the other one a white dome and wall with a bluish verandah. The cornice of the building is decorated with pink, yellow, red and white parallel stripes. The light pink stripe decorating the wall just above the cornice is carefully rendered with a meandering pattern of leaves and flowers. The red canopy with a green border is attached to the building over the doorway. Peacocks sit in the trees in front of the building.

Kṛṣṇa's circular dance, *rāsamaṇḍala*, takes place in the background behind the wall of the palace. Kṛṣṇa is surrounded by milkmaids dancing and playing various musical instruments. Those who sprinkle colored water in celebration of the season are shown in diminutive scale as if to convey spatial depth. The Rajput artists did become familiar with this aspect of spatial treatment through the Mughal artists, who in turn learned it from European examples. Both Rajputs and Mughals, however, used this treatment to create supernatural phenomena instead of the mundane reality of physical world.

Published: Chandra 1971: cat. no. 145; Raducha: cat. no. 2.45.

64

Portrait of Maharaja Ram Singh of Jodhpur

Marwar (Jodhpur), mid 18th century

Gouache and gold on paper, 9¾ x 5⅜ inches

1981.288

64

The primary intention of the artist is to create an exalted figure of the Maharaja through verticality. The length of the sword, linear pattern of the pleats, and the unusually tall turban emphasize the lofty and sublime personality of the monarch. The slightly arched back of the sitter expresses the pride of the Rajput king, an element first introduced by the Kishangarh school.

The main figure is identified on the verso in Devanāgarī script as the Maharaja Ram Singh (r. 1749–1772) of Jodhpur. He stands proudly, resting his right hand on a sword and holding the *jighā* in his other hand. A *jighā*, a spray of gems resembling plume used as turban ornament, is often presented to a friend or a courtier to express respect and gratitude, a custom that prevailed in the courts of both Mugahls and Rajputs. He wears a white pleated *jama*, matching tall turban, earring, and pearl necklace. His countenance is encircled with a nimbus.

Published: Chandra 1971: cat. no. 147; Raducha: cat. no. 2.63.

65

65

Jaina Monks Addressing the Laity, fragment of a *Vijñaptipatra*

Marwar school, Nagaur, mid 18th century

Gouache on paper, 20¾ x 7⅞ inches

1972.51

Such characteristics of early Jaina manuscript paintings as the red background, complete rejection of the three dimensionality of the architecture, linear treatment of figures without shading, and the use of primary colors in a contrasting manner are continued in this eighteenth-century work. Chandra determined that this painting was rendered in Naguar, a fief of Marwar, where a variation of the Marwar style developed (Chandra 1971: 91). Traditionally a well-to-do Jaina family, or an entire Jaina community, sends a formal invitation to a Jaina monk at the to perform the ritual of *paryuṣaṇa,* the rainy season retreat. The invitation is on a long scroll illustrated with auspicious symbols and the scenes of significant religious activities.

This painting is a section of such a scroll known as *vijñaptipatra* (a letter of invitation). Although the letter is missing, the illustration shows a high Jaina monk and his associates addressing different groups of laity inside a building. The high priest is seated in a colorful throne that resembles a shrine with a dome, a parapet, and a cornice. To the right of the throne an attendant dressed in Mughal fashion waves the *chowrie* to express respect to the priest who explains the Jaina text he holds in his left hand. Recitation and explanation of religious texts is part of the rainy season ritual. Apparently the priest belongs to the *Śvetāmbara* (clad in white robe) sect, rather than the *Digambara* (space-clad, i.e. naked) sect. He holds a broom on his lap. Even these days a Jaina monk, strictly adhering to the traditional belief in *ahiṃsā* (noninjury to men, animals, and insects), sweeps the path as he walks and covers his mouth and nose with cloth to avoid injury to insects. The mouthpiece is not shown, perhaps because he is preaching. Two noblemen attired in turban and *jama* listen to him with great attention and devotion.

Immediately below the high priest another Jaina monk in white garments sits on a low bench and addresses devotees, including a child. Yet another monk sits on the ground, per-

66

haps indicating his lower status, and teaches women including a widow dressed in white.

Published: Chandra 1971: cat. no. 148; Raducha: cat. no. 2.8.

66

Rāma's Army

Probably Marwar school, early 19th century

Gouache on paper, 3⅛ x 7⅝ inches

1982.165; see color plate 20

On the verso an unknown Brajabhāṣā text, associated with Rāma's legend, is given in Devanāgarī script. It is written with black ink on the buff-colored background.

Perhaps the significance of the painting is derived from the stylistic viewpoint, for the artist does an outstanding job of portraying the panoramic expanse of the scene within the narrow available space of the manuscript folio. Using the elongated configuration of the folio, the artist created a luminous horizontal line to suggest an immense space.

Rāma, the protagonist of the Hindu epic *Rāmāyaṇa*, spent fourteen years of exile in a forest with his wife Sītā and his brother Lakṣmaṇa. Their peaceful life was disturbed when the demon king Rāvaṇa abducted Sītā and imprisoned her on the island of Laṅka. Although Rāma and Lakṣmaṇa were great warriors, they could not fight the demonic host without an army. In the forest the only help that they could get was from Hanumān, the chief of the monkeys, and Sugrīva, king of the bears. With their help Rāma built the army of monkeys and bears, shown here brandishing trees and branches as their weapons and marching together in double file toward the battlefield. Both groups wear shorts, but they can easily be distinguished as the monkeys have red faces and flesh-toned bodies, whereas the bears are dark from head to toe but have sparkling eyes.

Rāma and Lakṣmaṇa each hold a bow and arrow and stand almost in the middle of the marching band. Rāma wears yellow *dhoti* specifically known as *pītāmbara* and his complexion is blue because both Rāma and Kṛṣṇa are considered incarnations of Viṣṇu. Lakṣmaṇa has fair complexion and wears a green *dhoti*. The crowned figures behind them are Sugrīva and Hanumān. The rest of the force moves ahead along the stylized pink, rocky ground. Another figure here is Prince Vibhīṣaṇa who marches with the army but apart on the grass. Vibhīṣaṇa wears a crown and carries a sword and shield. He was the brother of the demon king, but he could not condone the demonic attitude of his older brother. Therefore he abandoned him and became an ally of Rāma and Lakṣmaṇa.

Published: Chandra 1971: cat. no. 153; Raducha: cat. no. 2.26.

67

67
The Summer Season

Marwar, ca. 1825

Watercolor, gouache, and gold on paper, 14 x 9¾ inches

69.28.20; see color plate 21

In order to suggest the hot Indian summer, the artist, with a touch of humor, has shown here the monarch and animals trying to stay cool. In the middle of the picture stands a pavilion with a golden-tiered roof (surely not a thatched roof as Chandra suggested [1971: 93]). A bearded royal figure, perhaps Man Singh of Marwar (1803–1843) sits in the pavilion holding a flower, which seems to be an ancient Indic custom. In classical Sanskrit, kings and merchants are often described holding a lotus in their hand as a plaything. The head of the monarch is encircled with an apple-green nimbus bordered with golden rays. Several female attendants surround him, most waving fans to produce cool breezes. The ladies and the king wear similar pale yellow dresses figured with a brownish flower pattern, apparently summer dress in the nineteenth-century Marwar palace.

The thick vegetation with plantain trees, exotic birds behind the pavilion, and the flowering lotus pond in the foreground are rendered here to create an auspicious ambience (see introductory essay). They have nothing to do with the reality of the dry Indic summer because during this time of the year before the arrival of the rainy season most of the subcontinent becomes parched. Trees shed their leaves, and due to the lack of water in the pond lotuses fade away. Such a real summer is depicted in the background with bare hills, parched trees, and an elephant suffering from scorching rays descending from the golden solar disc shown at the upper right of center section. It is so hot that even the tiger, who is always hunting the elephant, is interested in only in cooling himself in the shade of the huge body of the elephant.

Published: Chandra 1971: cat. no. 154.

SIROHI

Sirohi, a small *thikānā* or fief located in the southwest corner of Rajasthan and bordering on Gujarat, Marwar, and Mewar, has long been a cultural center of Rajasthan. The medieval Jaina temple of that region attracts not only the followers of Jainism but also the students of architectural history. Most of the time Sirohi remained a part of Mewar state, but sometimes it slipped away. In recent investigations art historians have shown that around 1680 this *thikānā* developed a style of painting recognizably different from the other neighboring Rajasthani styles (Beach: 158). A distinctive feature of this style is the modeling of figures by means of heavy shading along the outlines.

68

The Worship of Durgā (Bhavānī)
[formerly The Worship of Bhairavī], folio 46
from a manuscript of the *Devīmāhātmya*

Probably Sirohi, late 18th century

Gouache on paper, 4½ x 9¹³⁄₁₆ inches

1982.166c verso; see color plate 17

This miniature is an illustration of the *Devīmāhātmya*, a Sanskrit text recited during the autumnal worship of the goddess Durgā. The Watson collection has three illustrated folios of the manuscript. It is written in Devanāgarī script with black and red ink on buff-colored paper. As usual red color is used only for the verse numbers and the lines that divide the areas for the text and illustrations. Durgā is also known as Bhavānī. According to the label at the right margin, "Bhavānī is doing a favor [for the devotees]."

Because of the heavy use of color, Chandra tentatively attributed this illustration to the Sirohi school (Chandra 1971: 95). Such a feature is visible in the modeling along the transitions between chins and cheeks and between eyebrows and upper lid with heavy shading. Another interesting feature of this miniature is an attempt to show the interaction between the divine figure and the human being, an element that became popular among the eighteenth century Rajput artists of Rajasthan and the Punjab hills.

Leaning against a red bolster, Durgā or Bhavānī, the goddess of autumn, sits on a golden throne equipped with a parasol. She wears a green sari, a red *coli*, a golden crown, and pearl ornaments. In her raised right hand she holds a cup and stretches it toward two devotees standing in front of her. They greet her, folding both hands in *namaskāra* gesture that enhances the aura of the interaction between the divine figure and the human beings. Both devotees appear to be the members of a royal family, as they are dressed in golden crowns and pearl necklaces and arm bands.

Published: Chandra 1971: cat. no. 157.

KISHANGARTH

Kishangarh, which lies between Ajmer and Jaipur, was established as a state in 1613 when Raja Kishan Singh, a prince from Marwar (Jodhpur), received the land from his famous father, Mota Raja Udai Singh (r. 1583–1594). The earliest identifiable paintings of this region are from the late seventeenth century (Beach: 185). They bear stylistic similarity to the contemporary Mughal painting. Some Kishangarh paintings of this phase are almost indistinguishable from Mughal works of the

68

69

same period. This phase continued until the middle of the eighteenth century, when a new Kishangarh style marked by expressively distinctive features replaced the earlier style. Catalogue number 69 is valuable because it was rendered just before the new Kishangarh style emerged.

The new Kishangarh style, befitting to Rajput style, showed strong reaction to the Mughalization of the early phase and placed more emphasis on capturing the abstract quality or essence of a subject than describing it as it appears. This reaction can be described as a return to the original concept of Rajput painting. The prominent figure responsible for beginning this new phase of Kishangarh school was Savant Singh (r. 1748–1757, died 1764), a remarkable Rajput prince who was born in 1699 as the eldest son of Raj Singh (r. 1706–1748). Like other Rajput princes, he served the Mughal emperor. When his father died in 1748, he was not in Kishangarh. In his absence his ambitious brother, Bahadur Shah announced himself the king of Kishangarh. Although Savant Singh was eventually enthroned in that year as the legitimate monarch of the kingdom, a terrible rivalry continued between these brothers until Savant Singh abdicated the throne in 1757. But Savant Singh was more than a monarch, he was a highly cultured person and a poet devoted to the cult of Kṛṣṇa. After he renounced the throne, he decided to retire in Brindavan with his beloved wife Bani-Thani, a lovely young woman with whom he fell in love in his stepmother's harem where she was a servant. She was a great dancer and an equally gifted singer. This romantic couple happily spent the rest of their life at Brindavan in imitation of the divine couple Rādhā and Kṛṣṇa. Savant Singh, under the name Nagari Das, composed devotional verse praising Kṛṣṇa. Bani-thani sang the verses and danced in front of Kṛṣṇa's shrine. Although Nagari Das himself was not an artist, he had a talented painter called Nihal Chand working for him. Inspired by Nagari Das's poem, the painter began to execute magnificent pictures in a lyrical style marked by such uniquely stylized physiognomic characteristics as pointed long noses, elongated curvilinear eyes with equally meandering eyebrows, and delicate skinny chins almost exactly as described in the poem. These features became the standard of idealized feminine beauty for the Kishangarh school, as exemplified by catalogue number 71. Male figures are, however, almost always shown with an arched back representing the masculine pride of the brave Rajputs (cat. no. 73).

69

A Musical Entertainment

Kishangarh, ca. 1735

Gouache and gold on paper, 9⅛ x 6⅝ inches

1985.323

The overall effect of the painting is an aura of tranquility. A viewer can almost hear the ongoing performance of the soothing music and the peaceful sound of the two fountains depicted in the foreground. An interesting feature of the Kishangarh school, which continued even after the new phase began, is the slender boats floating in the distant lake (cat. 71). Another such feature is the diaphanous *ghumghat* or the veil whose circular border resembles a nimbus. Here it is important to note that this miniature was painted before the second phase of Kishngarh school developed with an emphasis on abstract quality. Therefore the female physiognomical features such as pointed long noses, elongated curvilinear eyes, meandering eyebrows, and delicate skinny chins as described in Nagari Das's poem are absent here.

This is a scene in a palace situated on the bank of a navigable river, as indicated by the two boats on its water. The wall of the palace has two doors, one of which is slightly open, and the flight of stairs leading to the river is visible through the gap. To the middle of the wall is attached a Mughal-style pavilion with a swimming pool. The swirling white, thin cloud around the moon and its reflection in the pool show that it is a cool autumnal Indian night. The prominent lady reclines against a bolster under a square canopy and gestures animatedly with her left hand in response to music performed by two female musicians, one singing, the other playing the *tānpurā*, both seated in front of her on the ground. To the left of this prominent lady a female companion gracefully holds a wine cup and listens to the music, while a palace girl, standing close to the pole of the canopy and holding a tray full of various objects attends the ladies. All the figures are rendered with some degree of naturalism and an attempt to distinguish them through individual features such as dark and fair complexions, an artistic feature also seen classical painting.

Published: Chandra 1971: cat. no. 158; Vajracharya 1994: 57.

70
The Festival of Divali

Kishangarh school, mid 18th century

Gouache and gold on paper, 4 x 6 inches

1982.167

As Chandra pointed out, this picture is a fragment of an originally much larger composition, which survived only in this tiny section (Chandra 1971: 96). Despite its fragmentary and damaged condition, this painting still illustrates the highly stylized feminine beauty of the new Kishangarh school. A slender youthful body with delicate waist, long arms are the ideals of this style. Savant Singh (alias Nagari Das), the poet-king responsible for establishing the new Kishangarh school, compared the feminine beauty with the twig of an evergreen tree.

This is a scene of fireworks celebrating Divali, the festival of light held in the middle of the autumn. Originally it was a harvest festival when Lakṣmī, the goddess of wealth, was worshiped in the shrines of private houses. In this festive evening, people illuminated their entire residential area with oil lamps, apparently because in the cultural history of India splendor, glory, and light are associated with wealth. Thus after fireworks were introduced to India during the Islamic period, they also became part of the festival. The lady, wearing a yellowish green sari with a dark red, pleated middle section, holds a sparkler in her outstretched right hand. She stands close to the parapet of a waterfront terrace where the spectacular display of other fireworks is taking place.

Published: Chandra 1971: cat. no. 158; Vajracharya 1994: 68.

71
Ladies in a Landscape

Kishangarh, mid 18th century

Gouache and gold on paper, 8⅝ x 12 inches

1985.324

Although this is a small painting, it encompasses a huge landscape with a navigable river. The river serves as a major compositional device of the picture, as it flows horizontally and divides the scene into two sections: a forest in the background and the grassy land of a village in the foreground. Various wild animals inhabit the forest: water buffalo, rhinoceros, boars, and deer.

A royal hunt is in process. The riders of the elephants and horses pursue those animals. On this side of the river is the more relaxed life of a remote Indian village. In the nearest section of the picture six beautiful women, rendered with the same physiognomy, are the main attraction of the scene. They head toward the lake adjoining a white building. The girls are enjoying the walk as they exchange bunches of what looks like grass. The girl leading the group balances three water jars on her head, apparently going to fetch water from the lake.

Closer to the river a woman washes clothes; another woman dresses after her bath; yet another dries her sari while talking to a friend seated on the grass. Similarly two other women with water pitchers on their heads are involved in conversation. Not too far from them, to the right, is another lake fed by the fresh water of the river. On the grassy field near the lake men are engaged in training elephants and stallions.

Published: Chandra 1971: cat. no. 160; Watson: 39; Raducha: cat. no. 2.93; Vajracharya 1994: 58.

70

71

72

72
The Image of Śrī Nāthajī

Kishangarh, mid 18th century

Gouache on paper, 6%16 x 4¾ inches

1982.168

This is a pictorial representation of the image of Śrī Nāthajī enshrined in a niche, exposed by rolling up the velvety curtain. The real shrine of the god is located in Nathdwara in Rajasthan. The shrine is shown here within a pink compartment against a yellowish green wall. The yellow border of the oval niche, decorated with flowering vine, contrasts sharply with the bright red wall of the niche from which emerges the frontally projected image of the blue god. He stands on a pedestal in a traditional fashion with splayed-out feet, raising his left arm into the space to symbolize the mythical event when the god lifted the Govardhana mountain to shelter the cattle and cowherds from the torrential rain. Apparently the god holds a sword in his right hand, a deviation from original iconography where the hand is placed on the hip (compare cat. no.41).

The god wears a multistrand pearl garland and a yellowish brown turban decorated with a peacock feather, a feature of Kṛṣṇa's iconographical identity. He is dressed in a six-pointed transparent *cākdār jama* and striped trousers, Mughal dress that became popular during the reign of Akbar (r. 1556–1605). Indian art depicts a god almost always dressed as a king would be during the same time, but sometime of a slightly earlier time as exemplified by this illustration. In Rajput painting, illustrations of figures in a frontal position are rare. But an image of Śrī Nāthajī is always depicted frontally.

Published: Chandra 1971: cat. no. 161; Raducha: cat. no. 2.29.

73

73

Kṛṣṇa Sheltering Rādhā

Kishangarh, late 18th century

Gouache on paper, 4⅞ x 3$^{11}/_{16}$ inches

1982.170

Rādhā and Kṛṣṇa stand near a lotus pond, holding lotus flowers. Kṛṣṇa, with his right hand, spreads a silky blue scarf dotted with tiny speckles over Rādhā, as if he is lovingly protecting her from dust or harsh sunlight. As usual, Rādhā has a fair complexion, whereas Kṛṣṇa is blue. In this example, however, he is depicted in a light gray-blue color. Rādhā is clad in orange and green sari and her *coli* is blue. Kṛṣṇa wears a yellow *dhoti*, a flower garland reaching all the way to his knees and an elaborate tall headgear decorated with flower design. His head is encircled by a nimbus. Both of them have big eyes rendered in the imitation of a lotus, hence designated in Sanskrit as *kamalanayana* "lotus eye." The use of gold brightens their ornaments and delineates the edge of their dresses.

A thick row of plantain trees, most of them in flower, is in the background. In the foreground three white cranes in dark gray water are rendered in rudimentary fashion.

Published: Chandra 1971: cat. no. 166; Raducha: cat. no. 2.49; Vajracharya 1994: 59.

सकलऋतुसमयप्राप्त रिनकानिसपतिष्ठनेस घटकलसनीर ग
नतसमेस ६कदिवसप्राशरांधरखराज खुरसरितविविधिकंन्यासमा
ड तिहिनोंगा६समालीक सिध संडतविलासुखसकलसिध बंधा
नरागक्षत्रिविवेक सपछराकरतनाठक अनेक अवगाहगंगाज
ल्ष्रंगारंग मिनिकरतमनं६क्रीड़ामतंग इहिसमयरेनुकानीर आ

74 recto

नंदसरितसुजुतसमाज रिधरद्कालक बुसरितितीर आवरसुभाव ची
अवधीरअधीर पुनिव्रतनोरप्रसिषियापाद्र ग्रासमेतमघ सत्व आ
६ दोस सत्यवतीकीमातहा कीनोत्रित्रिविचार मुनिजकधौक्षित
निमतचरु यामट्क सुमअधिकार ६ग सतिवतीकेनिमतचरु कीनो
तोरिखेस मातासोचर सादलै कीनो
तव्षिसिध ६ सेधरसोचरखुत्रिक
नततनकौसमून विविकेके अंक
नमग्रया यावीर रैनमृल्ष्ण्ल्दर करि
आवेरिषनिसहत चरनहीपाथ्रेचां
नसत्यवंतीसोतिहिसमय पूछतभेद
निदांन ६ग्रीखाद्कोतवप्रीक कौ
रतेऱ्रामप्रसिष्ट मककरेहमझ्ष्च
रोसीक्रमनोरप्रसिषि ६ध बुंदप्दरी
तलकष्यारुरिषिर्मई संताप सन्त्रिष्याकष्टउप्देशामाप सतवती

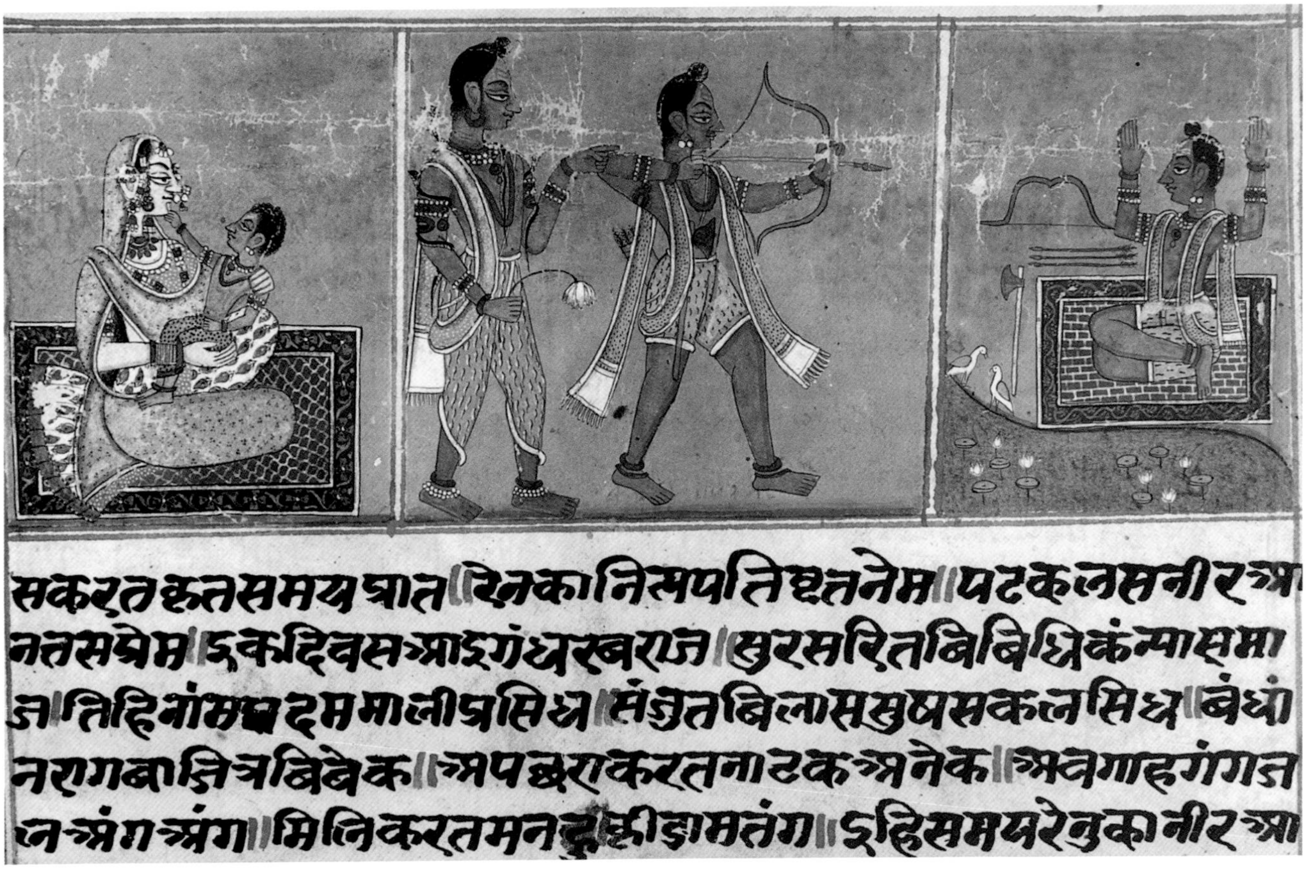

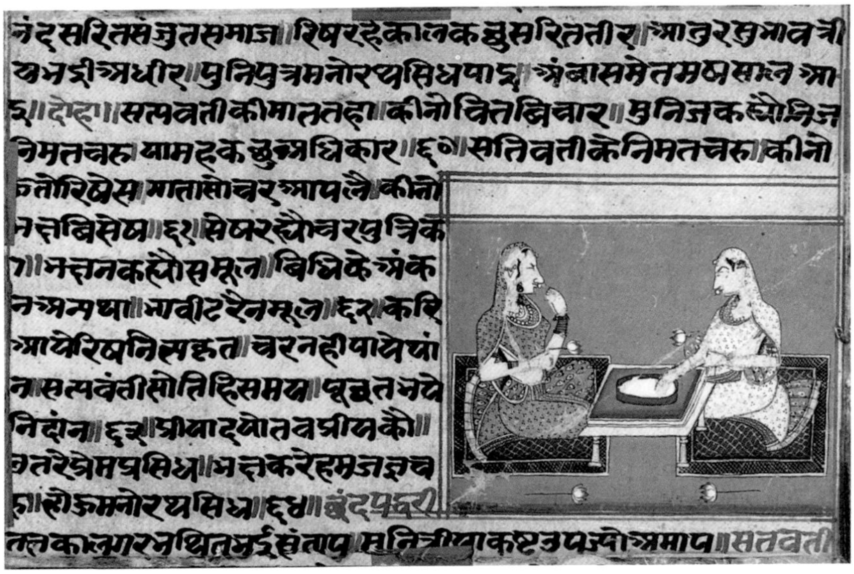

74 verso

74

The Story of Reṇukā and the King of Gandharvas [formerly folio from an unknown manuscript]

Kishangarh, mid 19th century

Gouache and gold on paper, 5⁵⁄₁₆ x 8⁹⁄₁₆ inches

1982.172

A fragment of a Sanskrit story from an unknown text is given immediately below the painting. The text is written in Devanāgarī script in black ink on the buff-colored paper. Red is sparingly used for some important words and marking the verse number. The verso of the folio also contains an illustration showing two women holding lotus flower in their hands; one of them is engaged in eating.

Although this is a late painting rendered long after the heyday of Kishangarh style, the physiognomy of male and female figures, the pointed nose and chin, and the unique shape of the eyes are still the immediately recognizable feature of the style. The figures also display arched backs.

According to the text Reṇukā was the devout wife of a hermit who lived on the bank of a river. One day a handsome king of the *gandharvas* known as Padumamālī, accompanied by beautiful *apsarās*, came to the river for bathing. In Indian myth the *gandharvas* are the male celestial singers and dancers. *Apsarās* are their women renowned for both beauty and skill in musical and theatrical performance. They traverse through the atmosphere playing variety of musical instruments.

When the *gandharva* king and his retinue were bathing in the river, Reṇukā arrived there to fetch water. She spent some time there watching their dalliance. Apparently this incident brought a disturbance in her peaceful conjugal love with her husband. Although the rest of the story is not available to us in this fragmentary text, very likely this is a version of Reṇukā and her jealous husband Jamadagni, a great hermit but infamous for his vehement anger toward his wife.

The textual description does not harmonize with the painting that shows three scenes against the green background. The first scene shows a fair-complexioned woman seated on a carpet with a blue child on her lap. However, the child is not necessarily Kṛṣṇa because in Rajput paintings the blue color is used to indicate dark complexion. The second scene depicts two noticeably blue male figures. One holds a lotus; the other shoots an arrow. The last scene leads us to a bank of a river full of lotuses and inhabited by a pair of aquatic birds. On the bank of the river an archer sits on a carpet in a yogic posture. He raises both his hands. His weapons, a battle-ax, a bow and arrows, are on the ground. Possibly this seated figure is Paraśurāma, Jamadagni's obedient son who chopped off his mother's head following his father's order. Paraśurāma's main attribute is a battle-ax, which lies in front of him.

Published: Chandra 1971: 170; Vajracharya 1994: 73.

BIKANER

Like Jodhpur, Bikaner is the capital city of a state situated on the border of the Thar desert in the northern section of Malwa, about 250 miles east of Delhi. It was established in the last quarter of the fifteenth century by a Rathor prince called Bika from Marwar (Jodhpur). He was the sixth son of Rao Jodha, the founder of the Jodhpur state. The political and social relationship of these two states was seldom cordial although the ruling families were so closely connected by blood.

In 1570, during Akbar's campaign to build his empire, Rao Kalyan Mall (1539–1571) submitted to imperial force and allowed his brother's daughter to marry the emperor. When Kalyan Mall's son Rai Singh (r. 1571–1612) became king, Rai's daughter was also given to Prince Salim (son of Akbar, later Emperor Jahangir, 1605–1627). Rai Singh's successors, Karan Singh and Anup Singh, continued to work for the Mughals and achieved a high status in the administration. Both of these princes deserve special attention in the history of the Bikaner school of painting. Around 1650 when Karan Singh was in Delhi serving the Mughal emperor, he hired the famous Muslim artist Ali Raza to paint for him a miniature depicting the god Viṣṇu and his consort Lakṣmī as they appeared in Singh's real dream (for a color picture see Khandalwala 1960: plate E). Although the painter was the master of Mughal-style painting, he rendered the miniature in accordance with the Rajput aesthetic, including hierarchical proportion, idealization of figures, and a background with a sharply contrasting color. Less than three decades later, in 1678, a stylistically more Mughalized version of the same subject matter was treated by another eminent Muslim artist, Ruknuddin (Beach: plate J). These seventeenth-century paintings set the tone for the Bikaner school of paintings. These paintings, however, display both the Mughal association and stylistic influence of the Deccani school. The reason is obvious. The rulers of Bikaner participated in the Deccan campaign for the Mughals and spent many years in such

75

Deccani regions as Daulatabad and Aurangabad. Raja Anup Singh, for example, served in the Deccan from 1680 to 1690 and even became governor of Bijapur. He collected Deccani paintings with which he enriched the traditional collection of the Lallgarh palace of Bikaner.

If Ali Raza was the *ustad* (the master) of Karan Singh's atelier, Ruknuddin was the *ustad* of his successor, Anup Singh, from 1680 to 1698 (Poster: 151). However, according to some scholars, Ruknuddin died in 1696 (Chaitnya: 3: 102). But his sons Ibrahim and Shahadin continued working for the Bikaner rulers. A valuable painting by Ibrahim in the Watson collection (cat. no. 75) exemplifies Ruknuddin's school of painting in rendering physiognomy and shading and its inheritance of the Deccani tradition.

The eighteenth-century paintings from Bikaner show a distinctive style that differs considerably from that of such neighboring schools as Marwar (Jodhpur) or Kishangarh. This style is characterized by comparatively small and naturalistic eyes (cat. no. 80), a tendency to depict a variety of physiognomies and differences of ages, and a combination of somber and vibrant colors (cat. no. 81).

75

Ibrahim, signed Number 29, album 86, the work of Ibrahim

Kṛṣṇa Waking the Sleeping Rādhā, folio from a series illustrating the *Rasikapriyā* of Keśavadāsa

Bikaner, dated V.S.1748 (A.D. 1691)

Gouache and gold on paper, 7 13/16 x 4 15/16 inches

1985.325

On the basis of either the inscription on the verso or the stylistic elements of the painting, the work can be safely attributed to Ibrahim, the son of prominent artist Ruknuddin. The short inscription in Devanāgarī script records: "an 29 jo 86 kam vrihma ro sam 1748" [Number 29, album 86, the work of Ibrahim, V.S. 1748/ A.D. 1691] (Chandra 1971: 105). To compare this style perhaps the most significant work of the same artist is "Nayika awaits her lover," dated 1692, housed in the Brooklyn Museum of Art (Poster: 150–51). The immediately striking similarity between these two paintings is in the physiognomy of Kṛṣṇa and the female figures. In addition Kṛṣṇa's crown and lower garment are almost identical as is the fashion of the short *colis* of Rādhā and her attendant figures. In the Brooklyn example, however, the facial features of the figures are much more deeply shaded than in the Watson example.

Furthermore the partial appearance of the tree at the upper left corner of the painting is a remarkable stylistic feature. Instead of showing the entire tree, the artist depicts only half of the trunk and the sections of the lower branches. The existence of the other half of the tree is left to the imagination of viewers, serving to magnify the scale of the subject. Such treatment of trees is often seen in Deccani painting (Binney 1973: 153) indicating that like other artists of Bikaner, Ibrahim was also exposed to the Deccani school. The composition of the picture, consisting of two registers, is rendered in the fashion of continuous narration, not unusual treatment in Rajput paintings. The painter does not strictly follow conventions, since he depicts the upper register as a mural on a yellow wall. The vertical line representing the corner of the room, together with the angle joining the border of the wall immediately below the line, creates the walls and floor of the room.

In the upper section Kṛṣṇa sits under a tree leaning against an orange bolster. He is bejeweled with a crown, earrings, pearl necklace, and arm bands and wears a white *dhoti*. In front of him stands a lady who gestures animatedly with her raised right hand. She wears a light pink sari and a short orange *coli*, and her head is partially covered with a scarf. She is a messenger. According to the superscript, she came to inform Kṛṣṇa that Rādhā is not feeling well. Thus the narration continues. Kṛṣṇa is shown again in the lower section of the painting holding Rādhā's hands and looking upward in perplexity. Rādhā is lying in the bed unable even to open her eyes. A female attendant sits on the ground near the bed. In the foreground two Brahmans perform the ritual of fire sacrifice with the hope that its magic will cure Rādhā.

Published: Chandra 1971: cat. no. 172; Raducha: cat. no. 2.39.

76

Attributed to School of Ruknuddin, fl. 1675–1700

A Lady at Worship

Bikaner, ca. 1690

Gouache and gold on paper, 5⅝ x 3⅛ inches

1985.326

Chandra (1971: 105) observed that this painting "is a product of the school of Ruknuddin which flourished in the last quarter of the seventeenth century." This attribution is apparently based on the body proportions, the facial features, and the adornments of the lady of this picture that bear similarities to the female figures of Ruknuddin and his son Ibrahim. Its origin becomes even more obvious if this painting is compared with catalogue number 75, which bears the name of the artist and date. This tiny painting is exceptional because of the artist's success in capturing the unlimited sky and the huge grassy land within the limited space of this painting and because of his approach in depicting the diminutive human figures in the lap of the all-covering, omnipresent, divine nature. This quality is often seen in Chinese painting but rarely in Indic works, where human figures usually dominate the scenes.

76

On a bank of a river under a tree, a white marble *Śivaliṅga* (a phallic representation of Śiva) and a *jalahari* (a drain to empty a libation) are set against the pink ground. A lady wearing a bright red and yellow sari kneels in front of *Śivaliṅga*, in a devotional position that became increasingly popular after

77

the sixteen century. She holds a ladle with her right hand to lustrate the water ritually on top of the *liṅga*. The water drains through the *jalahari* and runs toward the river. The entire scene is shown against the vast grassy land, gradually merging into a greenish blue sky.

Published: Chandra 1971: cat. no. 173; Raducha: cat. no. 2.12.

77
Lady and Tree

Bikaner, late 17th century

Watercolor, gouache, and gold on paper, 4½ x 2 inches

69.28.11; see color plate 6

Although this painting may be contemporary with two products of Ruknuddin's school Kṛṣṇa Waking the Sleeping Rādhā (cat. no. 75) and A Lady at Worship (cat. no. 76), it differs stylistically from them considerably. The most noticeable distinguishing features are the soft color scheme here replacing a bright one in the earlier two examples and the fine facial features here replacing the earlier broad ones.

A slender, elegant lady with a fair complexion sits on a lower branch of a fruit-bearing tropical tree—probably a kumquat—and leans against the branch, touching the ground only with her left foot. She holds a twig in her right hand and a freshly cut branch in her left. Apparently this is a seventeenth-century version of the ancient artistic motif of the *śālabhañjikā*, a young woman shown grabbing a branch. A woman with a tree is a popular subject in Indian art because it is a fertility symbol. Just as the subject is treated in classical art, the elegant lady wears many ornaments. Her tiara is a contemporaneous fashion, decorated with a plumelike crest. She is dressed in close-fitting purple trousers and a diaphanous tunic reaching from her waist to her ankles. She is barefoot. In the foreground runs a stream, its bank covered with green grass dotted with tiny white flowers. The pale green middle ground gradually merges into a gray sky covered with surging cloud patterns, which are accentuated by a flight of migrating birds.

Published: Chandra 1971: cat. no. 175; Raducha: cat. no. 2.60.

78
Gauḍa Malhār Rāga [formerly Rāginī Gauḍa Malhār]

Bikaner, ca. 1700

Gouache and gold on paper, 6¼ x 4$\frac{5}{16}$ inches

1986.56

This painting is from a *rāgamālā* series. A short inscription on the verso identifies the male figure as goḍa malhāra (Gauḍa Malhār), a masculine musical mode. He sits in a yogic position in a beautiful landscape with a lotus pond, mango trees, a flowering bush, and a banana plant. The tranquility of the place is accentuated by grassy land gradually turning into light gray ground and eventually culminating in a green and pink hilltop with three white buildings.

The musical mode is iconographically represented here as a yogi. He holds a rosary in his right hand and rests the other on a crutch. He is seated on lotus petals in the ubiquitous position utilized for a yogi and for divine figures throughout the history of Indic art. Usually in classical art such figures are depicted frontally. In this example, however, due to the

Rajput artists' fascination for the full profile, the head of the divine rāga is shown facing his right—our left—directly, and his torso is slightly turned toward that direction. His lower body remains frontal.

He wears a tiger skin around his waist and on his bare chest multiple pearl necklaces studded with rubies and gems. He has a mustache, and his long hair is neatly tied into a single lock behind the head. A pearl ornament tied to the lock comes all the way to his forehead. The round shape of his head, his curvilinear elongated eyebrow, long curly lashes, and the convex line forming the forehead and linked with diagonal contour of the nose are noticeable facial features creating the Bikaner type of physiognomy.

Published: Chandra 1971: cat. no. 177.

78

79
A Lady Adjusting Her Veil

Bikaner, early 18th century

Gouache on paper, 6¾ x 5$\frac{1}{16}$ inches

1982.174

The painting's apple-green background is a stylistic element often seen in Mughal and Rajput portraiture beginning with Jahangir's time (1605–1627). A tall, beautiful young woman has partially covered her head with the end of a diaphanous sari, a gesture of politeness and an expression of shyness. The light pink sari has a gold border, and its pleated middle section is white. Her palm and the soles of her feet are painted red. Her ornaments consist of a *bindi* (pendant worn on the forehead), *phulia* (nose ornament), earrings, a pearl necklace, armlets, and bracelets. Her upper body appears to be bare. The artist has given much attention to rendering her pretty face and youthful breasts, which are visible through her transparent sari. The rest of her body is rendered rudimentarily Although she is tall, her neck is quite short as a mark of beauty; women are never shown with long necks in Indic art. In accordance with the prevailing style of Bikaner painting her chin and neck are heavily shaded.

Published: Chandra 1971: cat. no. 178; Raducha: cat. no. 2.62.

79

80

80

Rāsamaṇḍala, Kṛṣṇa and Dancing *Gopīs*

Bikaner, early 18th century

Gouache and gold on paper, 6½ x 8¹¹⁄₁₆ inches

1986.57

As in most other examples, Rajput artists here do not depict the physical world realistically; The viewpoint is not consistent: The figures in the circular dance are depicted as if from above; however, the trees and Yaśodā and Nanda are shown in profile. Furthermore, the position of the two girls pouring the colored water can not be explained whether they are standing on the flat ground or in an elevated place. Such treatment, however, does not affect the clarity of the scene. The language of the painting is symbolic, not realistic, a prominent feature of Indic art throughout the history of the continent.

Surrounded by sumptuously dressed female companions, musicians, and dancers, Kṛṣṇa momentarily lifts his flute from his lips and flexes both his knees in a particular mode of dance to the beat of a drum. This is a scene of *rāsamaṇḍala*, the circular dance, mainly associated with the cult of Kṛṣṇa. It is depicted here against the green circular ground bordered by a thick line of darker tone separating it from rest of the picture. The Sanskrit word for the circular area is mandala, which is part of the name of the dance and symbolizes not only dance but also the celestial realm, both visualized here as circular. Although the painting is partially damaged and much of the upper right quarter missing, we can still see some of the dance and musical performance. Not only the bright colors of the saris such as orange, scarlet, pink, blue, and yellow, but also the suggestions of sounds of a drum, trumpets, a *vīṇā* and other musical instruments enliven the scene as the girls dance, clap their hands, or wave the *chowrie* around Kṛṣṇa in the rhythm of the music. The two girls on the top who pour colored water on Kṛṣṇa suggest that this dance is a part of the spring festival of Holi. Outside the circle on the left are Nanda and Yaśodā, Kṛṣṇa's foster parents, under mango and palm trees, watching the dance. Behind them, in the distance looms the rolling hill topped by round bushes and pointed cypresses.

Published: Chandra 1971: cat. no. 179; Raducha: cat. no. 2.43.

81

The Child Kṛṣṇa Playing with His Mother

Bikaner, early 18th century

Gouache and gold on paper, 10⅛ x 7⅜ inches

1986.58

Symmetrical organization, a favorite feature of many Rajput artists, is emphasized here by the display of the peacocks on the corners of the flat roof, the pointed cyprus trees together with lush vegetation flanking the building, the arrangements of figures and architectural elements, and the pattern of the formal garden. The three-quarter profile for one male and two female attendants, the abundance use of white, and Yaśodā's facial features together with a distinctive single curl confirm that this is an eighteenth-century Bikaner painting.

This scene takes place in the palace where Kṛṣṇa was brought up by his foster parents Nanda and Yaśodā, who are often depicted in Rajput art as a king and queen. The two-story white building shown here is not a residential superstructure or a harem, but a pavilion or audience hall with many pillars and open space. In the middle of the hall, located on the upper floor of the building, Nanda, attired in Mughal imperial fashion, leans against the pink balustrade. Surrounded by colorfully dressed attendants, the aged monarch receives the homage of a courtier who salutes him in Mughal fashion.

81

Immediately below the cornice of the upper floor, is a huge rolled-up curtain exposing three openings of the ground floor with engrailed arches and a stairway on the left. Although the somber blue sky and white color of the palace and the courtyard dominate the scene, the bright orange color of the curtain horizontally dissecting most of the painting vivifies the picture. Additional color is supplied by the sumptuously dressed women carrying regalia and toys for the child Kṛṣṇa who is led by Yaśodā, shown in the middle in hierarchic proportion. In the foreground a scarlet railing separates the courtyard from the garden.

Published: Chandra 1971: cat. no. 180; Raducha: cat. no. 2.42.

82

82

Rāmakarī Rāginī

Bikaner, early 18th century

Gouache and gold on paper, 6¼ x 4³⁄₁₆ inches

1986.59

As the introductory essay states, the subject matter depicted as Rāmakarī Rāginī itself provides evidence that some themes of *rāgamālā* painting date back at least to the fourth century A.D. The renowned poet Kālidāsa; in his work *Meghadūta* (The Cloud Messenger) describes a separated lover rendering a self-portrait kneeling at the feet of his lover to assuage her anger. Unfortunately no such painting of the classical period has survived.

According to inscriptions found on similar Rajput paintings, the lady seated on a low bench furnished with elaborate soft cushions is Rāmakarī Rāginī, the heroine. This example, however, has no inscription. Her well-dressed young lover kneels before her. She turns her face away from him in anger. The lover, to mollify her anger, bows down to her and in desperation holds her pendant leg. She does not accept this gesture of submission and courtesy and prevents him, with her hand, from inclining his head.

The episode takes place late at night, as suggested by the flaming candles on the bottom right, the dark sky with a crescent moon, and the dozing attendants in the bedroom. One attendant is still awake and tries to wake her friend, who is leaning against the window of the *chatri*. The three-quarter profile, employed here for both dozing figures, is a characteristic of Bikaner painting of this time. The feature derives from earlier works such as the late seventeenth-century painting "Kṛṣṇa Supporting Mount Govardhana" (Barrett and Gray: 156).

Published: Chandra 1971: cat. no. 181; Vajracharya 1994: 52.

83

Nathu Ahmad

Toḍī Rāginī

Bikaner, mid 18th century

Gouache and gold on paper, 5 x 3⅝ inches

1982.175; see color plate 11

A short inscription in Devanāgarī script, given on the back of the painting, reads: *kām nāthū amadjiro,* Nathu Ahmad's work. We do not know any other work of this artist.

Comfortably leaning against a purple bolster, a lady clad in a scarlet sari with floral designs sits cross-legged on an apple-green carpet with a blue border. With her right hand, she holds a golden *vīṇā*. Attracted by her music an opalescent fawn stands in front of her without fear. These iconographic elements, particularly the *vīṇā* and the deer, identify her as Toḍī Rāginī.

The artist has rendered her as a petite lady with diminutive body proportions. Her rounded hips and plump torso suggest youth and inner vitality often described as *prāṇa*, a prominent feature of Indian art discussed in detail in the introductory essay. Heavy shading indicates the transition between her neck and face and tear-duct and nose. Other noticeable stylistic elements are the dark green leaves with their upper section conspicuously turning white, the cypress tree marked by white lines, and stylized white clouds of peculiar shape.

The painting is colorful. Toḍī 's scarlet sari, the yellow floor with pink flowers, green carpet with blue border, mauve bolster, dark green vegetation inhabited by colorful birds, apple-green horizon and blue sky all show the artist's fascination with the Rajput conventions of color.

Published: Chandra 1971: cat. no. 182.

84
Malkauns Rāga

Bikaner, late 18th century

Gouache and gold on paper, 11 9/16 x 8 1/4 inches

1982.176

The affinity of Bikaner style with the Deccani tradition is still visible even in this late eighteenth-century painting, particularly in rendering the subtle transition from the forehead to the skull of the female attendant. Compare the treatment of her hair with that of the figures in cat. no. 125.

This shows musical entertainment in front of an impressive edifice with white and gray walls. The colorful curtains are rolled up along the walls just under the eaves. Behind the building a symmetrical row of palm trees and elongated cypress trees, barely visible against the dark blue sky, indicates nighttime.

In the middle ground is the yellow floor of the terrace and the bluish gray throne cushioned with pink pillows. The princely figure seated on the throne holds a flower in his right hand. He is dressed in a dark gray *jama*, a turban, and pearl necklaces, bracelets, armlets, and earrings. Attended by a *chowrie* bearer, he listens to the music performed by two female musicians, one playing a *tānpurā* and the other a drum. He is identified in the Devanāgarī inscription on the verso as the second rāga Malkauns.

Published: Chandra 1971: cat. no. 183.

83

84

85

85

Princess and Bird

Bikaner, late 18th century

Gouache on paper, 6⁹⁄₁₆ x 4⁷⁄₁₆ inches

1982.177

Unlike other Rajput artists, this painter is skillful in creating space through the device of diagonal line that meets with the vertical shaded line representing the corner of the wall. The bluish color background used for the wall of the balcony also contributes to creating spatial depth. The tall narrow openings flanking the balcony resemble the windows of modern architecture and are unprecedented in Indian painting. Furthermore, the subtle rendering of her hair around the neck and earlobe clearly indicates the artist's interest in realistic detail rendering, a feature often ignored by most Rajput artists.

Despite such sophisticated technique, the subject of the painting seems to be derived from classical tradition. The earliest examples of this subject are Kuṣāṇa / Mathura female figures with tamed birds perched on their arms (Dehejia: 64). In this example, a youthful lady stands facing left in an ivory white arched balcony that is sumptuously decorated with foliage and flowers. A little bird perches on her right hand and looks toward the lady. She wears a dark tunic and a colorful cap, both in European fashion. By the late eighteenth century elite Indians were exposed to western customs, although only some approved them. The artist of the present painting appears to be familiar not only with European fashion but also the painterly style of the west, which explains the appearance of new features in the painting.

Published: Chandra 1971: cat. no. 184; Raducha: cat. no. 2.69.

SAWAR (AJMER)

Sawar is a *thikānā* (fief) in Ajmer, located only a few miles south of Jaipur. Like Jaipur, Ajmer was a Rajasthani state near the Mughal capital of Delhi that was incorporated into the Mughal empire very early. Although the rulers of this tiny fiefdom did not play any important role in the political history, Archer, Binney, and others have shown that the paintings of this region possess an admirable style distinct from the pictorial idioms of neighboring schools, including Jaipur. Between the late seventeenth and early nineteenth centuries, the state of Sawar produced secular and religious paintings including the portraits of the members of the ruling family of Sawar and the romance of Kṛṣṇa and Rādhā. These painting are characterized by the use of unpainted areas to indicate space. As Chandra pointed out, this technique is derived from the Mughal *nim qalam* (partial coloration of drawing) (Chandra 1971: 114). Binney described this prominent feature of Sawar school as "not completely painted," noting " the unpainted background is not the result of failure to finish the picture but rather of concentration on the major decorative elements to the exclusion of non-essentials" (Portland: 47).

86

Two Ladies at Play

Sawar (Ajmer), early 18th century

Gouache on paper, $6\frac{3}{8}$ x $3\frac{15}{16}$ inches

1982.179

86

Usually an Indic miniature is painted on a well-prepared burnished surface. As we mentioned earlier, the painters of the Ajmer miniatures do not follow this convention; instead they paint their subject directly on the blank paper. In the present example, the blank paper is treated as the space representing the background and the foreground; thus the dancing figures appear to be dancing in space weightlessly.

Looking upward and holding each other's hands criss-crossed so as to balance themselves, two young girls dance rhythmically. The flying ends of their saris and *dupattās*, veils worn by women around the head and shoulders, indicate the cadence of their dance. The girl on the left wears pearl ornaments, a dark green *coli*, and a yellow sari with a blue black pleated middle section; the other girl is dressed in tight orange *pai jamas* (trousers), a transparent apple-green *jama*, pink *dupattā*, and pearl ornaments.

The theme of two girls dancing is a popular motif in Indic painting. Although this motif became popular in Rajasthani, Pahari, and Mughal painting beginning from the early eighteenth century, it originally goes back to the pre-Mughal tradition of Indic art. We know this from the decorative illustrations found in some fifteenth-century Gujarati manuscript paintings (Khandalavala, Chandra, and Chandra: fig.8)

Published: Chandra 1971: cat. no. 186.

87

87

Kṛṣṇa Leading Rādhā Through a Garden

Sawar (Ajmer), early 18th century

Gouache and gold on paper, 9⅞ x 5½ inches

1.1970.2

In the foreground of the painting is a small lotus pond with a duck at each end. Some lotuses are full-blown, others are about to bloom. As in the classical period, the ripples of the water are indicated by repeated semicircles. The flowers of the garden on the bank of the pond are blooming. Kṛṣṇa, attired in Mughal dress, leads Rādhā through the path of the garden, apparently heading to the hill in the background. Their two female companions have already reached the other slope of the hill. A row of plantains alternates with stylized trees with thick leaves on the top of the hill. A poem in Brajabhāṣā above the painting briefly describes the gently blowing cool breeze. Note the use of blank surface of the paper as the background of the painting as in catalogue no. 86, the previous work.

Published: Chandra 1971: cat. no. 187; Raducha: cat. no. 2.41; Vajracharya 1994: 46.

JAIPUR (AMBER)

Jaipur is located only about 160 miles south of Delhi and Agra, the capital cities of the Mughals. In the late sixteenth century when the Kacchawaha Rajput, Raja Bihar Mall, ruled the state of Amber, later also known as Jaipur, the Mughal emperor Akbar (r. 1556–1605) was expanding his empire systematically. Although Akbar was only a teenager at that time, he already had a vision; his master plan included assimilating the Rajput rulers of Rajasthan into his administration through intermarriage and by employing them in highly responsible positions. Raja Bihari Mall was the first Rajput ruler who realized the superiority of growing Mughal power in India and willingly or unwillingly supported Akbar's master plan. In 1562 he voluntarily submitted to Akbar and gave his daughter to the emperor in marriage. Later she became the mother of the crown prince Jahangir (r. 1605–1627).

Although this new trend of marriage of Rajput daughters with Mughal princes continued throughout the history of the Rajputs and the Mughals, it remained almost entirely political. Until recently scholars believed that close family relations with the Mughal court did not change the cultural and artistic spirit of the Rajput rulers at Amber. According to Chandra, the late sixteenth and early seventeenth century paintings from Amber do not show any interest in Mughal style (Chandra 1971: 116). Beach also suggests that even in the eighteenth century when the *rāgamālā* series was painted under the patronage and supervision of the renowned Maharaja Sawai Jai Singh (1700–1744) artists looked to earlier Rajput paintings for stylistic inspiration (Beach: 184–85). Although these statements are correct, recently Glynn (2000: 236) has shown that some artists of seventeenth century Amber did take interest in assimilating Mughal stylistic elements in their works. According to her, catalogue number 88, Portrait of a Nobleman, in the Watson collection is an example of this aspect of Jaipur painting.

After the death of Aurangzeb (1658–1707), which precipitated a chaotic situation in India, Maharaja Sawai Jai Singh engaged in the Hindu *Pad Padshahi*, a movement to reestablish Hindu independence on the ruins of the Mughal empire. In accordance with this movement, he endeavored to restore the glory of the ancient Indic tradition. He commissioned the construction of observatories based on the prescriptions given in Sanskrit texts on *jyautiṣa* (the sciences of astronomy and astrology) in his new capital Jaipur (the city of victory). Furthermore, with an intention to revive the architectural study of ancient India, the city of Jaipur itself was built following the city plan prescribed in ancient Indian texts. Although such elements as the rectangular grid plan resemble European models, they seem to be coincidental. This spirit of reviving the ancient glory might have inspired some contemporary painters of Jaipur to adhere to a traditional style that was little influenced by the Mughal atelier. No reliable sources indicate whether Jaipur artists studied ancient texts on pictorial representation as scientists did texts on architecture and astronomy. We do not encounter any dramatic upheaval in the history of Jaipur paintings as expected.

88

88

Portrait of a Nobleman

Jaipur (Amber), 17th century

Gouache and gold on paper, 8⅝ x 4¾ inches

1974.51; see color plate 5

Chandra thought that this Mughal painting was rendered in the late eighteenth century during Shah Alam's reign (1759–1806) rather than during the reigns of Jahangir (1605–1627) and Shah Jahan (1627–1658), because it is characterized by several stylistic features of a later time such as the yellow flesh tone instead of pink, the absence of luminosity of the jewels, lack of volume in showing the pleats of cloth at the wrist, and discordant elements such as the off balance six knobs on the shield. However, a comparative study of this portrait with the representation of Ram Singh (born in 1635), the raja of Amber, may suggest that this painting could be a contemporaneous portrait commissioned by the raja. Glynn has convincingly shown the existence of an Amber school of painting in the seventeenth century (Glynn 1996: 67–93) According to her research several portraits of Ram Singh, which were previously considered to be Mughal paintings, were in fact the works of the Rajput painters associated with the raja. In a more recently published article, Glynn suggests that this portrait of the nobleman may also be the work of an Amber artist that may represent Ram Singh's brother Kirat Singh (d. 1673) (Glenn 2000: 236). In that case the aforementioned stylistic elements should not be considered later development of Mughal painting but the characteristics of a school of early Jaipur (Amber) painting.

Under the blue sky, a tastefully dressed and armed nobleman stands on grass facing left. He brings his hands together, perhaps in a gesture of respect or supplication to his superior or a divine figure, who is not shown. Furthermore, just as in other portrait paintings of this type, the artist here makes no attempt to paint the background. He chose to eliminate all these elements of distraction and direct our full attention to the nobleman's handsome youthful figure silhouetted against the blue sky. Such treatment is a Mughal invention that began to appear during Jahangir's time.

The light brown turban of the nobleman is accentuated by a scarlet fold emerging from the inner section of the turban almost like an exotic flower bud. The turban is further enhanced with a ribbonlike flowery band that runs diagonally around the turban. Likewise his white, pleated *jama* is sumptuously accentuated with a golden sash whose flaring ends are decorated with red flowers and cascades below his waist. The pink stripe of the additional sash supports the dangling sword. The black shield with six knobs is held by a baldric over his right shoulder. His formal attire befitting his noble rank is complete with golden shoes and trousers adorned with pink flowers. Note also the pink pendant that resembles the shape of a bird. As Raducha noticed, the entire portrait is rendered with a finely handled brush.

Published: Chandra 1971: cat. no. 29; Raducha: cat. no. 2.66: Glynn 2000: fig. 7.

89

Āśavarī Rāginī

Probably Jaipur (Amber), early 18th century

Gouache and gold on paper, 8⅝ x 7 inches

1.1970.4

89

In the background is a steep mountain with a shrine on the summit. At the foot of the mountain, on a little pink hill, a young lady representing Āśavarī Rāginī, an Indian musical mode in a human form, holds a snake. She wears a yellow blouse and a skirt made of peacock feathers that seems to be her iconographical feature (see also cat. no. 53 depicting the same rāginī). In front of her, a bearded snake-charmer, wearing a Mughal type of headgear and dress, plays a pipe described in the superscript as *algojā*, which is usually made out of a gourd. His dress is made of multiple pieces of materials of a variety of colors sewn together. Snakes attracted by the music crawl closer to him. There are more snakes on the trunks of the trees at either side of the picture. The trees are delineated with the traditional stylization.

Published: Chandra 1971: cat. no. 189; Vajracharya 1994: 45.

90

90

Dhanaśrī Rāginī

Probably Jaipur (Amber), ca. 1700–1750

Gouache and gold on paper, 8½ x 7 inches

1.1970.4

According to the Devanāgarī superscript given in the bluish red margin, the lady is Dhanaśrī Rāginī. The Hindi verse given in the yellow register further describes her as a lonely lady separated from her beloved. In this case the equestrian princely figure accompanied by warriors must be her absent lover who is on an expedition, perhaps against an enemy stronghold. Dhanaśrī's complexion is supposed to be iconographically blue or green, but here she is shown as a lady of fair complexion.

On the ground floor of the white palace, Dhanaśrī paints a portrait of her lover. Holding a drawing board with her left hand, she sits in the traditional posture of an Indic artist. One of her maids stands behind her, waving the fly whisk, while the other sits in front of her. Another maid stands near the door holding a small object, perhaps a brush.

Published: Chandra 1971: cat. no. 190.

91

Mānavatī Rāginī [formerly Rāginī Rāmakali]

Probably Jaipur (Amber), ca. 1700–1750

Gouache and gold on paper, 9 x 6 inches

1.1971.68

The superscript written in Brajabhāṣā identifies the subject as Mānavatī, "a proud lady." Chandra had mistakenly identified this painting as Rāmakali Ragini, a secondary spelling for Rāmakarī Ragini. Mānavatī and Rāmakarī rāginīs are easily confused because they do not differ much. The main difference between them is this. The illustration of Rāmakarī Rāginī is characterized by the scene in which a man attempts to bow down to the feet of his lover, an extreme reaction in the context of traditional Indian society. No such extreme action appears in the Mānavatī Rāginī, and the man simply displays the *namaskāra* gesture folding both hands. Note also the fact that just as Mānavatī Rāginī, occasionally the Lalita Rāginī also includes a scene of a horse and a groom in the lower register (Barrett and Gray: 135). This scene is never associated with Rāmakarī Rāginī. Thus Mānavatī Rāginī seems to be created combining the features of Rāmakarī and Lalita. As we explained in the introductory essay, the iconographical features of these two raginis are based on the popular themes of ancient Indian art.

The main episode of the love story takes place inside a room of a palacelike house adorned with ornamental *chatris* on the roof. The wide-open space under the roof is divided into two rooms. The outer room has bluish green walls and yellow carpet on which two female musicians sit playing musical instruments. A female retainer who holds a *chowrie* stands near the post that divides the rooms. The retainer turns towards the musicians to avoid the lovers' quarrel. The couple sits on the green bed of the inner room, which has a white wall intercepted by a small door leading to another room or storage area. The nobleman is dressed in red *jama* and plumed turban and equipped with sword and shield, which indicate that he is about to leave home for an expedition. The lady, dressed in green *coli* and brownish yellow sari, turns away from the nobleman as he attempts to please her before he leaves. Her face is depicted in three-quarter profile, a rare feature in Rajput painting. Behind her stands another female retainer with a *chowrie* in her hand. A caparisoned black horse and a groom await the nobleman in the courtyard, which is accessible by a pink and yellow stairway. The courtyard is not delineated clearly. Apparently the blue background against which the stairway, the groom, and the horse are shown, stand for it.

91

Published: Chandra 1971: cat. no. 191.

॥राग हिंडोल॥दोहा॥मधुमाधौगं धार मिलि टोडी और देसाष बिलावल हिंडोल संग रा
गरंग जिवराष॥चौपई॥बृणेषं न बिबिरचे अमोला रतन जरित सुषरासि हिंडोला च
ढी हिंडोल पिय बीन बजावे नारी उमगि पेम धुनि गावे समो सुहागिनि रति सुषदाई
निरमल जलद जु किबर षालाई दामिनि देषि होत उजियारी राजत बाग पंकति सु
षकारी पियसौं प्रीति फंदे अति बाढी आनंद मगन झुलावत ठाढी दोहा राजत रंग
हिंडोल त्रिय झूलत बनिता संग पूरन आनंद मग हिय जततानततरंग १२

92

92
Hiṇḍola Rāga

Probably Jaipur (Amber), ca. 1700–1750

Gouache and gold on paper, 7¼ x 6 inches

1.1971.69

The subject matter of this painting is the Hiṇḍola Rāga, the musical mode associated with the swing festival. Kṛṣṇa and Rādhā sit in a swing gently rocked by two attendants. In front of them two female dancers dance to the music, while several female musicians standing immediately behind the plantain trees play cymbals, *dholaki* drums, and *sāraṅgi*, a stringed musical instrument. All the female figures show the same physiognamy. Two cows resting on the ground also seem to be enjoying the music and the dance. The lotus pond and the fountain in the foreground contribute to the pleasant surroundings.

The conventional apple-green middle ground changes dramatically into a cloudy sky illuminated by flashes of lightning and the flights of celestial nymphs known as *apsarās*. One nymph plays the *tānpurā*, while the other pours flowers from the sky over Kṛṣṇa and Rādhā. The traditional belief is that the *apsarās* are excellent musicians and also the most beautiful creatures in the world. As in this painting, they are depicted in the wall paintings of Ajanta (ca. sixth century A.D.) flying through the sky and playing musical instruments. In the Ajanta painting they are shown in classical costumes, whereas in the current example they are dressed in the eighteenth century Rajput costumes. In both cases the costumes are contemporaneous with the painting.

The word *hiṇḍola* means a swing. Thus the Hiṇḍola Rāga suggests the arrival of the spring or rainy season, for the swing festival of Kṛṣṇa is celebrated during the early month of that season, which is also the mating time of many species of Indian birds, including the peacocks. During the rainy season, the peacocks, enlivened by the thunderstorm, dance and sing. Thus, in addition to the dark rain clouds, the flashes of lightning, the peacocks perching in the branches and the swing are all shown here as the iconographical features of the Hiṇḍola Rāga.

While we cannot give a certain stylistic attribution for this painting, useful clues are the physiognomy of the cute diminutive figures, the particular way of delineating the plantain trees and other vegetation, the style of the cloud pattern, and the symmetrical arrangement.

Published: Chandra 1971: cat. no. 192; Raducha: cat. no. 2.44.

93

93

Ramkishan

The Month of Śrāvaṇa, illustration for the *Kavipriyā* of Keśavadāsa

Jaipur (Amber), ca. 1768

Gouache and gold on paper, 8¾ x 6 inches

1989.14

On a buff-colored paper, the bright red border with white and blue flowers is used as a rectangular frame of the painting. The upper section of the painting consists of three lines of text in Devanāgarī script. It is written in white and gold ink on black surface. The text is from Keśavadāsa's work *Kavipriyā* in the Brajabhāṣā language.

On the basis of stylistic similarity, Chandra convincingly identified the artist of this painting as Ramkishan, who also painted a *rāgamālā* series in 1786 at Malpura, a city between Bundi and Jaipur (Chandra 1971: 119). One leaf of the series is in the Harvard University Art Museums, another leaf in the Victoria and Albert Museum, London (Portland: 48).

This representation of the rainy season features Śrāvaṇa or the second month when it rains almost every day. The lakes and the rivers swell. In the rhythm of thunder and lightning, peacocks and cranes sing and dance in order to attract their mates. Fresh leaves make the world colorful. No expedition should be launched in this rainy season. Therefore the male members of a family are expected to stay at home, particularly if that family belongs to the castes of warriors or businessmen. In this miniature the artist has successfully captured this phenomenon.

Minimizing the architecture, the artist created a vast landscape of lakes, rivers, forests, and an expansive cloudy sky. He combined such colors as brilliant yellow for the tree and the banks of the rivers that blend with the blue sky and water; the white building is intersected by sparkling a red cornice, which echoes the elongated red boat on the blue water of the lake.

As part of the iconography of the season, a couple is seated near the window of the pavilion facing each other. Both wear multiple necklaces including some of pearls, and both stylishly hold a flower in their right hand. The pointed red turban of the male represents perhaps the contemporaneous fashion of Jaipur.

Published: Chandra 1971: cat. no. 194.

94

Maharaja Sawai Prithvi Singh (1768–1778) of Jaipur

Jaipur (Amber), ca. 1775

Gouache on paper, 7 1/16 x 4 13/16 inches

1982.181

Against an apple-green background bordered with bluish white clouds in a blue sky, a young maharaja stands facing right. He is dressed in a bright orange *jama* and turban that is decorated with a *jighā* (plumelike turban jewel) and scarlet *cappals* (pointed Indian sandals). He wears four strands of pearl necklaces. In accordance with the contemporary regal costume, he holds a sword and tiny flower in his hands. Chandra identified him as Prithvi Singh, the son of Madho Singh: "born in 1763 and ascended the throne when he was but five years of age. He died in 1778 at the age of fifteen" (Chandra 1971: 117).

The chubby figure of the child king is unusually naturalistic. Few representations of children in Indic miniature paintings show such successfully drawn childish features as the chubby cheek, short blunt nose, well-fed plump body that starts swelling immediately bellow the chest with smoothness and tightness and thus differs from the corpulent adult male torso with its bulging lower abdomen.

Published: Chandra 1971: cat. no. 193.

94

95

95

Dīpaka Rāga, from a *rāgamālā* series

Jaipur (Amber), ca. 1825

Gouache and gold on paper, 7⁹⁄₁₆ x 5¼ inches

1982.182

A five-line poem describing Dīpaka Rāga in the Braja language or Brajabhāṣā is given at the yellow upper panel. The Devanāgarī script is written here in black ink. The Watson collection has two folios of this *rāgamālā* series. This is number 19, the other 31 (1982.183). The painting is rendered within a frame projected against the purple surface. The frame is marked by green and yellow borders, the green border being decorated with golden vine motif.

A clarity of color and pattern seems to be the main concern of the artist. Thus he applies brilliant colors such as blue, orange, yellow, purple, and scarlet in rendering the sari, canopy, couch, and drum—all sumptuously decorated with patterns of flowers and leaves. The bluish white marble courtyard and the wall of the building accentuate the brilliancy of the colors. The profuse shading, particularly in the facial features, is used to render an ideal physiognomy rather than to create three-dimensionality. The artist has painted two-dimensional, paper-thin architecture.

In front of a one-storied white marble building, under a scarlet canopy, Kṛṣṇa and Rādhā sit comfortably on a couch leaning against purple cushions. Kṛṣṇa wears a yellowish brown robe that matches Rādhā's sari. His crowned head is encircled with a green nimbus bordered with double lines. He holds a mirror with his right hand and turns his head toward the female attendant who stands behind the couch holding a fly whisk made of peacock feathers. Rādhā is shy like a newly wed bride. Embraced by Kṛṣṇa, she gently touches his leg and gazes toward the ground. In front of the divine couple, female musicians play such musical instruments as the *dholaki* drum. The courtyard is illuminated by candlelight. The dark sky above the back garden indicates that it is night.

Published: Chandra 1971: cat. no. 195; Raducha: cat. no. 2.53.

96

Megha Malhār Rāga, from a *rāgamālā* series

Jaipur (Amber), ca. 1825

Gouache and gold on paper, 7⁹⁄₁₆ x 5⅛ inches

1982.183; see color plate 22

The similarity of script, language, and border decoration clearly indicates that this is another work by the Amber artist who painted the previous catalogue entry of the Dīpaka Rāga (cat. no. 95) and belongs to the same *rāgamālā* series, this being folio number 31. His interest in color and clarity is also apparent in this painting. This particular folio of the series depicts the Megha Malhār Rāga as Kṛṣṇa dancing to the rhythm provided by the female musicians who are playing a *vīṇā*, cymbals, and a *dholaki* drum. In the background is a dark blue cloudscape with a silver lining that resembles the semicircular flowering borders of the foliage below.

This musical mode traditionally is sung during the rainy season and believed to bring rain even during drought due to the failure or the monsoon, if correctly sung. Therefore the name Megha, is significant because it means cloud. This very old rāga helps us to study the gradual development of the iconography of the ragas. Although in the later period many ragas became associated with the cult of Kṛṣṇa, originally they had nothing to do with the god and the cult. An early depiction and description of Megha makes this clear. For instance, in a fifteenth-century illustrated Nepali manuscript of *rāgamālā*, the personified cloud is depicted in the middle of a cloudscape, and in the Sanskrit verse given in the illustration he is identified with Megharaja "the king cloud" (Kaufmann: pl. 33). This original identity was already lost at the beginning of Rajput painting. In the *rāgamālā* from around 1605 this musical mode is called Megharaga, "cloud rāga. He is depicted there as a dancer flanked by two female musicians (Pal 1978: fig. 5), although he has not yet been identified with Kṛṣṇa.

Published: Chandra 1971: cat. no. 196; Raducha: cat. no. 2.54.

96

BUNDELKHAND

Bundelkhand is located northeast of Malwa in central India. Orchha and Datia are the important political and cultural centers of the region. When the sultans ruled central India from their capital Mandu in Malwa, they controlled Bundelkhand. During the first and second quarters of the sixteenth century when the Malwa sultans were loosing their control and the Mughal dynasty was still struggling to establish dominance in northern India, a Hindu king, known as Raja Rudra Pratap, took advantage of this political situation to found an independent kingdom around Orchha. Although we have no Bundelkhand painting from this early period, art historians

97

believe—on the basis of the earliest dated work that can be epigraphically ascribed to Bundelkhand, such as the 1675 *Rāmāyaṇa* manuscript in the National Museum, New Delhi—that the early Hindu paintings of Bundelkhand show strong stylistic affinity with contemporaneous Malwa painting (Chaitanya, vol. 3: 89–90).

During the seventeenth century Raja Bir Singh Dev of Orchha was responsible for bringing prosperity to the region. Yet in Indian history the raja is an infamous person. A good friend of Emperor Jahangir (r. 1605–1627), he ingratiated himself more by assassinating Abu'l Fazel, the consular and chronicler of Akbar (r. 1556–1605) and was rewarded abundantly. The construction of beautiful palaces at Orchha and Datia after the assassination indicates this new wealth. The 1675 *Rāmāyaṇa* set in the National Museum was rendered in this milieu. In the eighteenth century Bundelkhand painting can be distinguished from Malwa by the hairstyle of female figures and the shape of the turban and voluminous sash of the male figures. Paintings in the Watson collection, such as cat no. 97, show evidence that in the beginning of the eighteenth century the school of Datia had developed a distinctively refined style, more advanced than that of Malwa. Courteous and graceful female figures of Datia are often completely devoid of archaistic features, such as tassels and striped skirts in women's clothing, that can be traced in Malwa school of painting (cat. nos. 55–58).

97
Mālaśrī Rāginī

Bundelkhand, Datia, early 18th century

Gouache and gold on paper, 9⅛ x 6⅛ inches

1981.281

Judging from such stylistic elements as "the bright red niche on the palace wall and the treatment of trees, creepers, birds, and monkeys in the background," Chandra considered this a painting of the advanced Malwa school that finally has "shed its archaistic mannerisms" (Chandra 1971: 84). However, I would attribute this painting to the Datia school on the basis of the following features: the figure type characterized by gentle and demure appearance, the pattern of sari often dotted with tiny speckles replacing earlier striped patterns, the avoidance of archaic elements such as the use of black tassels, and muted cool colors (Poster: 23, 194).

On a terrace of a white building adjoining a lush garden inhabited by monkeys, peacocks, and other birds, a princess, with radiant halo, leans against a bolster. She holds a *vīṇā* and a fully blossomed lotus. She wears a transparent yellow sari embellished with a white flower pattern. The blue, pleated middle section of her sari offers a pleasing contrast to the adjoining color of the red bolster as well as the rest of the sari. A female attendant, dressed in a dark red and green sari with light polka dots and dark flower pattern, approaches her holding a flower garland in her left hand. Both ladies have similar physiognomy marked by half-closed eyes and gentle appearance. On the floor are water jars, flowers, and other paraphernalia. At the right corner, close to the scarlet railing, an oil lamp burns. Such evening scenes with demure ladies enjoying musical amusements were popular subjects during the seventeenth and eighteenth centuries.

Published: Chandra 1971, cat. no. 135; Raducha cat. no. 2.91.

98

A Lady Waiting for Her Lover
from a series illustrating the verse of Matiram

Bundelkhand, late 18th century

Gouache and gold on paper, 9 x 7¼ inches

1.1970.8

At the upper yellow panel a two-line verse in Brajabhāṣā is given in Devanāgarī script. It is written mostly in black ink on buff-colored paper, but the first word of Matriam's verse and its verse number 195 at the end are in red ink. This miniature painting is one of the two examples in the Watson collection from a series illustrating the verses composed by Matiram, a medieval poet of the South Asian language Brajabhāṣā. The subject of the painting is the separation of lovers, a popular theme, which here shows two different scenes within a picture. One of them is represented in the foreground where a lady on a yellow carpet faces toward her friends. According to the verse given in the superscript, the lady eagerly anticipates the arrival of her lover. Her friends stand close to the pink wall of the courtyard on the left and indicate their deep concern with animated hand gestures. Adjacent to the courtyard is a one-storied building with *chatris*. The empty bed of the house, which symbolizes the absence of the lover, is prominently exposed to convey the intensity of situation. The background shows the absent lover, comfortably seated in a pavilion, smoking a hookah, and appearing to be unaware of the anguish of his beloved. These two scenes are rendered here not as chronological narration but as describing two simultaneous incidents within a picture. The style of continuous narration is seen even in the second century B.C. stone relief of Bharhut, whereas the style of simultaneous narration began to appear in the sixteenth century when the Mughal emperor Akbar (r. 1556–1605) established his atelier.

98

The absent lover is attired in royal dress: white turban and *jama* and bright yellow trousers. He also wears a voluminous sash loosely tied around his waist and hips. This typical sash, which reminds us of earlier sculptures of north India where the male figures are almost always shown with the sash dangling from their waist, is one of the main feature of Datia school. Another distinguishing feature is the flatness of their turbans. This observation becomes clearer if we compare the figure of the absent lover with the portrait figure of Rao Satrujit, the king of Datia (cat. no. 100), which is rendered in same style.

Published: Chandra 1971: cat. no. 202; Raducha: cat. no. 2.101.

99

99
A Lady Waiting for Her Lover by the Riverside from a series illustrating the verse of Matiram

Bundelkhand, late 18th century

Gouache and gold on paper, 9 x 7¼ inches

I.1970.9

The similarity of superscript, language, and the format of the painting suggests that this is another work by the Bundelkhand artist who painted the previous catalogue entry of A Lady Waiting for Her Lover (cat. no. 98) and belongs to the same series illustrating Matiram's verses. Given here is verse number 161, which is five lines, longer than the verse on the previous entry (195). Thus it overflows to the blue surface of the painting. It is written mostly in black ink on yellow paper, but the first word and verse number 161 at the end are in red ink.

Despite the many examples that show some similarity between the artistic and the literary representations of India, these two traditions are less two branches of the same tree than two different species of the same genus. Quite often knowledge of literature does not help to comprehend artistic expressions and vice versa. Around the eighteenth century, however, a group of artists came up with an interesting idea that brought artistic and literary traditions very close. This miniature painting is an excellent example of that artistic movement. Following the convention of the movement, here the artist has translated Matiram's verses into paintings literally representing the poetic imaginations and comparisons in figures. For example, Matiram, in his Brajabhāṣā verses that are given above the painting, poetically describes a young lady waiting for the arrival of her lover at the bank of the river Yamunā. The poet compares her beautiful eyes with the bees, fish, and the cakora birds frolicking by the riverside. In the painting, bees hover above the tree, fish emerge from water, and two cakora birds appear immediately behind them. The animals, like the woman, eagerly await the arrival of her lover. Thus the creatures are not only descriptive elements but also symbolic representations of her beautiful searching eyes.

Published: Chandra 1971: cat. no. 203.

100
Portrait of Rao Satrujit (1762–1801) of Datia

Bundelkhand, late 18th century

Gouache and gold on paper, 7⅝ x 5⅝ inches

I.1970.10

Rao Satrujit, the king of Datia, faces left within the sky-blue oval space which itself is enclosed within the pink rectangular background. The edge of the oval space is shaded by darker blue color, so that the oval surface appears to be convex. The bearded king holds a flower in his left hand and rests his right hand on a beautifully designed striped scabbard planted on the ground. He wears multiple pearl necklaces, armlets, and bracelets of deep blue sapphire and a yellow turban embellished with *jighā*. He is clad in a diaphanous *jama*, flowered black trousers, and matching shoes. Characteristically, a voluminous, bright yellow sash is loosely wound around his hip in the fashion of Datia.

The identity of this king is based on a Devanāgarī inscription given on the verso. It reads: *śrī mahārājādhirāja śrī mahārāja śrī rau rājā satrajit bahādura ju deva.*

Published: Chandra 1971, cat. no. 204; Raducha cat. no. 2.68.

100

101

Admiration of Beauty [formerly one of two paintings from a series illustrating the *Satsai* of Bihari]

Bundelkhand, late 18th century

Gouache and gold on paper, 6⅞ x 7⅞ inches

1.1970.12

This miniature is a folio of a series illustrating the *Satsai* of Bihari, written in the Brajabhāṣā language in Devanāgarī script. The black upper panel (not shown) contains a Satsai verse in red ink, which can be translated partially as follows: this lady of fair complexion is indeed admirably beautiful [particularly when] her smile dimples her cheek. A Brajabhāṣā label is given in white ink in the black upper left corner. Both these texts, in Devanāgarī script, indicate that the subject of the paintings is the hero's admiration for the heroine's beauty. They are designated here as *nāyaka* (hero) and *nāyikā* (heroine). Same information also derives from the six Brajabhāṣā lines in Devanāgarī script, written in black ink on the verso. The collection has one more painting from the series (1.1970.11).

The hero, dressed in light blue *jama,* patterned black trousers, pink sash, and turban of the Datia fashion, arrives at the rendezvous with his male companion, who wears similar *jama,* sash, and turban but in white. As the hero sees the young heroine standing on the grass, he must express his admiration for her beauty in a verse given in the superscript. The artist does not show dimples but has created a beautiful face. She faces the hero and his friend. She is sumptuously dressed in short green *coli* and flowered dark sari with a yellow middle section. Her head and shoulders are covered with the transparent greenish yellow end of the sari. She wears the contemporary Datia hairstyle, a diminutive knot of hair at the back of her head.

Published: Chandra 1971: cat. no. 206.

101

102

102

The Month of Agahan from a *Bāramāsā* series

Bundelkhand, late 18th century

Gouache and gold on paper, 6¼ x 9⅞ inches

1.1971.70

A ten-line inscription in Devanāgarī script is given on the verso. The inscription is written on the buff-colored paper with black and red ink and consists of six verses, from 48 to 54, of *Bāramāsā* in Avadhi language. The subject of the verses is a poetic description of a winter month of Agahana, which begins toward the end of November or beginning of December.

To indicate a cold winter night the artist represents not only the full moon and starry sky but also five individual scenes happening simultaneously in the different sections of the compound. Clockwise, beginning from lower left corner, the first scene depicts a lady greeted by a female retainer. They face each other on the terrace of a white building. The lady raises her hand, whereas the retainer folds both hands to show her respect to the lady. The empty bed just behind the lady symbolizes that she is without a lover. She is about to be shot by the flowery arrow of Kāmadeva, the god of love and desire, who is concealed in a nearby tree. Sanskrit literature relates that young men and women fall in love because the god of love shoots his arrows of flower at them. This story was originally related to spring and had nothing to do with winter.

The second scene shows a couple in a house on a bed bundled together in a blanket. The third scene takes place in the same house but in a different room where a man and woman warm themselves in front of a brazier. The forth scene describes two lovers on a terrace embracing. The last scene, in the courtyard of the compound, shows a bearded ascetic on a raised platform, warming himself before a fire. Another ascetic, perhaps his disciple, sits on the ground facing the bearded ascetic. A well-dressed nobleman, wearing a beautiful shawl, stands near the ascetic. Apparently the nobleman visited the ascetic as a gesture of veneration.

All scenes in the compound are symmetrically composed: The terraces and white edifices, similar in appearance, flank the courtyard; the trees and shrubs are balanced. In the foreground a river with fully blossomed lotuses runs horizontally. This is indeed a perfect example of the conventional approach of the Rajput artists, since these flowers do not bloom in the winter.

Published: Chandra 1971: cat. no. 210.

Pahari

The Punjab hills, locally known as *pahari* (mountainous), are located on the foothills of the Himalayas between two major river systems of the Indus and the Ganges. In the maps the region appears a short distance to the north of Rajasthan and northwest of Mughal capitals Agra and Delhi. Until quite recently, however, it was difficult to travel to or mount military expeditions from the plain to the Punjab hills, since the region was well protected by natural boundaries of high elevations. For the same reason the people of the Punjab hills were not always in close contact with Rajasthani or Mughal cultural/political centers. Just like in Rajasthan, the Hindu warriors who identified themselves as Rajputs ruled this hilly region, which consisted of thirty-five principalities.

The rulers of the Punjab hills occasionally did serve the Mughal emperors, but their relationship with the Mughals was not as close as that of Rajasthani Rajputs. For example, there was no intermarriage between the great Mughal emperors and the rulers of the hills. Thus, due to geographical and political isolation, the painterly tradition of the Punjab hills remained almost untouched by the sixteenth- and seventeenth-century advancement of Rajasthani and Mughal painting.

The earliest example of Pahari paintings is the *Caurapañcāśikā*-style Devīmāhātmya illuminations rendered around 1552. After more than a hundred-years gap, in ca. 1660–1670, two sets of paintings, the Rasamañjarī and Devī series, made a dazzling appearance in the painterly history of the hills. Both these series are executed in traditional archaic style, easily distinguished by vibrant warm colors, rustic energy, slanted big eyes with tiny pupils, and personal ornaments such as pearls rendered with so much pigment as to appear in relief and the trademark beetle wings (fragments from the iridescent wings of *Coleoptera cetonia aurata*). An earlier generation of scholars believed that this archaic style originated in a province known as Basohli, hence, named the style after the province. But this style was prevalent not only in Basohli but in many other provinces of the hills. Recently Goswami and Fischer have shown that both the Rasamañjarī and Devī series were the works of an artist who was a member of an artist family in Nurpur (Goswami and Fischer: 30).

After this initial phase, the Pahari traditional style went through a transitional stage (ca. 1700–1740) when the archaic intense colors and effusive display of beetle-wing ornaments diminished [cat. no. 105], and enchanting landscapes [cat. no. 103] were introduced. Within few decades this new spirit eventually culminated in the most sensuous lyrical style of India (1740–1780). Stylistically it is characterized by fine draftsmanship, subtle coloration, and idealized beautiful faces. At the height of this development, Nainsukh, an exceptional painter who died in 1779, painted by careful observation realistic portraits and actual physical settings, an isolated example in the history of mainstream Indian art. Yet at the same time Nainsukh set forth ideals of human beauty that were adopted by the succeeding generations. Pahari style continued to develop even after 1780, but the realistic approach found few followers. The younger generation of painters after Nainsukh took a much greater interest in creating a dreamlike, beautiful world with moonlit atmosphere, eye-pleasing coloration, and the flawless beauty of youthful figures (cat. nos. 110, 112, 116–118). Just like in other schools of Rajaput paintings, Pahari artists rendered an idealized portrait of the king with hierarchic proportion [cat. no. 113] and male and female figures as types without specific personalities. Due to political turmoil involving Nepalese invasion and Sikh control, the spirit of Pahari painting began to decline after 1850 but managed to survive until the last decades of the nineteenth century. Traditionally the last phase of the development of the Pahari school after 1780 is designated as Kangra style, a misleading term because it was prevalent not only in Kangra but in a much larger area.

103
Baz-Bahadur and Rūpamatī

Pahari style, ca. 1700 [formerly Basohli style]

Gouache and gold on paper, 6½ x 6 inches

1.1971.73a

The painting is partially damaged along the edges due to moisture. It is, however, an excellent example of Pahari painting of the early eighteenth century. Chandra considered this painting earlier than cat. no. 106 (Chandra 1971: 132, 137). This dating is based on the stylistic similarity with Rādhā and the Curd Pot, which Khandalawala attributed to ca. 1720 A.D. (Khandalavala: pl. C). The skillful overlapping of the animal and human figures and the lack of the traditional yellow background in the present example indicate stylistic advancement, which is also visible in rendering the eyes, forehead, and nose. Compare these features with those of the Lakṣmī and Viṣṇu painting (cat. no. 105). The archiac crown decorated with lotuses and the intense tonality found in cat. no. 105 have already been abandoned here. However, we should remember that in the transitional phase of stylistic development, both archaic and advanced styles of works would be expected to coexist.

Two lovers, sumptuously dressed and mounted on richly decorated, beautiful horses, meander across an open area of a forest. Baz-Bahadur is clad in an orange *jama* patterned with dark green leaves. The orange clothes sparkle against the white stallion. In addition to earrings and pearl necklaces, he wears a golden turban embellished with a plume. With his right hand he holds a thin rein and with his left hand he holds a rose. Rūpamatī, slightly ahead of him, rides a red horse and turns around to look intimately at her husband. She wears a striped red dress and an orange turban adorned with a white plume, thus echoing the tonality employed for the horse and the royal dress. Across the bluish green grassland in the distance, rows of trees are inhabited by *sārasas*, Indian cranes.

The love story of Rūpamatī and Baz-Bahadur is one of the most popular romantic themes of the Indic miniature paintings and literature. Baz-Bahadur was the musician-king of Malwa, contemporary with the great Mughal king Akbar (1556–1605). Rūpamatī, his queen, was famous for her extraordinary beauty. According to Muslim historian Badauni, in March, 1561, Akbar's army, led by the Mughal officer Adham Khan, invaded Malwa. Although Baz-Bahadur fought in the battle very bravely, he was easily defeated by the superior Mugal army. He fled to a neighboring country. The Mughal officer, who had heard of Rūpamatī's beauty, immediately seized Baz-Bahadur's harem and treasures and plundered Mandu, the capital of Malwa. Being unable to escape from such a cruel invader, Rūpamatī took poison to preserve her chastity, which was obviously more precious to her than anything else. The people of Maṇḍu believe that the souls of these separated lovers still reside in the ruin of their palace where they dance and sing every night.

Published: Chandra 1971: cat. no. 225; Watson, 43.

103

104

104
Raja Chatar Singh (1664–1690) of Chamba

Pahari style, early 18th century [formerly Basohli style]

Gouache and gold on paper, 6⅜ x 10⅛ inches

1.1970.21

Recently Goswamy and Fischer (129–31) studied contemporaneous portrait paintings of Chatar Singh in detail. They have convincingly shown that the present example is a later version of a seventeenth-century original painting in National Museum, New Delhi, depicting an almost identical scene in which the raja pours the liquid from a *surahi* and a hookah is ready for smoking. According to them this is a scene of a solemn vow taken by the raja on a particular occasion. However, the raja's informal gown and the phenomena of daily morning rituals shown in both examples make it difficult for me to accept their view that he is making a solemn vow. Indian texts on *vratas*, rites of taking vows, do not associate merely pouring water in a bowl and smoking a hookah with any ritual; the raja simply empties the water after the morning wash.

Chatar Singh, the raja of Chamba, sits on a white cloth spread on a striped carpet, attended by three retainers. One sits in front of the king holding a bowl; another stands far left holding the hookah; yet another stands immediately behind the king waving the fly whisk of peacock feathers. Apparently this depicts the everyday life of the raja. The king, dressed in a bright red morning gown, leans against a bolster painted in great detail. He is, however, fully arrayed with earrings, necklace, and a royal turban adorned with pearls and a plume. As we know from multiple examples, the representation of any unornamented figure, male or female, was considered inauspicious. Therefore in Indian miniature painting even a sleeping queen is fully bejeweled, and a male figure almost always wears headgear whether he is sleeping on the bed or engaged in other activities, including sexual intercourse. This is why

105

the raja is depicted here fully attired with royal crown although the composition shows him engaged in his morning ritual. In order to suggest that he has finished cleansing, he holds a golden *surahi* in inverted position, pouring the excessive water into a bowl held by the seated retainer. In his left hand, he holds a rosary indicating that after ritual cleansing, he will perform his daily morning prayer, then enjoy a relaxed moment smoking the hookah. The retainer is ready to offer him the hookah.

All the retainers wear white *jamas* with contrasting kamarbands and turbans. The scene has an apple-green background. The vertical stripes of the carpet create a kind of spatial depth that is not realistic and shows no familiarity with linear perspective, which does appear sometimes in the Mughal painting.

Published: Chandra 1971: cat. no. 226; Goswamy and Eberhard 1997: 129–31.

105
Lakṣmī and Viṣṇu [formerly Lakshmī-Nārāyaṇa]

Pahari style, ca. 1730 [formerly Basohli style]

Gouache and gold on paper, 7 x 4⅞ inches

I.1970.22

This painting displays several archaic stylistic features that continued even in the transitional phase (ca. 1700–1740) of Pahari paintings such as the petallike eye with tiny pupil placed close to the tear duct, thus exposing the white part. Often the end of eye is painted red in an effort to interpret the poetic expression "beautiful eyes resembling the lotus petal." Other stylistic features are the pointed heads, the angular poses, a palette of great intensity such as yellow and red, and the frequent use of emeralds in the ornaments.

The subject of this painting is a later version of a cosmogonic story from ancient Hindu myth. Emerging from the primordial ocean is a giant lotus on which Viṣṇu sits closely embracing Lakṣmī on his lap. During the late medieval period not only was Kṛṣṇa considered an incarnation of Viṣṇu but these two gods were considered almost identical. Therefore as in other contemporary examples, the blue complexion of Kṛṣṇa is regarded here iconographically appropriate for Viṣṇu as well. The other iconographical features of the god are his attributes—a club, a wheel, a conch, and a lotus displayed in his four arms clockwise from lower left. In addition he wears a crown embellished with pearls and emeralds. The pointed crests of the crown are decorated with three fresh lotuses, a feature that appears repeatedly in Pahari paintings from about 1660 to 1670. His other ornaments include pearl and emerald earrings, multiple necklaces, armlets, and bracelets. Lakṣmī also wears all these ornaments (except the crown) but with more emeralds than pearls to match with her dark green sari. Her red blouse resembles Viṣṇu's lower garment in color. In addition, she wears *phulia,* a nose ornament worn only by women, and she holds a lotus as her iconographical identity.

As in the early Pahari paintings (ca. 1660–1670), the figures of the god and goddess are shown against the yellow background traditionally used for writing manuscripts. A conventional blue sky appears above the yellow panel; in the foreground the dark blue water of the ocean is shown with sparkling white waves delineated with horizontal sinuous lines decoratively interspersed with floating white flowers. The green stalk of the lotus is rendered naturalistically showing the tiny thorns around it. Such naturalistic treatment of the stalk reminds of us ceiling paintings (ca. 850) from Sittanavasal, south India (Barrett and Gray: 40-41).

Published: Chandra 1971: cat. no. 229; Raducha: cat. no. 2.20.

106

Devagāndhārī Rāginī

Pahari style, ca. 1730 [formerly Basohli style]

Watercolor and gouache on paper, 6⅞ x 6⅞ inches

69.28.14

Although the pale palette departs from the traditional use of intense colors, some early features of the Pahari school are retained, such as the yellow background, the profuse use of emerald and pearls, and the angular skull and big eye with tiny pupil. The Tākri inscription that seems to be contemporaneous with the painting identifies this as a scene of Devagāndhārī Rāginī, wife of Malkauns Rāga. This seems to be a Pahari interpretation. In Rajasthani painting this musical mode is depicted as an emaciated man leading an ascetic life in a forest (Poster: 193). However, a clearly decipherable superscript in another Rajasthani painting describes the Devagāndhārī Rāginī as an ascetic woman, while the figure shown in that painting is a male ascetic with long beard and mustache (Kaufmann: pl. 22). This recurrent problem associated with a male versus a female musical mode can be solved partially if we realize that rāga and rāginī were the names of the background music associated with particular theatrical scenes. As we discussed in detail the introductory essay, artists customarily represented these theatrical scenes in paintings and wrote the name of the background music on the painting. Thus originally the rāga / rāginī have nothing to do with the gender of the protagonists shown in the paintings. Totally different local traditions of representing rāga and rāginī existed in the Deccan as well as in the Punjab hills, of which the present painting can be an example.

Here, against the yellow background, an elegant lady accompanied by a female attendant offers flowers to dark blue Śivaliṅga, the phallic symbol of Śiva. A structure like an hourglass supports the triangular *jalahari*, the drain carrying the water during the ritual of bathing. The pale structure with a dark blue ring in the middle is placed on a three-stepped dark blue pyramid emerging from the lotiform pale circular base. The whole structure represents the Kailāsa mountain where Śiva resides.

She shows her devotion to the god by bowing her head and upper back and reaching toward the image to place flowers on top of the Śivaliṅga. She wears a tiny green *coli* and a flowery pink sari with a red border and a white pleated middle section. With an end of the sari she covers the back of her head. Her fingers, toes, and soles are fashionably dyed red. Her ornaments consist of a *bindi,* earrings, *phulia*, necklaces, armlets, bracelets, and anklets.

The female attendant is shown much smaller than the lady, following the rule of hierarchic proportion. The attendant is, however, dressed elegantly, just like her mistress. She wears an orange *coli* and a dark blue sari with a green border. She holds a tray on her right hand and raises her left hand to wave the fly whisk, holding its metal handle carefully. Just above the fly whisk a white line indicates the horizon, which separates the yellow background from the bluish sky.

Published: Chandra 1971: cat. no. 230; Raducha cat. no. 2.14.

106

107

Rāgaputra Kanara

Pahari style, mid 18th century

Gouache and gold on paper, 8¼ x 6 inches

1.1970.23; see color plate 10

Inside a Rajput-style building that seems to be a music hall are two music lovers, one holding a lute in his left hand, the other clapping his hands rhythmically. The pink wall is tastefully decorated with numerous niches, for slender decorative glasses or flat flower-bowls.

The musician who holds the lute is depicted in three-quarter profile, the other in full profile facing toward the musician. Both sit on a white carpet adorned with flowery pattern. The musician wears pink *jama* and a turban with black and white stripes. The other figure, apparently representing the Rāgaputra Kanara himself, wears a green *jama* and a turban with orange and red stripes. Both have prominent mustaches and wear emerald and pearl ornaments.

Chandra had noted that the painting stylistically resembles the Berlin *Rāgamālā* paintings published in Ernst and Rose Leonore Waldschmidt, *Miniatures of Musical Inspiration* (Berlin 1967).

Published: Chandra 1971: cat. no. 232.

107

108

108

Portrait of Guru Haragovind

Pahari style, mid 18th century

Gouache and gold on paper, 7 9/16 x 5 1/16 inches

1984.1316

Haragovind (1595–1645) is one of ten gurus or teachers of Sikh, a sect of reformist Hindu founded by Nanak (1469–1538). He organized his followers into a military brotherhood and often fought with the ruling Mughal powers for religious freedom. Annoyed by his aggressive behavior, the Mughal emperor Jahangir (r. 1605–1627) imprisoned him for a decade. Despite this Mughal attitude, even these days the Sikhs honor Haragovind both as a teacher and as a courageous leader.

The bearded guru stands erect with a sword in his right hand. He wears a pink turban sustained by light-brown binding, above which emerges the flowerlike yellow striped knot. His *jama* is white but its upper part around the shoulder and chest is bright yellow, which accentuates the brightness of pearl necklaces he wears. His short *pai jama,* which is cut away diagonally exposing the ankles, is decorated with yellow and blue stripes. The vertical pattern of the *pai jama* contrasts with the horizontal green stripes of the hanging ends of the sash. The background is dark green. The scarlet scabbard held by Haragovind stands out conspicuously.

Published: Chandra 1971: cat. no. 233.

109

109

Indra, the King of the Gods

Pahari style, ca. 1750–1755

Gouache on paper, 6 3/4 x 6 1/16 inches

1984.1317

Indian artists are famous for creating expansive volume in a linear style rather than a painterly manner. Here, too, the artist has created a voluminous elephant using concave and sinuous lines while avoiding shading and modeling.

According to Hindu myth Indra, king of the gods, rides the white elephant Airavata. Because the animal is white instead of its natural gray color, we can identify the princely figure seated on the howdah as Indra. Usually the god holds a thunderbolt or an elephant goad as his principle attribute, but here he holds a fanlike obscure object. He wears a crown decorated with pearls and tiny lotus flowers, pearl earrings and necklaces, and a velvety red *jama* with gray stripes sustained by a bluish sash. A lock of hair dangles on his temple. The mustachioed face of the god has gentle and majestic appearance enhanced by his slightly closed somnolent eye. The purple howdah is slightly tilted toward the neck of the elephant, indicating the rhythmical movement of the animal's gently moving body.

An attendant just behind the howdah holds a flag and waves a partially visible fly whisk. His yellow *jama* has a leaf pattern; his other ornaments closely resemble those of the prince. The elephant also is highly adorned with a colorful cover, yak tails on either side of its earlobe, a bell hanging close to its stomach, and rows of rattling *ghuṅghurus* (small bells) around its neck, tail, and feet.

Published: Chandra 1971: cat. no. 235.

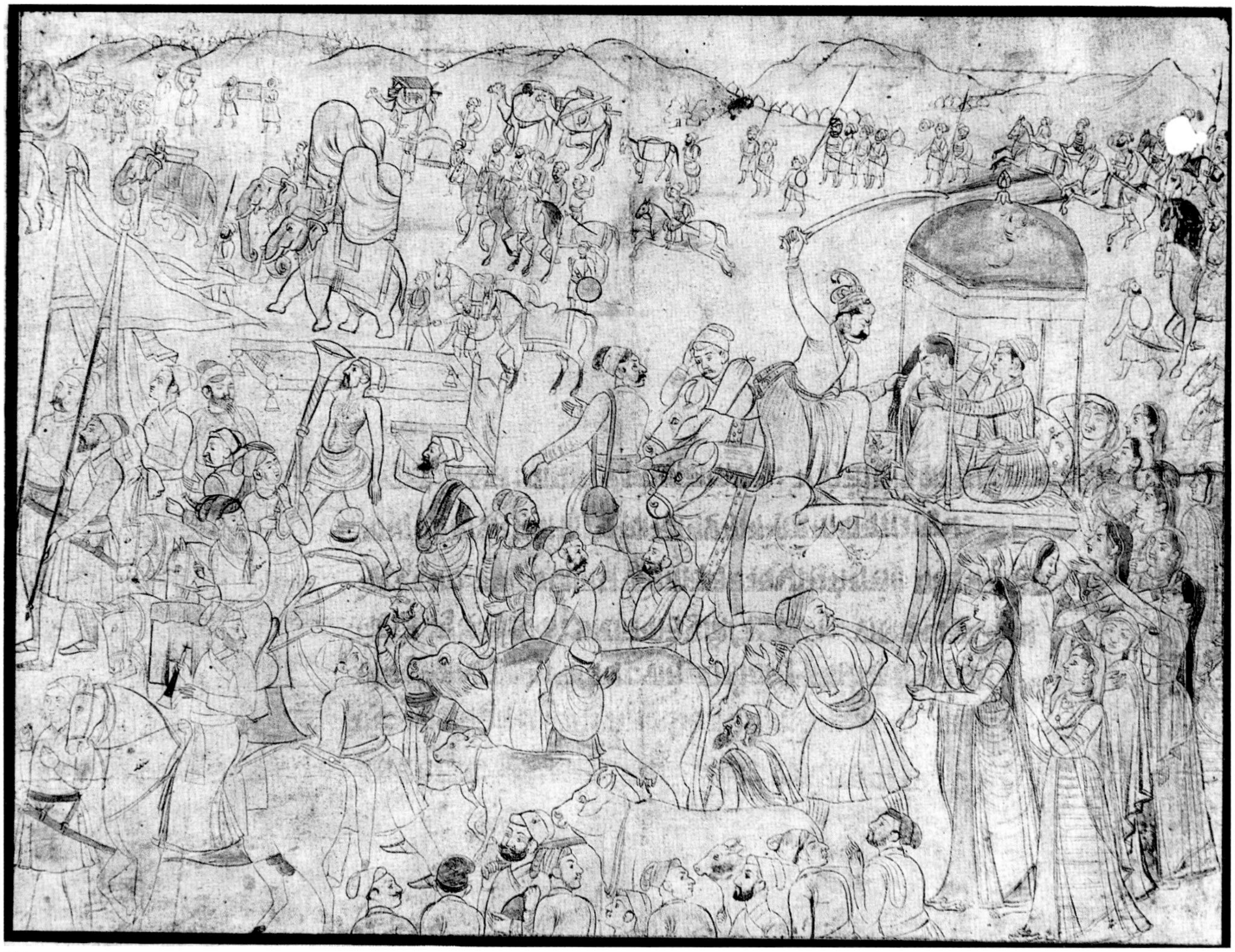

110

110
The Daughter of Ugrasena Threatened with Death

Pahari style, ca. 1780 [formerly Kangra style]
Watercolor and ink, 8¾ x 12 inches
1.1970.24

This is an excellent stylistic drawing of the Pahari school. Unlike in earlier works, figures are rendered here recognizably different in terms of age, physical characteristics, mental conditions, and personalities. The rhythmically sinuous lines define the tall and pretty female figures. The animals such as water buffalo, cows, bullocks, and horses are delineated naturalistically. Although the artist does not completely abandon the traditional use of hierarchic proportion, he successfully shows the objects in the distance growing smaller and more blurred as our eye travels into the background of the painting, a stylistic device recently introduced to the Rajput artists. Even more admirable is, however, the melodious quality that pervades the entire picture. The abrupt turn of the head is another stylistic element that appeared for the first time in Akbari painting, but is employed here meaningfully to describe the bewilderment caused by unexpected incident.

This is an episode of a well-known Hindu myth associated with Kaṃsa and his newly wed sister Devakī. The detailed

Sanskrit description of the scene on the verso of the painting states that Devakī and Vasudeva's wedding ceremony went very well without any obstacles, making King Ugrasena, Devakī's father, very happy. In accordance with custom the king gave his daughter a generous dowry consisting of cattle, water buffaloes, stallions, elephants, chariots, and hundreds of maids. The crown prince Kaṃsa also was in a happy mood. He himself drove the chariot of the newly wed couple during the groom's homecoming procession. But on the way Kaṃsa heard an incorporeal speech predicting that he was destined to be killed by his sister's son. This message triggered his anger, and he turned violent.

Kaṃsa grabs Devakī by her hair and brandishes the sword. She sits inside the chariot with her groom, who is vainly trying to protect her. The women following the chariot raise their hands, shouting for help and trembling with fear as they put their fingers close to their lips. Standard-bearers, musicians on horseback, cattle, and their caretakers move ahead of the chariot. Bewildered by this unexpected incident, many turn their heads toward the chariot. In the foreground spectators watch the procession; in the background elephants, camels, and people carry the dowry protected by a retinue of horse-riders.

Published: Chandra 1971: cat. no. 236.

III
A Hill Chief Adoring the Goddess

Pahari style, late 18th century [formerly Kangra style]

Gouache and gold on paper, 7⅝ x 4⅞ inches

I.1971.74

The female retainers are significant for stylistic analysis. The Pahari artist attempts to create a demure female figure. The Sanskrit noun for demureness is *namratā*, which literally means bending down; this adjectival form is often used to describe fruit trees, such as banana plants and mango trees, with branches weighed down with fruit. It is also use to describe a rain cloud heavy with water. A similar quality is expressed here through gentle faces, polite downward looks, and long shawls emphasizing the demureness of the female figures.

This scene is of a shrine of the Hindu goddess Tripurasundarī, who is worshiped here both by human devotees and prominent Hindu gods. As in other examples of Pahari works, the human beings and deities are depicted here as if they live in same world and interact. The golden shrine stands on four pillars and has a flat roof with a dome surrounded by cupolas in four corners. Inside the shrine the goddess, who symbolizes the female principle, sits on the supine body of Śiva, who represents the male principle. Hindus believe the entire universe is made of these two principles. The male principle remains inert as a corpse until it is revived by the active female principle. This concept is expressed here iconographically showing her seated on a giant male body.

The goddess wears a golden tiara encircled with a halo, orange *coli*, and sari. She has four arms holding arrows, a

III

112

noose, an ax, and a bow. Likewise, Śiva holds his attribute damaru (a tiny drum that resembles a hour-glass), but his other significant attribute, the trident, lies beside him on the blue surface of the huge hexagonal bench. They are attended by two female retainers, one holding a *chowrie* and a white towel, the other a fan and a *vīṇā*. Each wears a striped skirt and partially covers her head with a shawl that extends all the way to her knees. In front of the bench, prominent Hindu gods Brahmā and Viṣṇu on the left, and Śiva and Indra on the right are seated on the bright red carpet flanking the *pūrṇa kalaśa*, the full water vase, the auspicious symbol of the goddess. All gods except Brahmā fold both hands in the *namaskāra* gesture to greet the goddess.

Outside the shrine on the left stands a bearded devotee who wears a red tunic, a matching cap, and yellow trousers. His right hand is inside the yellow purse containing the rosary. On the right we see a female devotee kneeling on a small stool with the *namaskāra* gesture. Bushy plants surround the shrine, and two flowering plants in the background grow beyond the roof of the shrine.

Published: Chandra 1971: cat. no. 238; Raducha cat. no. 2.18; Vajracharya 1994, 56.

112

Rāma and Sītā with Raja Jagat Prakash (ca. 1770–1789) of Simur

Pahari style, late 18th century [formerly Kangra style]
Watercolor, gouache, and gold on paper, 9⅞ x 7⅞ inches
69.28.15; see color plate 18

This scene illustrates an important episode from the Hindu epic *Rāmāyaṇa*. In this timeless mythical event Raja Jagat Prakash participates as a devotee. According to the epic, Rāma and Sītā returned to the capital city after fourteen years exile in the forest. They were accompanied by the kings of monkeys and bears, who helped them to fight with the demon who abducted Sītā during the exile. Within a few days of his return, Rāma was crowned. He asked his friends to stay and participate in the coronation ceremony. This ceremony, depicted here, is Rāma's happiest moment.

The happy couple leans against the colorful red cushion in the hexagonal golden throne. Rāma's head is encircled with a golden nimbus. Like Kṛṣṇa he is blue, but he holds his distinctive attributes, a bow and an arrow. He is clad in a yellow *dhoti* that contrasts with Sītā's green sari. Rāma wears a crown and an elongated garland of wild flowers, *vanamālā,* whereas Sītā holds a huge lotus flower in her right hand. Both are richly embellished with ornaments befitting a recently crowed royal couple.

In front of them stands a royal priest chanting an auspicious Vedic mantra as indicated by his raised hand. His body is overlapped by the magnified representation of Raja Jagat Prakash, dressed in a white *jama* and a turban. Such magnification is a comparatively new development in Rajput painting that is not seen in early miniature paintings. This is symbolically different from the hierarchic proportion that we see throughout the history of the classical period. The main purpose of showing him in greater scale is to direct the attention of the viewers toward his portrait; thus his scale does not imply the greatness of his personality. Furthermore his large size is so isolated from the context of the painting that his presence does not seems to be noticed by anybody, including the three monkeys (light in color) and a bear (darker in color) standing adjacent to him.

To the left of Rāma and Sītā we see more bears among the crowd of divine and princely figures and long-haired bearded ascetics, all of them joining their hands in adoration to Rāma and Sītā. One ascetic is shown prostrate on the ground where he has placed his manuscript and staff momentarily. Immediately behind the throne stand Rāma's three brothers Bharata, Lakṣmaṇa, and Śatrughna, holding regalia such as the yak tail called *cāmara*, a fly whisk made of peacock feathers, and a sword encased in a red sheath. They are richly dressed in blue, yellow, and pink enhancing the polychromatic quality of the painting.

Published: Chandra 1971: cat. no. 239; Raducha: cat. no. 2.25.

113

Raja Bir Singh (ca. 1789–1846 of Nurpur)

Pahari style, late 18th century [formerly Kangra style]

Gouache and gold on paper, 7⅝ x 4⅝ inches

1.1970.25

Against the light blue background, Raja Bir Singh is depicted near a white marble window with a scalloped arch. The raja leans comfortably against the white bolster and holds the pipe of a hookah, which is concealed by the bolster. He has a pointed nose, elongated eyebrows, a goatee, and a smooth neck, a characteristic of Pahari painting. Clad in a dark blue *jama* and turban, he has shoulders partially covered by a bright red shawl. He wears a *jighā* on the turban, emerald earrings, a pearl necklace, and pearl bracelets.

He is attended by a bearded retainer who holds a *chowrie* with his right hand and a white towel in his left. He wears pink *jama* and turban, and a bright orange shawl diagonally across his torso. The artist pays equal attention to rendering the portraits of the raja and the retainer. Because these are idealized portraits, both figures share almost the same physiognomy, differentiated only by the type and extent of beard.

Published: Chandra 1971: cat. no. 240; Watson, 45; Raducha cat. no. 2.86.

113

114

114
Nobleman on a Terrace

Pahari style, late 18th century [formerly Kangra style]
Gouache and gold on paper, 8⅜ x 5½ inches
1984.1319

As we've often noted, Rajput artists seldom attempted a realistic work of art based on actual observation. Relying on tradition, they delineated even a portrait of a sitter in an idealistic fashion, not as he or she looks but as he or she is supposed to appear. Although Pahari artists did not abandon this traditional approach, they did produce some comparatively realistic portraits, such as this example.

An emaciated, aged nobleman holds the pipe of the hookah with his left hand. He wears a white *jama* and a turban with yellow stripes. He watches the falcon perched on his right hand protected by a brownish leather gauntlet. He is comfortably kneeling on a beautiful carpet embellished with flowers and a vine motif. At his back is a puffy bolster whose voluminous appearance intensifies the skinniness of his body. The detailed study of his pointed nose, wrinkles around the eyes, and frail-looking bony neck indicate that this portrait was rendered through observation. In the background is a white railing with latticed screen and symmetrical cloudscape against the blue sky.

Published: Chandra 1971: cat. no. 241.

115

115
Portrait of a Hill Raja

Pahari style, late 18th century
Gouache and gold on paper, 5$\frac{5}{16}$ x 6⅜ inches
1984.1320

Despite the partially soiled condition, Pahari-style physical features such as slim almost feminine wrists and hands, the rendition of forehead and nose with a slightly dented diagonal line, and the smooth neck are still discernable in the male figures of this miniature.

A bearded Pahari raja sits on a simple square bench with a blue seat. He wears a grayish blue turban with dark blue feather on the top, light pink *jama,* and brownish red shawl. Leaning against a yellowish brown bolster, the raja faces the retainer who is sits and holds a tray. The seated retainer wears light pink *jama* and a bright red turban. The standing retainer, clad in pink turban, a green *jama,* and red trousers, holds a *chowrie* with his raised left hand and a towel with his right; he stands behind the raja. The scene is rendered against pinkish cream color background with a rudimentarily rendered parapet and flowering plants.

Published: Chandra 1971: cat. no. 242.

116

Vilaval Rāga

Pahari style, late 18th century

Gouache and gold on paper, 8⁹⁄₁₆ x 5³⁄₈ inches

1984.1321; see color plate 19

116

The Devanāgarī superscript labels the painting as Vilaval Rāga, the son of Bhairava Rāga. None of the descriptions of Vilaval given in standard sources such as Ebling's *Ragamala Painting* (Ebling: 155, illustrated in pl. 17, and on 8, 215, 342, 376) matches the iconography of this example, perhaps because the Pahari tradition of representing the rāga / rāginī differs considerably from that of other parts of India.

Under the blue sky, in a courtyard flanked by twin white buildings linked by a tall gray wall with a parapet, sit a pretty woman and a handsome man. The woman offers him a *pān* (a mildly intoxicating delicacy made of betel leaves and spices) from the tray that she holds in her left hand. Leaning against the voluminous orange cushion he looks at her affectionately and plays on the *sarod.* He is clad in a green *jama* with a striped sash and a turban of matching color with a light yellow band. His ornaments consist of earrings, a necklace, bracelets and armlets, all made of sparkling pearls. She also wears all these ornaments in addition to a *phulia* and a *bindi* made of emeralds surrounding the ruby in the middle. Her blue sari, green *coli,* saffron *orhani,* and the red carpet on which she sits makes the picture admirably colorful.

Published: Chandra 1971: cat. no. 244.

117

117

Love Scene

Pahari style, ca. 1800 [formerly Kangra style]

Gouache and gold on paper, 8 5/16 x 5 1/4 inches

1984.1323

As we know from many other examples the love scene is a widely appreciated theme of Indian art and literature. The earliest representation of a love scene is found in the second century B.C. sculptures of Bharhut where a couple on an isolated rocky hill embrace. In the later period, this secular theme became the iconographical feature of various divinities including Śiva and Pārvatī. In Rajput painting it continued to be secular as well. Since it is derived from the same origin thematically, it is not different from the iconography of the divine couple.

Here we see a young couple in a well-furnished bedroom with niches and a red carpet. The inner view of the room is revealed through the wide window that makes a frame for the painting, although partially covered by a purple curtain. The wooden door, however, is closed. The couple sit on a bed with striped pillows and a flowery bedspread. A water pitcher and a spitoon are placed close to the bed. To the left on a low end table is a candlestick indicating nighttime. Both are richly dressed. He wears a white *jama* and green trousers and an elegant turban with an topknot and a plumelike crest decorated with pearls. She wears a purple sari and covers her head and body with a golden *orhani*. They are in an intimate mood. She is, however, shy and trying to reject, without much success, the advances of the young man who seeks to embrace and untie *ijār-band,* a string that sustains the petticoat and the sari. Cleverly she covers his eyes since the candlelight has not been put out yet. This favorite subject matter of Sanskrit literature is described elegantly by such renowned poets as Kālidāsa. In his well-known work *Kumāra-Saṃbhava* "The Birth of the Divine Prince Kumāra," the poet describes a humorous incident of the honeymoon night of Śiva and Pārvatī:

> In their intimate affair, she [Pārvatī] was experiencing a tremor [a sign of first experience]. She removed Śiva's hand as he touched around her navel area. . . . She closed both his eyes with her hands as he undressed her. But her effort was in vain because he was still watching her with his third eye on the forehead.—*Kumāra-Saṃbhava* (8. 4–7)

Although no such early painting has survived, the similarity that we see between this picture and classical writing clearly suggests the continuity of the ancient pictorial tradition.

Published: Chandra 1971: cat. no. 247; Watson, 46.

118

118

The Transfer of Babes

Pahari style, early 19th century [formerly Kangra style]

Watercolor, gouache, and gold on paper, 11¾ x 18⅞ inches

69.28.16

The technique of continuous narration is used effectively here. This admirable quality inherited from the classical tradition of Indic art sets Rajput art apart from the tradition of Indo-Persian and Mughal art.

The story of the miraculous birth of Kṛṣṇa is a well-known Hindu myth. According to the myth, the wicked king Kaṃsa imprisoned his pregnant sister Devakī and brother-in-law because of the prediction that the god Viṣṇu would incarnate as their unborn baby, Kṛṣṇa, in order to punish him. The parents of the baby knew that Kaṃsa had determined to kill Kṛṣṇa just after he was born.

The narration of the story begins from the upper left corner of the painting where Devakī and Vasudeva inside the walled prison discuss their plan to save the baby. The narration moves from left to right; in the next scene the newborn baby appears not as a human but as a god endowed with all the iconogrphic features of Kṛṣṇa but diminutive in size. Standing in front of the baby, the parents join their hands in adoration of their divine baby. In the heaven gods appear through the cloud and shower flowers on him to celebrate his birth. In the center of the painting Devakī and Vasudeva are shown once again discussing the plan that he should take the baby across the Yamunā river, to the nearby Gokula village and exchange it with Yaśodā's newborn daughter. Meanwhile the main gate of the prison, shown here in the center, opens miraculously. Vasudeva takes the baby and walks away from the prison. The guards are sleeping. But the Yamunā river, depicted here diagonally to the left, is flooded due to the heavy rain. Knowing this the serpent god Vāsuki comes out of the river and helps the father and baby to cross the river, sheltering them with his hood as shown here in the foreground. The entire Gokula village is sleeping. Vasudeva enters Yaśodā's room (bottom left corner) and successfully places the baby on Yaśodā's bed. We know that baby is Kṛṣṇa because of the bluish complexion. Vasudeva goes back to prison. The guards are still sleeping. Now at the upper right section of the miniature Vasudeva places the baby with a white complexion in the hand of Devakī. Clearly she is Yaśodā's daughter, not baby Kṛṣṇa. The story is not over yet. In the foreground the crowned, tall figure of Kaṃsa accompanied by his two attendants heads toward the prison, unaware that the babies have been interchanged.

Published: Chandra 1971: cat. no. 250; Watson, 47; Raducha cat. no. 2.51.

119

Waiting for the Lover

Pahari style, early 19th century [formerly Kangra style]

Gouache and gold on paper, 8¾ x 6½ inches

1.1970.27

The houses in the left middle ground are shown on a diminutive scale in order to indicate the distance. The trees cast shadows on the slope of the hills. Throughout the history of Indic art, artists never depicted shadows. Only at the height of the Pahari school did shadows begin to appear sparingly and continued even in the later period, which makes this miniature stylistically valuable. The oval format of this miniature is another remarkable feature that was dear to the later Pahari school after 1740. This painting, however, stylistically differs slightly from other early Pahari works such as cat. no. 110 that show much taller female figures. The women's noses are not as high near the tear-ducts due to the downward curve of the sinuous flow of the outline shaping the forehead and nose.

This is a romantic scene of a rapidly approaching storm. Dark blue and bluish clouds lit up by flashes of lightning are emerging from the horizon. Heavy rain is already falling in the distant landscape. Soon it will be raining hard on the terrace where we see a *dūtī*, a female messenger encouraging the love-sick heroine to come with her to meet her separated lover. The messenger is clad in a bluish green skirt and diaphanous shawl, whereas the heroine is dressed in royal blue skirt, orange trousers, momentarily exposed as she walks, and a light blue silky shawl with light brown stripes. She is shy and hesitant to follow her. Her friend is persistent, holding her by the end of the shawl.

The bluish gray ground and the wall suggests a gloomy day, which is considered romantic in the art and literature of the subcontinent. Similarly the empty bed inside the carpeted room indicates her loneliness, which has been intensified by the dark cloud of the rainy season. Just outside the terrace we see a plantain tree overlapped by a bushy tree inhabited by several birds including a sleepy peacock.

Published: Chandra 1971: cat. no. 252; Raducha cat. no. 2.102.

119

120

120
The Descent of the Ganges

Pahari style, early 19th century [formerly Kangra style]

Gouache and gold on paper, 9 x 6 inches

1.1970.28

Pārvatī's voluminous shawl and a facial contour marked by the slightly dented diagonal line representing the forehead and nose are noticeable stylistic features of the eighteenth- and nineteenth-century Pahari painting.

In front of an arched purple cave on the pink rocky mountain of the Himalayas, the divine couple, Śiva and Pārvatī sit on a tiger skin. Śiva's lower body is clad in a leopard's hide, and he wears a serpent around his neck as if it is a necklace. Śiva's vehicle, the gigantic bull, Nandī, stands in front of them, covered with an orange mantle. Pārvatī is dressed in a red sari and a bright yellow shawl. Just like the birds nestled on the trees, the divine couple expresses their intimacy with sensual gestures and the warmth of the physical closeness. Particularly elegant is the turn of Śiva's head and the gazing eyes of Pārvatī.

A stream of water, representing the heavenly river Ganges (Sanskrit Gangā), flows out of Śiva's matted hair. In the legend the Gangā is viewed as an arrogant celestial woman. The god, exasperated by her arrogance, once imprisoned the river goddess inside his matted hair. Such imprisonment of the river goddess caused long-lasting drought on the earth. At the foot of the mountain, the prince Bhagīratha, who has been practicing penance for many years by standing on one leg in order to persuade Śiva to release her, is delighted to receive the heavenly river on the earth. This is one of many Indic legends associated with drought and water.

Published: Chandra 1971: cat. no. 253; Raducha cat. no. 2.16; Vajracharya 1994, 56.

121

121

A Pensive Lady Listening to Music [*Proṣitabhartṛkā*]

Pahari style, early 19th century [formerly Kangra style]

Gouache and gold on paper, 8½ x 5¼ inches

1.1971.76

Proṣitabhartṛkā is a Sanskrit word for the *Nāyikā* "heroine" whose husband has gone abroad. Since a woman, in accordance with ancient Indic custom, is not supposed to decorate herself when her husband is far away, she is depicted here with undressed long hair falling loosely over her back. She wears a white sari with brown border and a light yellow *coli*. On the terrace leaning against a bolster, she sits on a light green couch embellished with foliage motif. She inclines her head and gazes steadily. Agonizing over the separation, she appears to be completely distracted and absentmindedly holds the pipe of the hookah with her right hand. The artist has successfully demonstrated the intense emotional situation of a separated lover as exactly described in literature. In front of her on the ground a female musician garbed in light pink sari plays on a *tānpurā* in order to divert her. Close to her stands a beautiful tall attendant, clad in a white sari, holding a sunshade attached to a long pole. Two more attendants dressed in white and pink saris stand behind the couch. Their gestures indicate that they are worried about the condition of the heroine. Behind the terrace a huge river flows rapidly in swirling motion. In distant landscape rolling hills are covered with trees, farms, and houses. Almost in the middle of the hills we also see a diminutive equestrian warrior garbed in red jacket and followed by another rider. Very likely the warrior represents the man whose return the love-sick heroine eagerly anticipates.

Published: Chandra 1971: cat. no. 254.

122

122

Entertainment During the Rainy Season

Pahari style, mid 19th century [formerly Kangra style]

Gouache and gold on paper, 8⅟₁₆ x 9¹⁵⁄₁₆ inches

1983.142; see color plate 24

Like the older generation this artist is still interested in variegated colors. The glowing moonlight-like effect of the colors is, however, the characteristic of the later Pahari school after 1740.

The subject matter of this painting is the swing festival of Kṛṣṇa, which is often identified as Hinḍola Rāga in the Rajasthani tradition. This appears to be a Pahari version of the same rāga because the Sanskrit word *hinḍola*, or *dolā*, means not only a swing but also a revolving wheel with swings attached to it as depicted here in the miniature. This festival is celebrated twice a year, in the spring and the rainy season. Note the dark cloudscape and the cātakas, the birds of the rainy season, flying in geometric formation, which indicate that the celebration is taking place during the rainy season rather than in spring. The lush vegetation and flowering creepers as shown here in the middle ground is, however, possible in the subcontinent during both seasons.

Due to the inventiveness of Pahari artists the works of their school often differ widely from other Rajput paintings. Kṛṣṇa, the protagonist, is not depicted here in the middle of the painting as we would expect in contemporaneous works of other schools; he is shown at the extreme left conversing with Rādhā. He is not represented in hierarchic proportion either; his presence is made significant by his distinctive position, slightly away from the group of pretty women riding the wheel. Their idealized beauty is enhanced by their demure and stately mannerism. The swirling rhythm of their silky saris and trailing diaphanous shawls heightens the poetic and lyrical quality of the painting.

Published: Chandra 1971: cat. no. 259; Raducha: cat. no. 2.55.

123

Four Illustrations on an unidentified manuscript

Pahari style, mid 19th century

Gouache and gold on paper, 8¾ x 6⅟₁₆ inches

1983.143

On the verso of the paintings are two columns of Persian writing in Arabic script, one vertical and one horizontal. The geographical manuscript deals with characteristics of climate on or near the equator, particularly hot and dry climates. The intellectual connection between the text and the images is not clear.

This painting consists of four illustrations. The illustration at top left depicts a man and a woman standing near a window of a brownish yellow building. The man wears a yellow *jama* and a red turban and the woman is clad in red. A stylized tree encircled with a heavy outline and undulating steep hills are behind the building. The blazing sun emerges behind the hill. In the foreground in front of the house is a blue lotus pond in which a woman is swimming nude. The square lotus pond is conspicuously fed by a stream directly descending from a dark blue cloud. Due to the celestial origin, the undulation of the hills has no effect on the flow of the stream. However, the cloud is not exactly a cloud but a cloud tree on which two monkeys jump from one branch to another. Furthermore, the stream is shown as if it is a trunk with several birds resting on it. Thus this illustration suggests that the story of riverine tree recorded in ancient Indian texts was still alive even in the mid-nineteenth century.

The second illustration on top right shows the same couple seated on a low bench in an open space. They are dressed exactly as before; a female *chowrie* holder attends them. Behind them is a one-storied house that partially blocks the view

123 recto

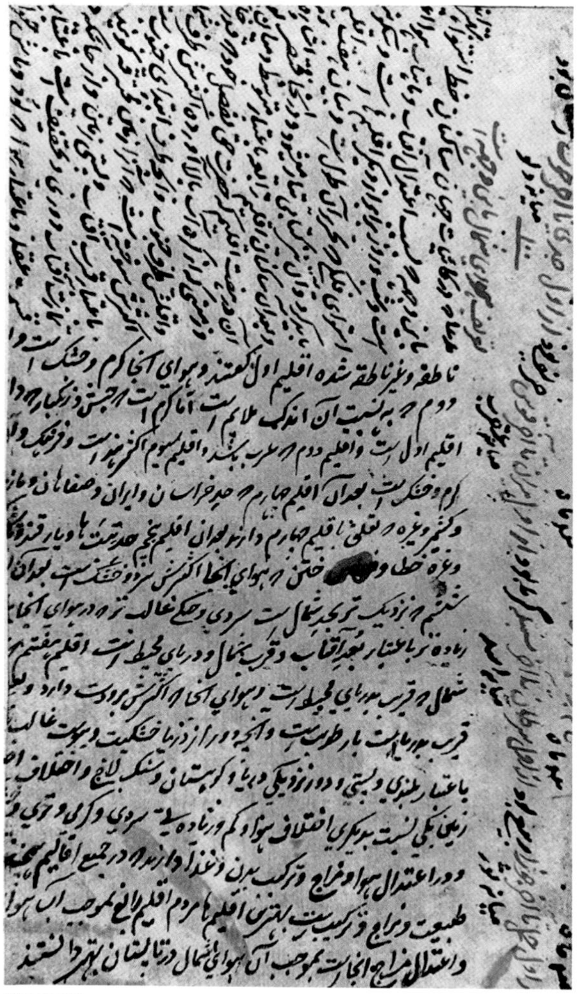

123 verso

of the tree and the hill in the background. Dark blue clouds and a flash of lightning cover the sky. On the left, once again, a green tree extends all the way to the dome of the sky weightlessly as if it is smoke or cloud. Two birds rest under the tree. Pink flowers adorn the foreground.

The third illustration, on bottom left, again shows the noble couple. Dressed in blue, they sit on a bench with red carpet inside a pavilion. The man smokes the hookah, and the woman smells the flower held in her right hand. Two female retainers in front of the pavilion are busy with outdoor cooking.

In the last illustration on bottom right the couple appears in front of a pomegranate plant naturally growing on an isolated green hill. The nobleman attired in a pink *jama* puts his left arm around the shoulder of his lady dressed in red and blue and extends his right hand to pick fruit from the plant. Just behind the couple on the right is a flowering big tree clasped by a grapevine. The enormous bunches of grapes project away from the tree. Both vegetation and human figures are silhouetted against the yellowish green abstract background with the starry blue sky above symbolized by the curved line at the top of each of the four images. In the foreground is a white bitch nursing and playing with four cute puppies. If there is any relationship between this scene and the riverine tree shown in the first illustration, it is not obvious.

Published: Chandra 1971: cat. no. 260.

Deccan and South India

The region south of the Narmadā river and north of the Krishna and Tungabhadrā rivers is designated as Deccan, a word of Persian origina meaning "south." Before the Deccani sultans of the Bahmani dynasty took over the region, it was under the control of the Hindu kings of the Vijayanagara empire. The sultans were Shi'a Muslim. They had a close cultural relationship and a thriving sea trade with the Arab world in general and admired their artistic tradition. The monarchs of the Vijayanagara empire inherited many artistic aspects of Pallava and Chola period. The Deccani sultans, as they took interest in art, hired both local and foreign artists. Thus in the Deccan a hybrid style of works began to emerge.

Although in the battle of Talikota in 1565 the Deccani sultans routed the Hindu king of Vijayanagara, they were not free from danger. The third Mughal emperor, Akbar (r. 1556–1605), and his successors were expanding their territory beyond north India. Fights between the Deccani sultans and the Mughals were inevitable. As Zebrowski (8–9) has pointed out, although both were Muslim, they belonged to different factions (the Mughals were Sunnis), and both were politically ambitious. The Deccani sultans maintained close cultural ties with Turkey and with western Iran through the sea route. The Mughals kept contact with eastern Iran and central Asia via the trade route that goes through the Hindu Kush. Furthermore, already in the sixteenth century the Portuguese had established their colony in Goa, which lies in the west coast of the Deccan, so that like the Mughal artists, the Deccani artists were also exposed to Western art through these newcomers.

Eventually the sixth Mughal emperor Aurangzeb (r.1658–1707) uprooted the Deccani sultans and extended his empire all the way to South India. But some sultans partially reestablished themselves in some parts of the Deccan when the Mughals lost their power in the region. Thus the Deccani sultanate style of painting continued to survive in several cultural and political centers of the Deccan including Hyderabad. An attempt to avoid the influence of Mughal art in the Deccani sultanate painting reflects their struggle with the Mughals.

The Rajput kings often assisted the Mughal emperors as military generals in their fight with the Deccani sultans and were appointed as governors to take care of the newly controlled Deccani region. As a result there was a fascinating stylistic interaction between Rajput and Deccani art. Thus in Deccani painting one can expect to see the artistic elements of the Pallava and Chola dynasty, the Arab and Western world, and the Mughals and Rajputs.

124

A Yoginī
Deccani style, early 17th century
Gouache and gold on paper, 5¼ x 2¹³⁄₁₆ inches
1973.34b

A yoginī, a female ascetic, is a favorite subject of Deccani artists. This representation, therefore, immediately reminds us of the contemporaneously celebrated Chester Beatty Library yoginī from Deccan. In both paintings the topknot and ash-hued bluish complexion are used as iconographical features to identify her as a yoginī. She is, however, depicted in both examples not as a typical ascetic who has abandoned all materialistic worldly possessions; rather she is shown as a youthful lady wearing a silky shawl or *orhani*, a four-pointed skirt contemporaneously known as *cākdār jama*, and gold and pearl necklaces. Very likely the artists have recorded here the style of the yoginis of their time, similar to the phenomena associated with Buddhist monks wearing elaborate robes.

Despite some iconographical similarities, the Watson yoginī differs stylistically from the other yoginī. She is shown here clasping her hands as she dances rhythmically. The rhythm is suggested by her curvilinear body position known as *tribhaṇga*, three-body-bends, which recalls the *sālabhañjikā* motifs of classical sculptures. Her green shawl, swirling and flaring out in the breeze over her shoulders, accentuates her movement. The artist of the Chester Beatty Library yoginī does not create such movement but endeavors to create a somber mood. The lack of background in the Watson example directs the viewer to the main theme of the painting, whereas the elaborate background endowed with rocky hills, flowering bushes, and huge buildings in other examples may distract from the main subject.

Published: Chandra 1971: cat. no. 62; Watson, 38; Raducha: cat. no. 2.58.

124

125

125

Ladies Relaxing on a Terrace

Deccani style (Hyderabad), early 18th century

Brush and pen, gray ink with traces of red, 9¼ x 5¾ inches

69.28.5

The facial features of the ladies indicate this picture definitely belongs to the Deccani school. Another characteristic of this school is the treatment of hair, thin around the forehead and becoming thicker near the upper section of the head. Compare this treatment with that of the Gujarati (cat. no. 28) and Mewar schools (cat. no. 32) where the transition of forehead to the head is marked by an abrupt hairline.

Leaning against the wall of a terrace, two elegantly dressed ladies enjoy the outdoor atmosphere. The terrace is covered with a huge carpet embellished with a flower pattern on which the ladies stand barefoot. The lady on the left holds a goblet from which she is about to drink. The other lady, whose face is depicted in three-quarter profile, turns toward her. Both wear diaphanous skirts revealing their youthful bodies. Furthermore, the sensuous hand gestures such as touching the hair or holding the edge of the wall gently, as well as the curvilinear standing posture emphasized by the crossed-leg position accentuate their feminine beauty as the artist seems to have intended. In the foreground is a fountain in the middle of a pool filled with fish and nearby are birds and with flowers on its bank. In the background is a garden of several different trees between two highly ornamented palatial buildings.

Published: Chandra 1971: cat. no. 67.

126

126
A Lady Receiving an Attendant

Deccani style, mid 18th century

Gouache and gold on paper, $5^{5}/_{8}$ x $3^{1}/_{4}$ inches

69.28.4b

Both the human figures and the rolling hills and vegetation are rendered here linearly. Color modulation is applied only in some places. Thus, at first glance the painting appears to be a monochromatic drawing. The furniture is rendered with reversed perspective. The drooping branches of weeping willow in a remote hillside reflect the somber facial expression of the lady seated under the same tree.

She holds a flower in her hennaed hand and comfortably leans against the bolster on a stool. She converses with a man who stands in front of her, gesturing animatedly with his hands. His bejeweled turban and flowery *jama* suggest that he may be an authority of high rank. A female attendant with a gentle look stands behind her holding a tray. The physiognomy of the lady and the female attendant does not differ much since they are derived from a Deccani type. Their demure facial expressions are an artistic feature to which Indian artists give a great deal of attention.

Published: Chandra 1971: cat. no. 64.

127

127

Kṛṣṇa Playing the Flute

Deccani style, late 18th century

Gouache and gold on paper, 9⅞ x 7⅛ inches

1975.34

Kṛṣṇa is not only a great dancer but also a divine flute player. The sound of his flute enchants the world including the cattle, milkmaids, and cowherds. Kṛṣṇa's stories associated with this belief are often described in texts in great detail. The same theme is expressed here visually.

Kṛṣṇa sits beneath a huge tree. Some birds fly around the tree, others nestle on the branches. The blue sky in the background contrasts with the green grassland below. The tree is situated above the grassland on a purple rocky, stylized hilltop. The hill, which is greener than the grassland, is dotted with flowering plants; below is a lotus pond in the foreground. Various aquatic birds inhabit the jagged bank of the pond.

Kṛṣṇa is depicted here in three-quarter profile. His hair, fashioned into a topknot, is decorated with a tiny peacock's feather. He holds the flute in both hands and sits comfortably on the rock with his right ankle on his left knee. To the viewer's right, a milkmaid who came to fetch the water stands with her left hand on her hip. She carries a water jar on her head and balances it with her right hand. Enchanted by the sound of the flute, she stands still. To the left a cowherd whose head and torso are covered with a dark blue blanket folds his hands in adoration to the flute-player. Even the cattle seem to realize the significance of the divine music. Some of them sit on the ground, others stand still looking toward Kṛṣṇa attentively. The calves, however, are busy with sucking.

Published: Chandra 1971: cat. no. 70.

128

128

Śiva and Pārvatī on Mount Kailāsa

Deccani style, early 19th century

Gouache and gold on paper, 9⅝ x 6¾ inches

1975.35

Perhaps the most interesting aspect of this painting is the continuity of several artistic elements from the classical period. First, the subject of the divine couple originated in the ancient motif of the loving couple (see introductory essay for detail). Second, the style of holding attributes derives from traditional Deccani and South Indian works in which Hindu deities hold their attributes with two raised fingers. This feature differs considerably from that of north India where gods grab their attributes in their fists. Third, the artist indicates his familiarity with the convention of the peaceful hermitage with the ascetics and beasts living together. Some elements of classical art survived even into the nineteenth century.

On top of the snow-capped Kailāsa mountain, the prominent Hindu deities Śiva and Pārvatī rest under a tree on a tiger skin. The iconographical features of Śiva are easily recognizable: He has matted hair, a third eye, and four arms. He wears serpents around his neck. His upper hands hold a trident and an antelope. Śiva's bull Nandī crouches in front of the divine couple. Their elephant-headed son Gaṇeśa stands on their left fanning them with a *chowrie*. Ascetics and beasts inhabit the caves of the mountain. Bellow the mountain, in the foreground, runs a river horizontally. The background consists of grassland, pink rolling hills, and a stripe of blue sky.

Published: Chandra 1971: cat. no. 72; Raducha: cat. no. 2.15.

SOUTH INDIA

The tip of the Indian peninsula, lying south of the Krishna river, is known as South India. Because ancient India usually came into contact with foreign cultures through the Hindu Kush mountain range, this region often did not respond to the sophisticated artistic movements of north India immediately. Usually newcomers, including Islamic rulers, established themselves in the Indus valley and Gangetic valley, and then they moved to the Deccan and South India. Due to the isolation in this region the elements of classical art survived much longer than in other parts of India. However, South India did have occasional contact with foreign civilizations that arrived through the sea route.

129

Scenes from the *Rāmāyaṇa*

South India (probably Tanjore), 18th century

Gouache and gold on paper, 6⅜ x 4 13/16 inches

1983.149

This is a fragment of a larger painting depicting the episodes of the epic *Rāmāyaṇa* in four registers. The top register contains two scenes: On the left a female figure falls to the ground. Raducha identifies this figure as an ogresses with whom Rāma and his companions waged battles in the forest (Raducha, 87). The second scene on the right is associated with a main episode of the epic in which Rāma's wife Sītā was abducted by the powerful demon king Rāvaṇa. In the middle of the forest, the only allies Rāma could get for his fight with the demon were monkeys and bears, who are depicted here behind Rāma under a tree. Rāma's brother Lakṣmaṇa stands in front of Rāma with the greeting gesture and confirms that Sītā is now in the palace of the demon. This he learnt from Vibhīṣaṇa, the demon king's younger brother who was furiously opposed to Sītā's abduction. In the painting Vibhīṣaṇa, immediately behind Lakṣmaṇa, is accompanied by three mustachioed demons, one carrying a trident. Reading from the left, the first scene of the second register shows Rāma receiving gifts from a charioteer who takes the trays and baskets from a chariot and places them in front of Rāma. The second scene on the right depicts the charioteer driving away after the delivery. At the left of third register, Rāma, accompanied by his usual companions, sits under a tree and receives reports from Vibhīṣaṇa and a trident holder. To the right Rāvaṇa, the abductor of Sītā, sits in a chamber of the palace, where three women greet him. The wall and the gate of the palace are symbolically shown as vertical elements, eschewing perspective, exactly as in early Jaina paintings or Buddhist Thanka paintings. After Sītā was rescued, she had to undergo the test of fire to prove her chastity during long captivity in the palace of the demon. This is the subject of the last register, which shows Sītā standing in the middle of fire. Various divinities float above the cloud; Rāma sits under tree; a crowd of monkeys, bears, and people including Lakṣmaṇa and Vibhīṣaṇa watch Sītā's trial. To the right is a winged chariot that originally belonged to the demon king but is now possessed by the victorious prince Rāma, who proudly watches it.

Bright colors such as yellow, orange, blue, green, pink, and brown adorn the troops of monkey and bears. Rāma is depicted here as green, because the Sanskrit word for dark complexion, *śyāma,* is translated in painting sometimes as blue other times as green. The narration of the story sometimes, but not always, moves from left to right, then back to left for the next register. Yet according to the *Rāmāyaṇa* the episode of the winged chariot (shown on the right) happened before Sītā's test of fire (shown on the left). Such multidirectional narration is often found in classical stone relief as well.

Published: Chandra 1971: cat. no. 268; Raducha: cat. no. 2.22.

129

Glossary

ahiṃsā: noninjury to men, animals, and insects
algojā: gourd, ground pipe
āmalaka: fruit
amir: nobleman, rich person
apsarā: winged nymphs

bhakti: reverence
bindi: a pendant suspended from the forehead

cakora: bird
cākdār jama: four-pointed tunic
cakravartī: the universal monarch,
cāmara: yak tail, Sanskrit for fly whisk
cappals: sandals
caupar: a game
chatri: kiosk with an umbrellalike dome
chowrie: fly whisk
coli: blouse

darśana: see essay for author's theory of
dholaki: drum
Digambara: "space-clad," i.e. naked, a division of Jains
dupattā: scarf covering shoulders and bosom

gairikācala: red chalk hill
ghumghat: bubblelike transparent the veil covering the head
ghunghurus: small bells
gopī: milkmaid

howdah: seat placed on back of an elephant

jaladharajāla: patterns of rain clouds
jalahari: drain to empty a libation
jama: robe covering shoulder to ankles
jighā: turban jewel
jizya: tax
jyautiṣa: astronomy

kālāpaka: "time of peacock's scream"
kamarband: a cloth sash or leather belt worn around the waist
kṣatriya: warrior caste in India

lalitāsana: a royal figure seated on a throne with right leg resting on left knee and left foot on the floor

mithuna: married couple

namaskāra: gesture of greeting
nim qalam: partial coloration of drawing

orhani: scarf for head and torso

paryūṣaṇa: rainy season retreat of Jainas,
patka: sash worn over the *jama*
pechwai: backdrop painting behind main image of shrine
phikdani: spitoon
phulia: woman's nose ornament
pītāmbara: yellow garment
pūjā: worship

rāga: classical musical mode personified as a male and associated with particular times of the day
rāginī: classical musical mode personified as female
rāgamālā: a garland of melodies
rājalīlāsana: the position of royal ease
rājāṅgana: front courtyard
rāsamaṇḍala: a circular dance
ratha: chariot

śakti: female principle
śālabhañjikā: a standing posture in which a female figure holds a branch of a tree
saṃvasarana: gathering or assembly
sāraṅgi: musical instrument
sari: outer garment of length of material with one end wrapped around waist and the other draped over the shoulder or head
Śivaliṅga: a phallic representation of Śiva
śikhara: a vertical element of the architecture of north India intended to suggest a Himalayan mountain peak
Śrāvaṇa: second month of the rainy season
Śrīvatsa: an auspicious symbol
subhikṣa: prosperous time
surāhi: ewer
svastika: auspicious symbol and the posture imitating it
Śvetāmbara: clad in white robe, Jaina sect

tānpurā: stringed instrument of Turkish origin
tapovana: hermitage
thanka: Tibetan and Nepali painting on cloth
thikānā: fief

uṣṇīṣa: the cranial protuberance of the Buddha
ustād: master

vanamālā: elongated garland of wildflowers
vijñaptipatra: letter of invitation
vikramaśīla: a monastery
vīṇā: stringed instrument of Indic origin

References Cited

Agrawala, Prithvi K. *Mithuna: The Male-Female Symbol in Indian Art and Thought*. New Delhi: Munshiram Manoharlal, 1983.

Archer, W. G. *Central Indian Painting*. London: Faber and Faber, 1958.

Archer, W. G. *Visions of Courtly India: The Archer Collection of Pahari Miniatures*. Washington, D.C.: International Exhibitions Foundation, 1976.

Banerjea, Jitendra Nath. *The Development of Hindu Iconography*. New Delhi: Munshiram Manoharlal, 1974.

Barrett, Douglas, and Basil Gray. *Painting of India*. New York: Rizzoli, 1978.

Beach, Milo Cleveland. *Mughal and Rajput Painting. The New Cambridge History of India* I:3. Cambridge: Cambridge University Press, 1992.

Bhattacharya, Sachidananda. *A Dictionary of Indian History, vol. 1*. New Delhi: Cosmo Publications, 1994.

Bhattacharyya, Dipak Chandra. *Studies in Buddhist Iconography*. Delhi: Manohar, 1978.

Binney III, Edwin. *Indian Miniature Painting from the Collection of Edwin Binney, 3rd. The Mughal and Deccani Schools*. Portland, Ore.: Portland Art Museum, 1973.

Bussagli, Mario and Calembus Sivaramamurti. *5000 Years of the Art of India*. New York: Abrams, 1971.

Chaitanya, Krishna. *A History of Indian Painting*, vol. 3. New Delhi: Abhinav, 1982.

Chandra, Pramod. *Indian Miniature Painting: The Collection of Earnest C. and Jane Werner Watson*. Madison: Elvehjem Art Center/ University of Wisconsin Press, 1971.

Chandra, Pramod. "Ustad Salivahana and the Development of Popular Mughal Art." *Lalit Kala* 8 (October 1960): 25–46.

Coomaraswamy, Ananda K. "Art of Eastern Asia." In *Coomaraswamy* edited by Roger Lipsey, vol. 1, 107. Princeton, N.J.: Princeton University Press, 1977.

Coomaraswamy, Ananda K. *History of Indian and Indonesian Art*. New York, Dover, 1965.

Coomaraswamy, Ananda K. *The Transformation of Nature in Art*. New York: Dover, 1956.

Craven, Roy C. *Indian Art: A Concise History*. London: Thames and Hudson, 1976.

Dehejia, Vidya. *Indian Art*. London: Phaidon, 1997.

Ebeling, Klaus. *Ragamala Painting*. New Delhi: Ravi Kumar, 1973.

Eck, Diana. *Darśan: Seeing the Divine Image in India*. Chambersburg, Pa: Anima, 1985; Columbia University Press, 1996.

Frater, Alexander. *Chasing the Monsoon*. New York: Knopf, 1991.

Glynn, Catherine. "Evidence of Royal Painting for the Amber Court." *Artibus Asiae* 56, 1-2 (1996): 67-93.

Glynn, Catherine. "A Rajasthani Princely Album: Rajput Patronage of Mughal-Style Painting." *Artibus Asiae* 60, 2 (2000): 222–64.

Goswamy, B. N., and Eberhard Fischer. *Pahari Masters: Court Painters of Northern India*. Delhi: Oxford University Press, 1997.

Grünwedal, Albert. *Buddhist Art in India*, trans. A. C. Gibson. 2nd ed. London: Susil Gupta, 1965.

Harle, James C. *The Art and Architecture of the Indian Subcontinent*. London: Penguin, 1990.

Huntington, Susan L. *The Art of Ancient India: Buddhist, Hindu, Jain*. New York: Weatherhill, 1985.

Jaina, Pravinacandra, and Darabarilal Kothia. *Jaina Purana-kosa* [Hindi]. Varanasi, India: Jainavidya Samsthana, 1993.

Kaufmann, Walter. *The Ragas of North India*. Bloomington: Published for International Affairs Center by Indiana University Press, 1968.

Khandalavala, Karl J. *Pahari Miniature Paintings*. Bombay: New Book, 1958.

Khandalavala, Karl, Moti Chandra, and Pramod Chandra. *Miniature Painting: A Catalogue of the Exhibition of the Sri Motichand Khajanchi Collection Held by the Lalit Kala Akademi*. New Delhi: Lalit Kala Akademi, 1960.

Kramrisch, Stella. *The Art of India: Traditions of Indian Sculpture, Painting and Architecture*. London: Phaidon Press, 1965.

Leach, Linda York. *Indian Miniature Paintings and Drawings: The Cleveland Museum of Art Catalogue of Oriental Art*. Cleveland: Cleveland Museum of Art/ Indiana University Press, 1986.

Lee, Sherman E. *Rajput Painting*. New York: Asia Society, 1960.

Losty, Jeremiah P. *The Art of the Book in India*. London: British Library, 1982.

Majmudar, M. R., ed. *Madhavanala-Kamakandala Prabandha*. Baroda, India: Oriental Institute, 1942.

Mukerjee, Radhakamal. *The Culture and Art of India*. London: Allen and Unwin, 1959.

Pal, Pratapaditya. *The Art of Nepal: A Catalogue of the Los Angeles County Museum of Art Collection*. Berkeley: Los Angeles County Museum of Art in association with University of California Press, 1985.

Pal, Pratapaditya. *The Classical Tradition in Rajput Painting from the Paul F. Walter Collection*. New York: Pierpont Morgan Library and the Gallery Association of New York State, 1978.

Pal, Pratapaditya. *The Peaceful Liberators: Jain Art from India*. New York: Thames and Hudson in association with Los Angeles County Museum of Art, 1994.

Portland Art Museum. *Rajput Miniatures from the Collection of Edwin Binney, 3rd*. Portland, Ore.: Portland Art Museum, 1968.

Poster, Amy G., S. R. Canby, Pramod Chandra, and J. M. Cummins. *Realms of Heroism: Indian Paintings at the Brooklyn Museum*. New York: Hudson Hills with The Brooklyn Museum, 1994.

Raducha, Joan A. and Blenda Femenias. *Two Faces of South Asian Art: Textiles and Paintings*. Madison: Elvehjem Museum of Art, 1984.

Rogers, J. M. *Mughal Miniatures*. London: British Museum, 1993.

Rowland, Benjamin. *The Art and Architecture of India: Buddhist, Hindu, Jain*. Baltimore: Penguin, 1974.

Smith, Vincent A. *The Oxford History of India*. London: Oxford University Press, 1961.

Sohoni, Sridhara V., ed. *Mahavamsatika*. Patna: Nava Nalanda Mahavihara, 1971.

Spink, Walter M. *Krishnamandala, A Devotional Theme in Indian Art*. Ann Arbor, Mich.: Center for South and Southeast Asian Studies, The University of Michigan, Special Publications, no. 2, 1971.

Swali, Haridas. "Vasudhara in Late Medieval Jaina Manuscripts." In *Indian Art and Connoisseurship: Essays in Honour of Douglas Barrett*, ed. John Guy. New Delhi: Indira Gandhi National Centre for the Arts in association with Mapin, 178–87.

Tod, James. *Annals and Antiquities of Rajasthan, or the Central and Western Rajpoot States of India,* vol. 1. Reprint: New Delhi: M. N. Publishers, 1978.

Upaniṣads. Translated by Patrick Olivelle. Oxford: Oxford University Press, 1996.

Vajracharya, Gautama V. "The Adapatation of Monsoonal Culture by Rgvedic Aryans: A Further Study of the Frog Hymn." *Electronic Journal of Vedic Studies* 3, 2 (1997): 4–20.

Vajracharya, Gautama V. "Atmospheric Gestation: Deciphering Ajanta Ceiling Paintings and Other Related Works (Part 1–2)," *Marg* (forthcoming).

Vajracharya, Gautama V. "Symbolism of Ashokan Pillars: A Reappraisal in the Light of Textual and Visual Evidence." *Marg* 51, 2 (December 1999): 53–78.

Vajracharya, Gautama V. "Tradition and Change in Rajput Painting from the Watson Collection." Elvehjem Bulletin (1994): 43–60.

Viṣṇudharmottarapurāṇa. Edited and translated by Priyabala Shah, vol. 2. Baroda: Oriental Institute, 1961.

Waldschmidt, Ernst, and Rose Leonore Waldschmidt. *Miniatures of Musical Inspiration in the Collection of the Berlin Museum of Indian Art*. Pt. 2, *Ragamala Miniatures from Northern India and the Deccan*. Berlin: Museum für Indische Kunst, 1975.

Watson, Jane Werner. "Down the Lotus-Petal Path." *The Connoisseur* (September 1972): 37-47.

Welch, Stuart Cary. *A Flower from Every Meadow: Indian Paintings from American Collections*. New York: Asia Society, 1973.

Williams, Joanna, and J. P. Das. "Raghunatha Prusti: An Oriya Artist." *Artibus Asiae* 48, 1–2 (1987): 131–59.

Wilkinson, J. V. S. *The Lights of Canopus: Anwar-i-Suhaili*. London: Studio Limited, 1929.

Zebrowski, Mark. *Deccani Painting*. Berkeley: University of California Press, 1983.

Index